Inventing the Enemy

Umberto Eco has written works of fiction, literary criticism and philosophy. His first novel, *The Name of the Rose*, was a major international bestseller. His other works include *Foucault's Pendulum*, *The Island of the Day Before*, *Baudolino*, *The Mysterious Flame of Queen Loana* and *The Prague Cemetery*, and several brilliant collections of essays, such as *Kant and the Platypus*, *How to Travel with a Salmon*, *On Literature*, and *Turning Back the Clock*.

D1082427

ALSO BY UMBERTO ECO

Fiction

The Name of the Rose
Foucault's Pendulum
The Island of the Day Before
Baudolino
The Mysterious Flame of Queen Loana
The Prague Cemetery

Non-fiction

Faith in Fakes
Five Moral Pieces
Kant and the Platypus
Serendipities
How to Travel With a Salmon and Other Essays
On Literature
On Beauty
Turning Back the Clock
On Ugliness
The Infinity of Lists

UMBERTO ECO

Inventing the Enemy

And Other Occasional Writings

TRANSLATED FROM THE ITALIAN
By Richard Dixon

VINTAGE BOOKS
London

Published by Vintage 2013

2 4 6 8 10 9 7 5 3

First published in Great Britain in 2012 by
Harvill Secker

Vintage
Random House, 20 Vauxhall Bridge Road,
London SW1V 2SA

www.vintage-books.co.uk

Addresses for companies within The Random House Group Limited can be
found at: www.randomhouse.co.uk/offices.htm

The Random House Group Limited Reg. No. 954009

A CIP catalogue record for this book is available from the British Library

ISBN 9780099553946

Illustrations credits
Page 150: *Series of observations of the planet Satern*, 1656, Oxford, Science
Archive. © 2011. Foto Scala Firenzel/Heritage Images (Italian text p. 238).
PAges 210-211: Bourgainville, Louise-Antione de (1729-1811), *Développement
de la route faite autour du monde par les vaisseaux du roy La Boudeuse et
L'Etoile*, © BnF (Italian text pp.318-319)

MIX
Paper from
responsible sources
FSC® C016897
www.fsc.org

Printed and bound in Great Britain by Clays Ltd, St Ives plc

CONTENTS

Introduction

THE TITLE OF this collection ought to have been the subtitle, *Occasional Writings*. It was only my publisher's proper concern — that such a pompously modest title might not attract the reader's attention, whereas the title of the first essay may arouse curiosity — that determined the final choice.

What are occasional writings and what are their virtues? They are generally on topics about which the author had no specific interest. He was, instead, encouraged to write each one after being invited to contribute to a series of discussions or essays on a particular theme. It captured the author's interest and encouraged him to reflect on something he might otherwise have ignored — and often a subject imposed from outside turns out to be more fruitful than one arising from some inner whim.

Another virtue of occasional writing is that it does not demand originality at all costs, but aims to entertain the speaker as well as the listener. In short, occasional writing is an exercise in baroque rhetoric, as when Roxane sets challenges for Christian (and through him, for Cyrano), such as "speak to me of love."

At the end of each essay (all written over the past decade) I note the date and occasion. To emphasize their occasional nature I should mention that "Absolute and Relative" and "The Beauty of the Flame" were presented during the Milanesiana festival of literature, an event centered on a specific theme. It provided an interesting opportunity to talk about the Absolute at a time when the controversy over relativism was blowing up, though the second essay was quite a challenge, as I had never before felt, shall we say, fired by such a topic.

"No Embryos in Paradise" is based on a lecture I gave in 2008 in Bologna at a conference on the ethics of research, which was then included in a book titled *Etica della ricerca medica e identità culturale europea,* edited by Francesco Galofaro (Bologna: CLUEB, 2009).

Thoughts on the poetics of excess in Victor Hugo bring together three different essays and lectures. I brazenly presented my entertainment called "Imaginary Astronomies" in two different versions at two different conferences, one on astronomy and the other on geography.

"Treasure Hunting" gathers various contributions on cathedral treasuries; "Fermented Delights" was presented during a conference on Piero Camporesi. "Censorship and Silence" was delivered almost off the cuff at the conference of the Italian Semiotics Association in 2009.

Three essays appeared in three different issues of the *Almanacco del bibliofilo,* in three different years, and are pieces of real entertainment, inspired by three set themes: "In search of new utopian islands" was the theme for "Living by Proverbs," "Sentimental digressions on readings from earlier times" for "I Am Edmond Dantès!," and "Late reviews" for "*Ulysses:* That's All We Needed . . ."

The penultimate essay, "Why the Island Is Never Found," appeared in the 2011 issue of the *Almanacco del bibliofilo* and is the text of a lecture given on islands at a conference in Sardinia in 2010.

"Thoughts on WikiLeaks" is the reworking of two articles, one that appeared in *Libération* (December 2, 2010) and the other in *L'Espresso* (December 31, 2010). Finally, returning to the first essay, "Inventing the Enemy" was delivered as one of a series of lectures on the classics organized at the University of Bologna by Ivano Dionigi. These few pages seem rather scant, now that Gian Antonio Stella has so splendidly developed the whole question over more than three hundred pages in his book *Negri, froci, giudei & co.: L'eterna guerra contro l'altro* (Milan: Rizzoli, 2009), but never mind—it would have been a shame to let it sink into oblivion, seeing that making enemies is a continual and relentless occupation.

INVENTING THE ENEMY

Inventing the Enemy

SOME YEARS AGO in New York I found myself in conversation with a taxi driver whose name I had difficulty in placing. He was, he explained, Pakistani and asked where I came from. Italy, I replied. He asked how many of us there were and was surprised we were so few and that our language wasn't English.

Then he asked me who our enemies were. In response to my "Sorry?" he explained patiently that he wanted to know who were the people against whom we have fought through the centuries over land claims, ethnic rivalry, border incursions, and so forth. I told him we are not at war with anyone. He explained that he wanted to know who were our historical enemies, those who kill us and whom we kill. I repeated that we don't have any, that we fought our last war more than half a century ago — starting, moreover, with one enemy and ending with another.

He wasn't satisfied. How can a country have no enemies? Getting out of the taxi, I left a two-dollar tip to compensate him for our indolent Italian pacifism. And only then did it occur to me how I should have answered. It is not true that we Italians have no enemies. We have no outside enemies, or rather we are unable to agree on who they are, because we are continually at war with *each other* — Pisa against Lucca, Guelphs against Ghibellines, north against south, Fascists against Partisans, mafia against state, Berlusconi's government against the judiciary. It was a pity that during that time the two governments headed by Romano Prodi had not yet fallen; otherwise I could have explained to the taxi driver what it means to lose a war through friendly fire.

Thinking further about the conversation, I have come to the conclusion that one of Italy's misfortunes over the past sixty years has been the absence of real enemies. The unification of Italy took place thanks to the presence of Austria, or, in the words of Giovanni Berchet, of the *irto, increscioso alemanno* — the bristling, irksome Teuton. And Mussolini was able to enjoy popular support by calling on Italy to avenge herself for a victory in tatters, for humiliating defeats in Abyssinia at Dogali and Adua, and for the Jewish plutodemocracy, which, he claimed, was penalizing us iniquitously. See what happened in the United States when the Evil Empire vanished and the great Soviet enemy faded away. The United States was in danger of losing its identity until bin Laden, in gratitude for the benefits received when he was fighting against the Soviet Union, proffered his merciful hand and gave Bush the opportunity to create new enemies, strengthening feelings of national identity as well as his own power.

Having an enemy is important not only to define our identity but also to provide us with an obstacle against which to measure our system of values and, in seeking to overcome it, to demonstrate our own worth. So when there is no enemy, we have to invent one. Look at the generous flexibility with which the skinheads of Verona would, just to identify themselves as a group, choose anyone not belonging to their group as their enemy. And so we are concerned here not so much with the almost natural phenomenon of identifying an enemy who is threatening us, but with the process of creating and demonizing the enemy.

In the *Orations Against Catiline,* Cicero had no need to convince the Roman senators that they had an enemy since he had proof of Lucius Catiline's plot. But nonetheless he builds up a picture of the enemy in the second oration, where he describes Catiline's friends, reflecting on the main accusation: that they were tainted with moral perversity.

Individuals who spend their time feasting, in the arms of loose women, torpid with wine, sated with food, crowned with wreathes, oiled with unguents, weakened by copulation, belch out in words that all good citizens must be killed and the city must be set on fire . . . You have them under your very eyes: not a hair out of place, smooth-faced or with a well-trimmed beard, dressed in tunics down to their ankles and with long sleeves, wrapped in veils and not togas . . . These "youths," so witty and refined, have learned not only to love and be loved, not only to dance and sing, but also to brandish daggers and administer poisons. (oration 2, sections 1–10)

Cicero's moralism was much the same as Saint Augustine's, who condemned pagans because, unlike Christians, they attended circuses, theaters, and amphitheaters, and celebrated orgiastic feasts. Enemies are *different* from us and observe customs that are not our own.

The epitome of difference is the foreigner. In Roman bas-reliefs the barbarians appear as bearded and snub-nosed, and as is well known, the word itself alludes to a defect in language and therefore in thought (*bar-bar,* "they are stuttering").

From the very beginning, however, the people who become our enemies often are not those who directly threaten us (as would have been the case with the barbarians), but those whom someone has an interest in portraying as a true threat even when they aren't. Rather than a real threat highlighting the ways in which these enemies are different from us, the difference itself becomes a symbol of what we find threatening.

See what Tacitus has to say about the Jews: "All things that are sacred for us are profane for them, and what is impure for us is lawful for them" (which brings to mind how the English dismiss the French as frog eaters or how the Germans condemn the Italians for excessive use of garlic). The Jews are "strange" because they abstain from eating pork, do not put yeast in bread, rest on the seventh day, marry only among themselves, are circumcised — not (of course) for hygienic or religious reasons but "to show they are different from others" —

bury their dead, and do not venerate our caesars. Having demonstrated how certain real customs are different (circumcision, Sabbath rest), the writer can further emphasize his point by adding legendary customs to the picture (they make sacred images of a donkey and despise their parents, children, brothers, their country, and the gods).

Pliny the Younger can find no particular allegations against the Christians, since he has to admit they are not involved in committing crimes; in fact, their actions are virtuous. Nonetheless he sends them to their death because they do not sacrifice to the emperor, and this stubbornness in refusing something so obvious and natural establishes their difference.

Then, as contact between peoples becomes more complex, a new form of enemy arises: he is not just the person who remains outside and exhibits his strangeness from a distance, but is also the person within, among us — today we would call him the foreign immigrant — who behaves differently in some way or speaks our language badly. He appears in Juvenal's satire as the cunning, swindling, brazen, lecherous Greek, capable of debauching even his friend's grandmother.

The Negro, due to the color of his skin, is a stranger wherever he goes. The entry for "Negro" in the first American encyclopedia, published by Thomas Dobson in 1798, states:

> In the complexion of negroes we meet with various shades; but they likewise differ far from other men in all the features of their face. Round cheeks, high cheek bones, a forehead somewhat elevated, a short, broad, flat nose, thick lips, small ears, ugliness, and irregularity of shape, characterize their external appearance. The negro women have the loins greatly depressed, and very large buttocks, which gives the back the shape of a saddle. Vices the most notorious seem to be the portion of this unhappy race: idleness, treachery, revenge, cruelty, impudence, stealing, lying, profanity, debauchery, nastiness, and intemperance, are said to have extinguished the principles of natural law, and to have silenced the reproofs of conscience. They are strangers to every sentiment of

compassion, and are an awful example of the corruption of man when left to himself.

The Negro is ugly. The enemy must be ugly because beauty is identified with good (*kalokagathia*), and one of the fundamental characteristics of beauty has always been what the Middle Ages called *integritas* (in other words, having all that is required to be an average representative of a species; by this standard those humans missing a limb or an eye, or having lower-than-average stature or "inhuman" color were considered ugly). That is why the giant one-eyed Polyphemus and the dwarf Mime immediately provide us with a model for identifying the enemy. Priscus of Panion in the fifth century describes Attila the Hun as small in stature, with a broad chest and large head, small eyes, a thin graying beard, a flat nose, and — a crucial feature — a swarthy complexion. But it is curious how Attila's face is similar to the physiognomy of the devil, as Rodolfus Glaber described him more than five centuries later — gaunt face, deep black eyes, forehead furrowed with wrinkles, flat nose, protruding mouth, swollen lips, thin narrow chin, goatish beard, hairy pointed ears, straight disheveled hair, canine teeth, elongated skull; he was also of modest stature, with a slender neck, protruding chest, and humped back (*Histories,* book 5, part 3).

When Liutprand of Cremona is sent by Emperor Otto I as envoy to Byzantium in 968 and encounters a hitherto unknown civilization, he finds the Byzantine emperor devoid of *integritas:*

> I came before Nicephorus, a monstrous being, a pygmy with an enormous head, whose small eyes gave him the appearance of a mole, with an ugly short broad thick graying beard, a neck as long as a finger . . . the color of an Ethiopian, "whom you wouldn't want to bump into in the middle of the night," fat belly, thin loins, thighs too long for his small stature, short legs, flat feet, and dressed in a fetid, threadbare peasant's garment faded with use. (*Relatio de legatione Constantinopolitana*)

Fetid. The enemy invariably stinks, as the French psychologist Edgar Bérillon wrote at the beginning of the First World War (1915) in *La polychésie de la race allemande.* In this volume he demonstrated that the average German produced more — and fouler smelling — fecal material than did the Frenchman. If the Byzantine stank, so too did the Saracen. In *Evagatorium in Terrae sanctae, Arabiae, et Egypti peregrinationem,* the fifteenth-century monk Felix Fabri notes that "the Saracens exude a certain horrible stench, for which they perform continual ablutions of various sorts; and since we do not smell, they do not care if we bathe together with them. But they are not so indulgent with the Jews, who smell even more . . . Thus the stinking Saracens are pleased to find themselves in the company of those like us who do not smell."

For Giuseppe Giusti, it was the Austrians who stank. Arriving at the Basilica of Sant'Ambrogio in Milan, he recorded these impressions:

> I enter, and find it full of soldiers,
> those soldiers from the north,
> Bohemians and Croatians,
> lined up like poles in a vineyard.
>
> . . . .
>
> I drew back; since standing there
> amid that rabble, I must admit
> a feeling of disgust, of suffocation,
> of filthy breath, which, by your calling,
> you can scarcely feel: even the candles
> (excuse me, your Excellency)
> on the altar of that fine house of God,
> seemed to reek of tallow. (*Sant'Ambrogio,* 1845)

The gypsy inevitably stinks, given that he feeds on carrion, as Cesare Lombroso tells us in *L'uomo delinquente* (1876, volume 1, chapter 2), and so does James Bond's enemy Rosa Klebb in Ian Fleming's *From Russia, with Love* (1957). She is not only a Soviet Russian but, worse still, a lesbian:

Outside the anonymous, cream painted door, Tatiana already smelled the inside of the room. When the voice told her curtly to come in, and she opened the door, it was the smell that filled her mind while she stood and stared into the eyes of the woman who sat behind the round table under the centre light.

It was the smell of the Metro on a hot evening — cheap scent concealing animal odours. People in Russia soak themselves in scent, whether they have had a bath or not, but mostly when they have not . . .

Tatiana was still cheerfully reviewing the situation when the bedroom door opened and "the Klebb woman" appeared . . . wearing a semi-transparent nightgown in orange crêpe de chine . . . One dimpled knee, like a yellowish coconut, appeared thrust forward between the half-open folds of the nightgown in the classic stance of the modeller . . . Rosa Klebb had taken off her spectacles and her naked face was now thick with mascara and rouge and lipstick . . .

She patted the couch beside her.

"Turn out the top light, my dear. The switch is by the door. Then come and sit beside me. We must get to know each other better." (chapter 9)

The Jew has been described as monstrous and smelly since at least the birth of Christianity, given that he is modeled on the Antichrist, the archenemy, the foe not only of man but of God:

This is how he looks: his head is like a burning flame, his right eye is bloodshot, his left is a cat-like green and has two pupils, his eyelids are white, his lower lip is large, his right femur is weak, his feet large, his thumb flat and elongated. (*Syriac Testament of Our Lord Jesus Christ,* fifth century, volume 1, part 4)

The Antichrist will be born from the Jewish people . . . from the union between a father and a mother, like other men, and not, as some say, from a virgin . . . At the beginning of his conception the devil will enter the mother's uterus, by virtue of the devil he will be nurtured in the mother's womb, and the power of the devil will always be with him. (Adso of Montier-en-Der, *Letter on the Origin and Time of the Antichrist,* tenth century)

He will have two flaming eyes, ears like those of a donkey, the nose and mouth of a lion, so that he will set men to acts of most criminal folly amid the fires and most shameful voices of contradiction, making them deny God, spreading into their senses the most horrible fetor, mutilating the institutions of the church with the most ferocious greed; sneering with an enormous grimace and showing horrible teeth of iron. (Hildegard of Bingen, *Liber scivias,* twelfth century, volume 3, part 1, section 14)

If the Antichrist comes from the Jewish people, his model must inevitably reflect the image of the Jew, whether in terms of popular anti-Semitism, theological anti-Semitism, or the bourgeois anti-Semitism of the eighteenth and nineteenth centuries. Let us start with his face:

They generally have a bluish face, hooked nose, deep-set eyes, protruding chin, and strongly pronounced constrictor muscles around the lips . . . Jews are also prone to diseases which indicate a corruption of the blood, such as leprosy in the past and now scurvy, which is akin to it, scrofula, bleeding . . . It is said that Jews always have bad breath . . . Others attribute these effects to the frequent use of strong-smelling vegetables such as onion and garlic . . . Yet others say it is goose meat, to which they are very partial, that makes them dark and melancholic, given that this food is thickly coated with sticky sugar. (Baptiste-Henri Grégoire, *Essai sur la régénération physique, morale, et politique des juifs,* 1788)

Later, the composer Richard Wagner was to complicate the picture with his considerations of voice and manner:

There is something foreign about the outward aspect of the Jew that makes this nationality supremely repugnant; instinctively we wish to have nothing in common with a man who looks like that . . . It is impossible to imagine the representation of an antique or modern stage-character by a Jew, be it as hero or lover, without feeling instinctively that there is something incongruous, indeed ridiculous, in such a performance . . . But what repels us above all else is the particular tone with which the Jew speaks . . . Our ears are particularly offended by the shrill, sibilant, strident sounds of this idiom. The Jew uses words and constructs his phrases in a way quite contrary to the spirit of our national language . . . When we listen to him, our attention dwells involuntarily on how he speaks rather than on what he says. This point is of the greatest importance in explaining the expression produced by the musical works of the Jews. Listening to a Jew talking, we are inevitably offended by the fact of finding his discourse devoid of all truly human expression . . . It is natural that the inherent aridness of the Jewish character which we find so distasteful finds its greatest expression in song, which is the liveliest, most authentic manifestation of individual feeling. We might recognize the Jew's artistic aptitude for any other art except that of song, which nature herself seems to have denied him. (*Judaism in Music,* 1850)

Hitler proceeds with a greater delicacy, bordering almost on envy: "In regard to young people, clothes should take their place in the service of education . . . If the beauty of the body were not completely forced into the background to-day through our stupid manner of dressing, it would not be possible for thousands of our girls to be led astray by Jewish mongrels, with their repulsive crooked waddle" (*Mein Kampf,* 1925, translated by James Murphy).

From facial appearance to customs: this brings us to the Jewish enemy who kills young children and drinks their blood. He appears very early, for example, in Chaucer's *Canterbury Tales,* where there is a story, much like that of Saint Simonino of Trento, of a young boy seized while passing through the Jewish quarter while singing "O alma redemptoris mater." His throat is slashed and his body thrown into a pit.

The Jew who kills young children and drinks their blood has a very complex genealogy: the same model existed earlier in Christianity, in the creation of the enemy within — the heretic. A single example is enough:

> In the evening, when we light the lamps and commemorate the passion, they take young girls initiated into their secret rites to a particular house, they snuff out their lamps as they wish no one to witness the indecencies about to take place, and give vent to their licentious practices on whomever it might be, even upon sister or daughter. Indeed they believe they are pleasing the demons by violating the divine laws that forbid union with those of the same blood. Once the ritual is over, they return home and wait for nine months to pass: when the time comes for the godless children to be born of a godless seed, they assemble once again in the same place. Three days after the birth, they seize the wretched children from their mothers, cut their tender limbs with a sharp blade, fill cups with the blood that spurts forth, burn the newborns while they are still breathing by throwing them on a pyre. Then they mix blood and ash in cups to obtain a horrible concoction with which they contaminate food and drink, secretly, like someone poisoning mead. Such is their communion. (Michele Psello, *De operatione daemonum,* eleventh century)

The enemy is sometimes seen as different and ugly because he belongs to a lower class. In *The Iliad,* Thersites ("crooked, lame in one foot; his shoulders rounded and bent over his chest; his head pointed and sprouting tufts of hair," book 2, line 212) is socially inferior to Agamemnon and Achilles, and is therefore jealous of them. There is little difference between Thersites and Edmondo de Amicis's character Franti in his novel *Cuore (Heart,* 1886): whereas Odysseus attacks Thersites, drawing blood, society punishes Franti with imprisonment.

> (25 October): And beside him there's a tough, cheeky-looking fellow called Franti who has already been expelled from another school . . . (21 January): Only one boy could laugh while Derossi was talking about the king's funeral, and that was Franti. I hate him. He's evil. When a father comes to school to reprimand his son, [Franti] thinks it's funny; when a boy cries, he laughs. He's

frightened of Garrone, and thumps the builder's son because he's small; he torments Crossi as his arm is paralyzed; he taunts Precossi, whom everyone likes; he even pokes fun at Robetti, in the second year, who walks on crutches after having saved a young child. He goads everyone who's weaker than him, and when it comes to blows, he gets vicious and hurts people. There's something repulsive about that low forehead, those dark eyes, which he keeps half-hidden beneath the peak of his waxed cotton cap. He fears nothing, laughs in the teacher's face, steals when he can, lies brazenly, is always arguing with someone, brings large pins to school to prick his classmates, he rips buttons off his jacket and off those of other boys, and plays with them, and his school bag, exercise books, textbooks are all crumpled, torn, dirty, his ruler dented, his pen chewed, his nails raw, his clothes creased and torn from fighting . . . The teacher sometimes pretends not to see his mischief, and that makes him worse. When he tried to treat him kindly, he insulted him; when he scolded him, he covered his face with his hands, as if he were crying, and he was laughing.

The born criminal and the prostitute are obvious examples of ugliness, due to their social position. But with the prostitute we enter another world, that of sexual enmity or what might be called sexual racism. For the male who dominates and writes, or by writing dominates, the woman has always been portrayed with hostility from the earliest times. Let us not be deceived by angelic descriptions of women. On the contrary, precisely because great literature is dominated by sweet, gentle creatures, the world of satire — which is that of the popular imagination — continually demonizes the woman, from antiquity, through the Middle Ages, and up to modern times. From antiquity, I will limit myself to one example from Martial: "You, Vetustilla, who have outlived three hundred consuls; you have but three hairs and four teeth and have the chest of a grasshopper, the legs and color of an ant. You walk about with a forehead more wrinkled than your gown and breasts like cobwebs . . . Your eyesight is like that of owls in the morning and you smell like he-goats; your buttocks are like those of a withered duck's bottom . . . Only the funeral torch can penetrate this vagina" (*Epigrams,* book 3, no. 93).

And who could be the author of this passage? "The female is an imperfect animal, stirred by a thousand passions that are disagreeable and loathsome even to think about, let alone to discuss . . . No other animal is less clean than she: not even the pig, wallowing in mud, is as ugly as they are, and if anyone should wish to deny this, let him examine their parts, let him search out the secret places where, in shame, they hide the fearful instruments with which they remove their superfluous humors." If someone as irreligious and bawdy as Giovanni Boccaccio (in *The Crow*) could think such a thing, then imagine what a medieval moralist must have thought and written to emphasize the Pauline principle that, if such temptation could be avoided, it would be better never to experience the pleasures of the flesh. The churchman Odo of Cluny recalled in the tenth century that

> the beauty of the body is only skin-deep. If men could see beneath the flesh, with the power of the Boeotian lynx to penetrate visually within, they would be nauseated just to look at women, for all this feminine charm is nothing but phlegm, blood, humors, gall. Consider what is hidden in the nostrils, in the throat, in the stomach: everywhere, filth . . . and we are repelled to touch vomit and ordure even with our fingertips. How then can we ever want to embrace what is merely a sack of excrement! (*Collationes,* book 3, chapter 133, col. 556 and 648)

From what might be called this "normal misogyny" we come to the creation of the witch, a masterpiece of modern civilization. The witch was certainly also known in classical antiquity, and I will mention only the witches in Apuleius's *Golden Ass* and in Horace: "I myself saw Candia, wrapped in a black gown, barefooted and hair disheveled, howling with the elder Sagana. Pallor had rendered both of them horrible to behold" (*Satires,* book 1, no. 8). But in antiquity, as in the Middle Ages, witches and wizards were generally linked to popular beliefs and were thought to represent fairly infrequent instances of possession. Rome at the time of Horace did not feel threatened by witches, and witchcraft in the Middle Ages was still regarded as a phenomenon of autosuggestion — in other words, the witch was someone who believed she was a witch, as the ninth-century *Canon episcopi* stated:

> Certain depraved women, having turned to Satan and been led astray by his illusions and seductions, believe and claim they have ridden certain beasts at night, in the company of a multitude of women, following Diana . . . Priests must constantly preach to God's people that these things are all raised in the minds of the faithful not by the divine spirit but by the force of evil. Satan, in fact, is transformed into an angel of light and takes possession of the mind of these poor women and rules over them due to their lack of faith and their incredulity.

And yet, at the dawn of the modern age, witches were said to meet in sects, to celebrate their sabbaths, to fly, to transform themselves into animals, and thus become the enemies of society, and as such to merit inquisitorial trials and death at the stake. This is not the place for examining the complex problem of the "witchcraft syndrome" — whether it represented a way of finding a scapegoat at a time of profound social crisis or the influence of Siberian shamanism or the phenomenon of eternal archetypes. What interests us here is the recurring model for the creation of an enemy — similar to the treatment of the heretic or the Jew. And it is not enough for men of science, such as Gerolamo Cardano in the sixteenth century, to raise their sensible objections:

> They are poor women of miserable condition, who scrape a living in the valleys feeding on chestnuts and herbs . . . Thus they are emaciated, deformed, ashen in color, with protruding eyes, and their gaze reveals a melancholy and bilious temperament. They are taciturn, distracted, and hardly distinguishable from those who are possessed by the devil. They are so firm in their opinions that any-

one listening to their stories alone would be quite sure the things they say with such conviction were true, things that have never happened and will never happen. (*De rerum varietate,* book 15)

A new wave of persecutions began in response to the spread of leprosy. Carlo Ginzburg, in his *Ecstasies: Deciphering the Witches' Sabbath* (1991, translated by Raymond Rosenthal), records that lepers were burned to death throughout France in 1321 because they had been convicted of trying to kill the whole population by poisoning water supplies, fountains, and wells: "Leprous women who had confessed to the crime spontaneously, or as a result of torture, were to be burnt, unless pregnant; in that eventuality, they must be kept segregated until their confinement and the weaning of their offspring—and then burnt."

It is not difficult to identify here the origins of every persecution of those thought to be spreading plague. But Ginzburg describes yet another aspect of this phenomenon: the contagious lepers were automatically identified with Jews and Saracens. Various chroniclers relate stories that accuse the Jews of aiding and abetting the lepers, and many of them were sent to the stake with the afflicted: "The local population took justice into their own hands, summoning neither priest nor bailiff: they closed the people in their homes, together with their livestock, goods, and chattels, and set fire to them."

One leader of such a group confessed he had been bribed by a Jew, who had given him some poison (made with human blood, urine, three herbs, and pieces of the consecrated host) placed in a sack that was weighted so it would easily sink to the bottom of a drinking fountain. But, he said, it was the king of Granada who had gone to the Jews—and another source also added the sultan of Babylon to the plot. Three traditional enemies—the leper, the Jew, and the Saracen—were thus brought together in one fell swoop. Reference to the fourth enemy, the heretic, was provided in a detail: the assembled lepers had to spit on the host and trample on the cross.

Rituals of this kind were later said to be practiced by witches. The fourteenth century saw the appearance of the first manuals for the trial of heretics by inquisition, such as the *Practica inquisitionis hereticae pravitatis* by Bernardo Gui and the *Directorium inquisitorum* by Niccolao Emeric, and in the fifteenth century (while Marsilio Ficino is translating Plato in Florence on the orders of Cosimo de' Medici and, according to a well-known schoolboys' ditty, people were preparing to sing "At last, at last, the Middle Ages are past!") John Nider's *Formicarius,* written between 1435 and 1437 and published in 1473, speaks for the first time in a modern vein about the various practices of witchcraft.

Innocent VIII wrote about these practices in the papal bull *Summis desiderantes affectibus* of 1484:

> It has recently reached our ears — to our great distress — that in certain regions of Germany . . . persons of both sexes, heedless of their own well-being and straying from the Catholic faith, have no hesitation in giving themselves carnally to devils incubus and succubus, letting the progeny of women, animals, fruits of the earth, die or perish . . . by means of spells, charms, incantations, and other odious magical practices . . . Seeking, as our office requires of us, by way of appropriate remedies, to prevent the scourge of heretical depravity from spreading its poison to the detriment of innocent people, the aforementioned inquisitors Sprenger and Kramer are permitted to exercise the inquisitorial office in those lands.

And Sprenger and Kramer, inspired also by the *Formicarius,* published their infamous *Malleus maleficarum* (*Hammer of the Witches*) in 1486.

The records of the inquisition in 1477 against Antonia, of the parish of Saint-Jorioz in the diocese of Geneva, provide one of a thousand examples of how a witch was created:

> The accused, having abandoned her husband, went with Masset to the place known as "laz Perroy" near the stream . . . where a synagogue of heretics was held, and found there a large number of men

and women, who courted, capered, and danced backwards with her. He then showed her a demon, called Robinet, who had the appearance of a Negro, saying: "Here is our master, to whom we must pay homage if you wish to have all you desire." The defendant asked him what she had to do . . . and the said Masset replied: "Disown God your creator, and the Catholic faith and that adulteress the Virgin Mary and accept this demon called Robinet as your lord and master and do whatever he wishes of you . . ." Having heard these words, the accused began to feel regretful and refused at first to comply. But she eventually disowned God her creator, saying: "I disown God my creator and the Catholic faith and the Holy Cross, and accept you, Demon Robinet, as my lord and master." And she paid homage to the demon by kissing his foot . . . Then in contempt of God she threw a wooden cross to the ground, trampled it under her left foot, and broke it . . . She was transported on a staff one and a half feet long; to reach the synagogues she had to lubricate it with the ointment contained in a pyx, which was filled with it, and place the staff between her thighs, saying: "Go, go to the devil!" and she was immediately transported swiftly into the air to the place of the synagogue. She also confesses that in the aforesaid place they ate bread and meat; they drank wine and danced again; the said demon, their master, having then transformed himself from a man into a black dog, they honored and worshiped him, kissing him on the behind; finally the demon, having doused the fire that was burning there with green flames illuminating the synagogue, exclaimed loudly: "Meclet! Meclet!" and upon that cry the men lay bestially with the women and she with the aforesaid Masset Garin. (quoted in *La civiltà delle streghe* by Giuseppina and Eugenio Battisti, 1964)

This testimony, with its various details about spitting on the cross and kissing the anus, is almost identical to the testimony given in the trial of the Knights Templar, which took place a century and a half before. What is surprising in this fifteenth-century trial is that not only are the inquisitors guided in their lines of questioning by what they have read of the earlier trials, but also, at the end of the interrogation, which seemed fairly summary, the victim is herself convinced of the truth of the accusations made against her. At the witchcraft trials, not only is a picture built up of the enemy, and not only does the victim in the end also admit to doing what she hasn't done, but through the act of confessing she becomes convinced that what she is saying is true. You will remember how a similar procedure is described in Arthur Koestler's *Darkness at Noon* (1940) — and how, during the trials under Stalin, a picture was first built up of the enemy and the victims were then persuaded to recognize themselves in that picture.

Even those who might otherwise hope to be viewed in a favorable light are induced, in this way, to become the enemy. Theater and literature provide us with examples of the "ugly duckling" who, having been scorned by his equals, adapts to the image they have of him. I will quote Shakespeare's *Richard III* as an example:

> But I — that am not shap'd for sportive tricks,
> Nor made to court an amorous looking glass —
> I . . . that am curtail'd of this fair portion,
> Cheated of feature by dissembling nature,
> Deform'd, unfinish'd, sent before my time
> Into this breathing world scarce half made up,
> And that so lamely and unfashionable
> That dogs bark at me as I halt by them —
> Why I . . . have no delight to pass away the time,
> Unless to spy my shadow in the sun
> And descant my own deformity.
> And therefore, since I cannot prove a lover
> To entertain these fair well-spoken days,
> I am determined to be a villain. (act 1, scene 1)

It seems we cannot manage without an enemy. The figure of the enemy cannot be abolished from the processes of civilization. The need is second nature even to a mild man of peace. In his case the image of the enemy is simply shifted from a human object to a natural or social force that in some way threatens us and has to be defeated, whether be capitalistic exploitation, environmental pollution, or third-world hunger. But though these are "virtuous" cases, even hatred of injustice, as Brecht reminds us, "makes the brow grow stern."

Is our moral sense therefore impotent when faced with the age-old need for enemies? I would argue that morality intervenes not when we pretend we have no enemies but when we try to understand them, to put ourselves in their situation. Aeschylus has no resentment toward the Persians, whose tragedy he experiences with them and from their point of view. Caesar treats the Gauls with great respect: at worst, he makes them appear rather wimpish each time they surrender. And Tacitus admires the Germans, crediting them with fine complexions and complaining only about their dirtiness and their reluctance to undertake heavy work as they cannot cope with heat and thirst.

Trying to understand other people means destroying the stereotype without denying or ignoring the otherness.

But let us be realistic. These ways of understanding the enemy are the prerogative of poets, saints, or traitors. Our innermost impulses are of quite another kind. In 1967 *Report from Iron Mountain on the Possibility and Desirability of Peace* was published in America by a certain "John Doe" (someone even suggested it was Galbraith).[1] It was clearly a pamphlet against war, or at least a pessimistic lament on its inevitability. But since, in order to wage war, we need an enemy to fight, the inevitability of war is linked to the inevitability of identifying and creating an enemy. In the pamphlet it is thus suggested with extreme seriousness that the reconversion of the whole of American society to a state of peace would be disastrous, since only war provides the basis for the harmonious development of human societies. Its organized wastage provides a valve that regulates the effective running of society. It resolves the problem of supplies. It is a driving force. War enables a community to recognize itself as a "nation"; a government cannot even establish its own sphere of legitimacy without the contrasting presence of war; only war ensures the equilibrium between

---

1. Edited by Leonard C. Lewin (New York: The Dial Press, 1967).

classes and makes it possible to locate and exploit antisocial elements. Peace produces instability and delinquency among young people; war channels all disruptive forces in the best possible way, giving them a "status." The army is the last hope for outcasts and misfits; the system of war alone, with its power over life and death, induces people to pay a blood price for institutions far less central to social organization than war, such as the motor car. From the ecological point of view, war provides a release valve for surplus lives; and though, until the nineteenth century, only the most courageous members of society (soldiers) were killed in war while worthless members survived, current technology has made it possible to overcome this problem with the bombardment of urban centers. Bombardment limits the population boom better than ritual infanticide, monasticism, sexual mutilation, extensive use of capital punishment . . . War makes it possible, at last, to develop a truly "humanistic" art in which conflicted situations predominate.

If this is so, the cultivation of the enemy must be intensive and continuous. George Orwell provides an excellent example of this in *Nineteen Eighty-four* (1949):

> The next moment a hideous, grinding speech, as of some monstrous machine running without oil, burst from the big telescreen at the end of the room. It was a noise that set one's teeth on edge and bristled the hair at the back of one's neck. The Hate had started.
>
> As usual, the face of Emmanuel Goldstein, the Enemy of the People, had flashed onto the screen. There were hisses here and there among the audience. The little sandy-haired woman gave a squeak of mingled fear and disgust. Goldstein was the renegade and backslider who once, long ago . . . had been one of the leading figures of the Party . . . He was the primal traitor, the earliest defiler of the Party's purity. All subsequent crimes against the Party, all treacheries, acts of sabotage, heresies, deviations, sprang directly out of his teaching. Somewhere or other he was still alive and hatching his conspiracies . . .
>
> Winston's diaphragm was constricted. He could never see the face of Goldstein without a painful mixture of emotions. It was a

lean Jewish face, with a great fuzzy aureole of white hair and a small goatee beard—a clever face, and yet somehow inherently despicable, with a kind of senile silliness in the long thin nose near the end of which a pair of spectacles was perched. It resembled the face of a sheep, and the voice, too, had a sheep-like quality. Goldstein was delivering his usual venomous attack upon the doctrines of the Party—. . . he was demanding the immediate conclusion of peace with Eurasia, he was advocating freedom of speech, freedom of the press, freedom of assembly, freedom of thought, he was crying hysterically that the revolution had been betrayed . . .

Before the Hate had proceeded for thirty seconds, uncontrollable exclamations of rage were breaking out from half the people in the room . . .

In its second minute the Hate rose to a frenzy. People were leaping up and down in their places and shouting at the tops of their voices in an effort to drown the maddening bleating voice that came from the screen. The little sandy-haired woman had turned bright pink, and her mouth was opening and shutting like that of a landed fish . . . The dark-haired girl behind Winston had begun crying out "Swine! Swine! Swine!" and suddenly she picked up a heavy Newspeak dictionary and flung it at the screen. It struck Goldstein's nose and bounced off: the voice continued inexorably. In a lucid moment Winston found that he was shouting with the others and kicking his heel violently against the rung of his chair. The horrible thing about the Two Minutes Hate was not that one was obliged to act a part, but that it was impossible to avoid joining in . . . A hideous ecstasy of fear and vindictiveness, a desire to kill, to torture, to smash faces in with a sledgehammer, seemed to flow through the whole group of people like an electric current, turning one even against one's will into a grimacing, screaming lunatic. (part 1, chapter 1)

We do not have to reach the excesses of *Nineteen Eighty-four* to recognize ourselves as beings who need an enemy. We are witnessing the fear that can be caused by new influxes of migrants. In Italy today, Romanians are being portrayed as the enemy by extending to a whole ethnic culture the characteristics of a few of its marginalized members, thus providing an ideal scapegoat for a society that, caught up in change — including ethnic change — is no longer able to recognize itself.

Sartre provides the most pessimistic vision in this respect in *No Exit*. We can recognize ourselves only in the presence of an Other, and on this the rules of coexistence and submission are based. But it is more likely that we find this Other intolerable because to some degree he is not us. In this way, by reducing him to an enemy, we create our hell on earth. When Sartre locks up three people who have died, who didn't know each other in life, in a hotel bedroom, one of them realizes the terrible truth: "Wait! You'll see how simple it is. Childishly simple. Obviously there aren't any physical torments. You agree, don't you? And yet, we're in hell. And no one else will come here. We'll stay in this room, the three of us, for ever and ever . . . In short, there's someone absent here, the official torturer . . . It's obvious what they're after — an economy of manpower . . . each of us will act as torturer of the two others" (translated by Stuart Gilbert).

[Lecture given at Bologna University on May 15, 2008, as part of a series of evenings on the classics, published in *Elogio della politica*, edited by Ivano Dionigi (Milan: BUR, 2009).]

Absolute and Relative

I F YOU ARE HERE this evening in spite of the terroristic title of my talk, that means you are prepared for anything – though a serious lecture about Absolute and Relative ought to last at least two and a half thousand years, as long as the debate itself. The title of this year's Milanesiana festival is "Conflict and the Absolute," and naturally I have been wondering what these words mean. It's the most basic question any philosopher must ask.

Since I haven't been to the festival's other events, I did a search on the Internet for pictures by artists who refer to the Absolute, and there I found Magritte's *La connaissance absolue,* as well as various works by others I needn't name – *Painting the Absolute, Quête d'absolu, In Search of the Absolute, Marcheur d'absolu* – and several advertisements like the one for Absolut vodka. The Absolute, it seems, is selling well.

The notion of Absolute also brought to mind one of its opposites, namely, the notion of Relative, which has become rather fashionable ever since leading churchmen, and even some secular thinkers, began a campaign against what they call relativism. It's a term that has become derogatory, used for almost terroristic ends, like Berlusconi's use of the word *communism*. But here I will limit myself to confounding your ideas rather than clarifying them, suggesting how each of these terms—depending on the circumstances—means many different things, and that they shouldn't be used as baseball bats.

According to dictionaries on philosophy, Absolute means anything that is *ab solutus,* free from ties or limits, something that does not depend on something else, which has its own inherent reason, cause, and explanation. Something therefore very similar to God, in the sense that he describes himself as "I am who I am" (*ego sum qui sum*), to which everything else is contingent and therefore does not have its own inherent cause and—even if it happens to exist—it could just as well not exist, or not exist tomorrow, as is the case with the solar system or with each one of us.

As we are contingent beings, and therefore destined to die, we desperately need to think there is something to fasten onto that will not perish, in other words, an Absolute. But this Absolute can be transcendent, like the biblical divinity, or immanent. Without discussing Spinoza or Giordano Bruno, with the idealist philosophers we ourselves enter to become part of the Absolute, since the Absolute (for example, in Schelling) would be the indissoluble unity of the conscious being and of such things that were once considered extraneous to the individual, such as nature or the world. In the Absolute we identify with God, we are part of something that is not yet fully complete: a process, a development, infinite growth, and infinite self-definition. But if this is how things are, we can never define or know the Absolute since we are part of it, and trying to understand it would be like Baron Munchausen pulling himself out of the swamp by his own hair.

The alternative, then, is to think of the Absolute as something that we are not, and that is elsewhere, not dependent on us, like the god of Aristotle, who thinks of himself as thinking, and who, according to Joyce in *A Portrait of the Artist as a Young Man,* "remains within or behind or beyond or above his handiwork, invisible, refined out of existence, indifferent, paring his fingernails." Back in the fifteenth century, in fact, Nicholas of Cusa in *De docta ignorantia* wrote, "Deus est absolutus."

But since God is Absolute, said Nicholas, he can never fully be reached. The relationship between our knowledge and God is the same as that between a polygon and the circumference into which it is drawn: as the sides of the polygon gradually increase, it comes closer and closer to the circumference, but the polygon and the circumference will never be the same. God, said Nicholas, is like a circle whose center is everywhere and whose circumference is nowhere.

Is it possible to imagine a circle with its center everywhere and no circumference? Obviously not. And yet we can describe it, which is what I am doing now, and each of you understand that I'm talking about something to do with geometry, except that it is geometrically impossible and unimaginable. There is therefore a difference between whether or not we can imagine a thing and whether we can nevertheless name it, give it some meaning.

What does it mean to use a word and give it a meaning? It means many things.

A. *To have instructions for recognizing such an object or situation or event.* For example, the meaning of the word *dog* or *stumble* includes a series of descriptions, also in the form of images, for recognizing a dog and distinguishing it from a cat, and differentiating a stumble from a jump.

B. *To have a definition or classification.* Definitions and classifications are given to a dog but also to events or situations such as voluntary manslaughter, as opposed to involuntary manslaughter.

C. *To know about other properties, facts, or encyclopedic details of a given entity.* For example, I know that dogs are faithful and good for hunting or guarding; I know that a conviction for voluntary manslaughter can lead to a particular sentence of imprisonment, and so forth.

D. *Where possible, to have instructions on how to produce the corresponding object or event.* I know what *vase* means since I know how a vase is produced even though I am not a potter—and the same is true for terms like *decapitation* or *sulfuric acid*. Whereas for a word like *brain*, I know meanings A and B, and some of the properties in C, but I do not know how to produce one.

A magnificent case in which I know properties A, B, C, and D is offered by C. S. Peirce, who defines *lithium* as follows:

If you look into a textbook of chemistry for a definition of *lithium*, you may be told that it is that element whose atomic weight is 7 very nearly. But if the author has a more logical mind he will tell you that if you search among minerals that are vitreous, translucent, grey or white, very hard, brittle and insoluble, for one which imparts a crimson tinge to an unluminous flame, this mineral being triturated with lime or witherite rats-bane, and then fused, can be partly dissolved in muriatic acid; and if this solution be evaporated and the residue be extracted with sulphuric acid, and duly purified, it can be converted by ordinary methods into a chloride, which being obtained in the solid state, fused, and electrolyzed with half a dozen powerful cells, will yield a globule of pinkish silvery metal that will float on gasoline; and the material of *that* is a specimen of lithium. The peculiarity of this definition—or rather this precept that is more serviceable than a definition—is that it tells you what the word *lithium* denotes by prescribing what you are to *do* in order to gain a perceptual acquaintance with the object of the word. (*Collected Papers,* volume 2, paragraph 330)

This is a good example of a complete and satisfactory representation of the meaning of a term. But other expressions have a hazy and imprecise meaning—and lesser degrees of clarity. For example, even the expression "the highest even number" has a meaning, since we know it would have to have the property of being divisible by two (and we would therefore be able to distinguish it from the highest odd number), and we also have a vague instruction on how to generate it, in the sense that we can imagine counting higher and higher numbers, separating odd from even . . . Except that we realize we will never get there, as in a dream wherein we think we can grasp hold of something without ever managing to do so. But an expression like "a circle whose center is everywhere and whose circumference is nowhere" doesn't suggest any rule for producing a corresponding object. Not only does it fail to support any definition, but it frustrates every effort to imagine one, apart from making us feel dizzy. An expression like Absolute has a definition that is, all in all, tautological (a thing is absolute when it is not contingent; it is contingent when it is not absolute), but it does not suggest descriptions, definitions, and classifications; we cannot think of any instructions for producing anything corresponding to it, nor do we know any of its properties, except to suppose that it has everything and it is probably what Saint Anselm of Canterbury described as *id cujus nihil majus cogitari possit* (something beyond which nothing greater can be thought), which brings to mind the saying attributed to the pianist Arthur Rubinstein: "Do I believe in God? No, what I believe in is something much greater." What we can imagine at most in trying to conceive of God is the classic night in which all cows are black.

It is certainly possible not only to name but also to represent visually what we cannot conceive. But these images do not represent the unimaginable: they simply invite us to try to picture something unimaginable, and then frustrate our expectation. What we experience in trying to understand them is that very sense of impotence expressed by Dante in the last canto of *Paradise* (no. 33, lines 82–96, translated by Mark Musa), when he wants to describe to us what he saw at the moment when he fixed his gaze on the Divinity, but all he can say is that he cannot tell us, and resorts to the intriguing metaphor of a book with an infinite number of pages:

> O grace abounding and allowing me to dare
> to fix my gaze on the Eternal Light,
> so deep my vision was consumed in It!

I saw how it contains within its depths
all things bound in a single book by love,
of which creation is the scattered leaves:

how substance, accident, and their relation
were fused in such a way that what I now
describe is but a glimmer of that Light.

I know I saw the universal form,
the fusion of all things, for I can feel,
while speaking now, my heart leap up in joy.

One instant brings me more forgetfulness
than five and twenty centuries brought the quest,
that stunned Neptune when he saw Argo's keel.

And the sense of impotence is no different when expressed by
Leopardi seeking to describe infinity ("my mind sinks in this immensity: / and foundering is sweet in such a sea").[1]

This is why it is artists who have come here, to this festival, to talk
about the Absolute. Pseudo-Dionysius the Areopagite wrote that,
since the Divine One is so distant from us that he can be neither understood nor reached, he must be spoken of through metaphors and
allusions, but above all, as an indication of the paucity of our language,
through negative symbols, contrasting expressions: "And they extol It
also with names of the most remote things, sweet-smelling ointment,
cornerstone, and they also clothe It in the form of a wild beast, attaching to It the characteristics of a lion and a panther, and saying that
It will be like a leopard and an angry bear" (*Celestial Hierarchy*, chapter 2).

Certain naive philosophers have suggested that poets alone can describe Being or the Absolute; but in fact they express only the indefinite. The poet Mallarmé spent his life trying to express an "orphic explanation of the earth": "I say: a flower! and out of the oblivion where

---

1. Giacomo Leopardi, *L'infinito*, c. 1819 – translation by Jonathan Galassi.

my voice relegates all context, insofar as something other than known calyxes is musically raised, an idea itself and gentle, the absence of all fragrance (*Crise de vers,* 1895).

This passage, in truth, is untranslatable. It tells us only that a word is chosen, alone in the white space that surrounds it, and it inevitably unleashes the totality of the non-said, but in the form of an absence. In fact, "to *name* an object, this means suppressing three-fourths of the enjoyment of the poem, which involves working it out little by little: to *suggest,* that is the dream" (*Sur l'évolution littéraire: Réponse à l'enquête de Jules Huret,* 1891).

Mallarmé pursued this dream throughout his life, but it eluded him. Dante had taken such elusion for granted from the very beginning, well aware that it is diabolic pride to claim that infinity can be expressed in finite terms, and he had avoided this inadequacy of poetry by making poetry out of such an inadequacy: his is not poetry that seeks to say the unsayable, but rather poetry about the impossibility of saying it.

It should be remembered that Dante was a believer (as were Pseudo-Dionysius and Nicholas of Cusa). Can you believe in an Absolute and claim it is unimaginable and indefinable? Certainly, provided the impossible thought of the Absolute is replaced by a feeling of the Absolute and therefore by faith, as "the substance of those hoped-for things and argument for things we have not seen" (Dante, *Paradise,* canto 24, lines 64–65). Elie Wiesel, during this festival, recalled the words of Kafka: that it is possible to talk with God, but not about God. If the Absolute is philosophically a night in which all cows are black, then for the mystic who, like John of the Cross, perceives it as a "dark night" ("O night that guided me / O night more lovely than the dawn"), it is a source of ineffable feeling. John of the Cross expresses his mystical experience through poetry: in the face of the indescribability of the Absolute, we may feel reassured by the fact that this unsatisfied tension can be materially resolved in a finished form. This enabled Keats, in his "Ode on a Grecian Urn," to see Beauty as a substitute for the experience of the Absolute: " 'Beauty is truth, truth beauty,' — that is all / Ye know on earth, and all ye need to know."

And that is fine for those who have decided to follow an aesthetic religion. But John of the Cross would have told us that it was only his mystical experience of the Absolute that assured him of the only possible truth. This has led many men of faith to the conviction that those philosophers who reject the possibility of knowing the Absolute are automatically rejecting every criterion of truth, or by rejecting such a thing as an absolute criterion of truth, they are rejecting the possibility of experiencing the Absolute. But it is one thing to say that a philosophy rejects the possibility of knowing the Absolute, and another thing to say that it rejects every criterion of truth — even that relating to the contingent world. Are truth and experience of the Absolute then so inseparable?

Confidence that something is true is fundamentally important for the survival of human beings. If we were unable to consider that what others tell us is either true or false, society would not be possible. We wouldn't even be able to exclude the possibility that a box with ASPIRIN written on it didn't in fact contain strychnine.

A specular theory of truth is that it is *adaequatio rei et intellectus,* as if our mind were a mirror that, provided it works properly and is not distorted or misted, must truly reflect things as they are. It is a theory supported, for example, by Thomas Aquinas, but also by Lenin in *Materialism and Empirio-criticism* (1909), and since Aquinas could not have been a Leninist, it ought to follow that Lenin was a neo-Thomist — without, of course, realizing it. In reality, other than in states of ecstasy, we are obliged to say what our mind reflects. Nevertheless, we define as true (or false) not the things themselves but the assertions we make about how things are. Alfred Tarski's famous definition says that the statement "Snow is white" is true if, and only if, snow is white. Let us leave aside for the moment the whiteness of snow, which is more and more open to dispute, and consider another example: the statement "It is raining" (set between quotation marks) is true only if outside it is raining (without quotation marks).

The first part of the definition (between quotation marks) is a verbal statement and represents nothing other than itself, but the second part should express how things in fact are. Nevertheless, something that ought to be a state of things is expressed once again in words. To avoid this linguistic mediation we ought to say that "It is raining" (between quotation marks) is true if there is that thing there (and, without saying anything, we point to the rain that is falling). But although this way of indicating the evidence of the senses can be used with rain, it would be more difficult to do the same with the statement "Earth revolves around the sun" (since, if anything, the senses would tell us quite the opposite).

To establish whether the statement corresponds to a particular set of circumstances, it is necessary to have interpreted the word *rain* and to have formed a definition of it. It needs to have been established that (a) to talk of rain it is not enough to feel drops of water falling from above (as there could be someone watering flowers on a balcony above), (b) the drops must be of a certain consistency (otherwise we would talk of mist or frost), (c) the sensation must be continuous (otherwise we would say it was trying to rain but had come to nothing), and so forth. Having decided this, we have to pass on to an empirical test, which in the case of rain can be done by anyone (all we have to do is hold out our hand and trust our senses).

But in the case of the statement "Earth revolves around the sun," the ways for testing it are more complex. What meaning does the word *true* have for each of the following statements?

1. I have a stomachache.
2. Last night I dreamed that Mother Teresa appeared to me.
3. Tomorrow it will certainly rain.
4. The world will end in 2536.
5. There is life after death.

Statements 1 and 2 express a subjective fact, but the stomachache is a clear and irrepressible sensation, whereas when I recall a dream I had last night, I may not be sure the memory is accurate. What is more, the two statements cannot be directly verified by other people. A doctor would, of course, have certain ways of checking whether I actually have gastritis or whether I'm a hypochondriac, but a psychoanalyst would have more difficulty if someone tells him she has seen Mother Teresa in a dream, since she could easily be lying.

Statements 3, 4, and 5 are not directly verifiable. But whether it will rain tomorrow can be verified tomorrow, whereas whether the world will end in 2536 is rather more of a problem (and here we distinguish between the reliability of a weather forecaster and that of a prophet). The difference between statements 4 and 5 is that 4 will become true or false in 2536, whereas 5 will continue to remain empirically undecidable *per saecula saeculorum*.

Now let's consider these statements:

6. The sum of the angles of a triangle is 180 degrees.
7. Water boils at 100 degrees Celsius.
8. The apple is an angiosperm.
9. Napoleon died on May 5, 1821.
10. We reach the coast following the path of the sun.
11. Jesus is the Son of God.
12. The correct interpretation of the holy scriptures is decided by the teachings of the church.
13. An embryo is already a human being and has a soul.

Some of these statements are true or false according to the rules we have stipulated: the sum of the angles of a triangle is 180 degrees only in the context of a Euclidean system of postulates; that water boils at a hundred degrees at standard atmospheric pressure, that is, at sea level, is true not only if we accept a law of physics elaborated through inductive generalization, but also on the basis of the definition of degrees centigrade; an apple is an angiosperm only on the basis of certain rules of botanical classification.

Some require us to trust facts ascertained by others before us: we believe it is true that Napoleon died on May 5, 1821, because we accept what the history books tell us, but we must always recognize the possibility that an unpublished document discovered tomorrow in the British naval archives might show that he died on another date. Sometimes for utilitarian reasons we adopt an idea as true that we know to be false: for example, to find our way in the desert, we behave as if it were true that the sun moves from east to west.

As for statements of a religious nature, we shall not say they are undecidable. If the evidence of the Gospels is accepted as historical, the proof of the divinity of Christ would be accepted as such by a Protestant. But this would not be so for the teachings of the Catholic Church. The statement regarding embryos having a soul depends entirely on stipulating the meanings of expressions such as *life, human,* and *soul.* Thomas Aquinas, for example (see the essay "No Embryos in Paradise"), claimed that, like animals, they had only a sensitive soul and therefore were not yet human beings equipped with a rational soul, and would not participate in the resurrection of the flesh. Today he would be accused of heresy, but at that very civilized time they made him a saint.

It is therefore a matter of deciding each time which criteria for truth we are using.

It is on the very recognition of various degrees of verifiability or acceptability of a truth that our sense of tolerance is based. I may be obliged, from a scientific and educational point of view, to fail a student who claims that water boils at ninety degrees, like the right angle — as was apparently once suggested in an exam — but even a Christian ought to accept that for some people there is no other god than Allah and Muhammad is his prophet (as we likewise ask Muslims to do for Christians concerning Christian doctrine).

And yet, in light of recent controversies, it seems that this distinction between different criteria of truth, typical of modern thought and in particular of logical scientific thought, produces a relativism that is seen as a historical malaise of contemporary culture, which rejects all idea of truth. But what do anti-relativists mean by relativism?

Some encyclopedias of philosophy tell us there is a cognitive relativism, by which objects can be known only under conditions determined by human faculties. But in this sense Kant would also have been a relativist, and he certainly didn't reject the possibility of setting out laws of universal value — and what is more, he believed in God, if only on moral grounds.

Yet in another philosophical encyclopedia we find that relativism means "every idea that does not admit absolute principles in the field of knowledge and action." But it is a different matter to reject absolute principles in the sphere of knowledge or the sphere of action. There are people who are prepared to assert that the statement "Pedophilia is evil" is a truth relative only to a particular system of values, seeing that it was or is accepted or tolerated in certain cultures, but who are nevertheless prepared to assert that the Pythagorean theorem must be valid for all times and all cultures.

No one could seriously include Einstein's theory of relativity under the label of relativism. To say that a measurement depends on the conditions of movement of the observer is regarded as a valid principle for every human being in every time and place.

Relativism, as a philosophical doctrine as such, came into existence with nineteenth-century positivism, together with the claim that the Absolute is unknowable and, at most, is a movable limit of ongoing scientific research. But no positivist has ever claimed it is not possible to arrive at scientific truths that are objectively verifiable and valid for all.

A philosophical position that, on a cursory reading of the textbooks, might be defined as relativistic is so-called holism, according to which every statement is true or false (and acquires a meaning) only within an organic system of assumptions, a given conceptual scheme, or, as others have said, within a given scientific paradigm. A holist claims (rightly) that the notion of space has a different meaning in the Aristotelian system than it does in the Newtonian system, so that the two systems are incommensurable, and that one scientific system is as valid as the other to the extent to which it succeeds in explaining a series of phenomena. But the holists are the first to tell us there are systems that cannot actually explain a series of phenomena, and that

some are far better because they succeed better than the others in doing so. Thus even the holist, in his apparent tolerance, has to deal with
matters that require explanation and, even when he doesn't say so, follows what I would call a minimal realism: the belief that things exist or
behave in a certain way. Perhaps we will never understand it, but if we
don't believe it exists, our research would make no sense, and it would
make no sense to go on trying out new systems to explain the world.

The holist is usually said to be a pragmatist, but here again it is
better not to be over-hasty in reading the textbooks: the true pragmatist, such as Peirce, did not say that ideas are true only if they prove to
be effective, but that they show their effectiveness when they are true.
When he supported fallibilism, namely, the possibility that all of our
ideas could always be revoked in case of doubt, at the same time he
stated that through the continual correction of its knowledge the human community carries forward "the torch of truth."

What gives rise to a suspicion of relativism in these theories is
the fact that the various systems are incommensurable. Certainly the
Ptolemaic system is incommensurable with the Copernican system,
and only in the first do the notions of epicycle and deferent assume a
precise meaning. But the fact that the two systems are incommensurable does not mean they are not comparable, and it is precisely by com-
paring them that we understand what are the celestial phenomena that
Ptolemy explained with the notions of epicycle and deferent, and we
understand that they were the same phenomena that the Copernicans
wanted to explain according to a different conceptual scheme.

The holism of philosophers is similar to linguistic holism, wherein
a given language, through its semantic and syntactic structure, is said
to impose a particular vision of the world in which the speaker is, so
to speak, a prisoner. Benjamin Lee Whorf, for example, pointed out
that there is a tendency in Western languages to consider many events
as objects, and an expression such as "three days" is grammatically
equivalent to "three apples"; whereas some Native American languages focus on the process — they see events whereas we see things.
For this reason, the Hopi language would be better equipped than

English for defining certain phenomena studied by modern physics. And Whorf also pointed out that the Eskimos have four different
words for snow, depending on its texture, and they would therefore
see different things where we see only one. Leaving aside the fact that
this suggestion has been disputed, a Western skier knows nevertheless
how to distinguish between various textures of snow, and it would be
quite enough for an Eskimo to meet us to understand perfectly well
that when we say "snow" for the four things that he supposedly describes in different ways, we are behaving in the same way as a Frenchman who uses the word *glace* for ice, glacier, ice cream, mirror, and
window glass—and the Frenchman isn't such a prisoner of his own
language that he shaves in the morning looking at himself in an ice
cream.

Finally, apart from the fact that not all contemporary thought accepts the holistic approach, holism follows the line of those perspec-
tive-based theories of knowledge according to which reality can be
given different perspectives and each perspective matches one aspect of it, even if it doesn't exhaust its unfathomable richness. There
is nothing relativistic in claiming that reality is always defined from a
particular point of view (which does not mean subjective and individual), nor does the assertion that we see it always and only under a certain description stop us from believing and hoping that what we picture is always the same thing.

Alongside cognitive relativism, the encyclopedias refer to cultural
relativism. First Montaigne, then Locke, had begun to understand, at
a time when Europe was coming into more significant contact with
other peoples, that different cultures not only have different languages
or mythologies but also different conceptions of morality (all reasonable in their own context). It seems indisputable that certain primitive people in the forests of New Guinea, even today, regard cannibalism as legitimate and commendable (while an Englishman would not),
and it seems similarly indisputable that certain countries treat adulterous women in a manner different from ours. But, first, recognizing the
variety of cultures does not mean denying that certain types of con-

duct are more universal (for example, a mother's love for her children, or the fact that people generally use the same facial expressions to express disgust or delight), and second, it does not automatically imply that this recognition is tantamount to moral relativism, the idea that since there are no ethical values valid for all cultures, we can freely adapt our behavior to fit our personal tastes or interests. Recognizing that another culture is different, and must be respected in this, does not mean abdicating our own cultural identity.

How then has the specter of relativism come to be built up as a standard ideology, the canker of contemporary civilization?

There is a secular critique of relativism, directed mainly against the excesses of cultural relativism. Marcello Pera, who presents his arguments in a book titled *Senza radici* (*Without Roots,* 2004), written jointly with the then Cardinal Ratzinger, is well aware that there are differences between cultures, but claims there are certain values of Western culture (such as democracy, the separation between church and state, and liberalism) that have proved superior to those of other cultures. Now, Western culture has good reason to regard itself as more developed than others in terms of these ideas, but in claiming that such superiority ought to be universally evident, Pera uses a dubious argument. He says, "If members of culture B freely show they prefer culture A and not vice versa—if, for example, there is a migrant influx from Islamic countries to the West and not vice versa—then it is reasonable to believe that A is better than B." The argument is weak when we recall that the Irish in the nineteenth century did not immigrate en masse to the United States because they preferred that Protestant country to their beloved Catholic Ireland, but because at home they were dying of starvation as a result of potato blight. Pera's rejection of cultural relativism is dictated by the concern that tolerance for other cultures degenerates into acquiescence, and that the West is giving way under the pressure of immigration to the demands of outside cultures. Pera's problem is not the defense of the Absolute but the defense of the West.

Giovanni Jervis, in his book *Contro il relativismo* (2005), gives us a portrait of a relativist—a strange blending of a late Romantic, post-modern thinker of Nietzschean origin with a follower of New Age thinking—that seems to be constructed to support his arguments. This person's relativism appears irrational, unscientific. Jervis denounces a reactionary quality in cultural relativism: to claim that every form of society is to be respected and justified, and even idealized, encourages the segregation of populations. Moreover, those cultural anthropologies that, rather than seeking to identify a continuity of biological characteristics and behavior between populations, have instead emphasized their diversity due to culture alone—giving too much importance to cultural factors and ignoring biological ones—and have indirectly supported once again the primacy of the spirit over matter, thereby supporting the arguments of religious thought.

It is therefore not clear whether relativism is contrary to the religious spirit or whether it is a disguised form of religious thought. If only the anti-relativists would agree among themselves. But the fact is that different people mean different things when they talk about relativism.

For some Christians there is a double fear: that cultural relativism necessarily leads to moral relativism, and claiming there are different ways of verifying the truth of a proposition casts doubt on the possibility of recognizing an absolute truth.

On cultural relativism, Cardinal Ratzinger, in various doctrinal notes of the Congregation for the Doctrine of the Faith, saw a close relationship between cultural relativism and ethical relativism, regretting that various people claim ethical pluralism to be the condition for democracy.

Cultural relativism does not, as I have already said, imply ethical relativism. Cultural relativism allows a Papuan from New Guinea to put a spike through his nose and yet, by virtue of an ethical principle that our group does not hold in question, it does not allow an adult (not even a priest) to abuse a seven-year-old child.

As for the contrast between relativism and truth, Pope John Paul II, in his encyclical *Fides et ratio,* stated that "abandoning the investigation of being, modern philosophical research has concentrated instead upon human knowing. Rather than make use of the human capacity to know the truth, modern philosophy has preferred to accentuate the ways in which this capacity is limited and conditioned. This has given rise to different forms of agnosticism and relativism that have led philosophical research to lose its way in the shifting sands of widespread skepticism."

And Ratzinger, in a homily of 2005, said that "a dictatorship of relativism is being established, which recognizes nothing definite or allows as a single lone measure the personal self and its wishes. Yet we have another measure: the Son of God, the true man" ("Missa pro eligendo romano pontefice," April 18, 2005).

Here are two opposing notions of truth, one as a semantic property of what is said and the other as a property of divinity. This is due to the fact that both notions of truth appear in the holy scriptures (at least according to the translations through which we know them). Truth is sometimes used as a correspondence between something said and the way in which things are ("Verily, verily, I say unto you," in the sense of "That's truly what I'm saying") and sometimes truth is an intrinsic property of divinity ("I am the way, the truth, and the life"). This led many fathers of the church to positions that Ratzinger would now define as relativistic, since they said it was not important to worry about whether a given statement on the world corresponded to the way in which things were, provided it focused attention on the only truth worthy of such a name — the message of salvation. Saint Augustine, when faced with the dispute over whether the earth was round or flat, seemed inclined to think it was round, but recalled that such knowledge did not help to save the soul, and therefore took the view that in practice one was much the same as the other.

It is difficult to find among Cardinal Ratzinger's many writings a definition of truth that does not invoke the truth revealed and embodied in Christ. But if the truth of faith is truth revealed, why contrast it with the truth of philosophers and scientists, which is a concept of another sort, with other purposes and character? It would be enough to follow Thomas Aquinas, who, in *De aeternitate mundi*, knowing perfectly well that to support Averroës's view about the eternity of the world was a terrible heresy, accepted through faith that the world was created, but admitted that from the cosmological point of view it could not be rationally demonstrated either that it was created or that it was eternal. For Ratzinger, however, in his contribution to a book entitled *Il monoteismo* (2002), the essence of all modern philosophical and scientific thought is as follows:

> Truth as such—so it is thought—cannot be known, but we can gradually advance only by small steps of establishing what is true and false. There is a growing tendency to replace the concept of truth with that of consensus. But this means that man becomes detached from the truth and thus also from the distinction between good and evil, submitting completely to the principle of the majority . . . Man plans and "builds" the world without pre-set criteria and thus necessarily exceeds the concept of human dignity, so that even human rights become problematic. In such a conception of reason and rationality there is no space left for the concept of God.

This extrapolation, which passes from a prudent concept of scientific truth as an object of continual investigation and correction, to a declaration of the destruction of all human dignity, is unsustainable. That is, unsustainable unless all modern thought is identified with this line of reasoning: there are no facts but only interpretations, which leads to the declaration that existence has no basis and therefore that God is dead, and finally that if there is no God, then anything is possible.

Now, Ratzinger and the anti-relativists are, generally speaking, neither fantasists nor conspiracy theorists. Quite simply, the anti-relativists whom I shall describe as moderate or critical identify in their enemy that specific form of extreme relativism whereby facts do not exist, only interpretations; those anti-relativists I shall call radicals extend this claim to the whole of modern thought, committing an error that — at least when I was at university — would have failed them in their history of philosophy exam.

The idea that there are no facts but only interpretations began with Nietzsche and is explained very clearly in "On Truth and Lies in a Non-Moral Sense" (1873). Since nature has thrown away the key, the mind works on conceptual fictions that it calls truth. We believe we are talking about trees, colors, snow, and flowers, but they are metaphors that do not correspond to the original entities. When faced with the multiplicity of individual leaves, there is no primordial "leaf," the model upon which "all leaves were perhaps woven, sketched, measured, colored, curled, and painted — but by incompetent hands." A bird or insect perceives the world in a different way than we do, and it is quite meaningless to say which perception is more accurate, because to do so we would need to have the criterion of "correct perception," which does not exist. Nature "knows no forms and no concepts, nor even any species, but only an X which for us remains inaccessible and indefinable." Truth then becomes "a movable host of metaphors, metonyms, anthropomorphisms," of poetical inventions that have become rigid knowledge, "illusions whose illusory nature has been forgotten."

Nietzsche, however, avoids considering two phenomena. One is that, by adjusting to the constraints of our dubious knowledge, we manage to some extent to reckon with nature: when someone has been bitten by a dog, the doctor knows what sort of injection to give, even if he knows nothing about the actual dog that bit the person. The other is that every so often nature compels us to expose our knowledge as illusory and to choose an alternative (which is then the problem of the revolution of cognitive paradigms). Nietzsche is aware of the existence of natural constrictions, which appear to him as "terrible forces" that continually press in upon us, conflicting with our "scientific" truths. But he refuses to conceptualize them, sensing that it was to escape from them that we built our conceptual armor, as a defense. Change is possible, not in the form of reorganization, but as a permanent poetic revolution: "If each of us had a different kind of sensuous perception, if we ourselves could only perceive things as, variously, a bird, a worm, or a plant does, or if one of us were to see a stimulus as red, a second person were to see the same stimulus as blue, while a third were ever to hear it as a sound, nobody would ever speak of nature as something conforming to laws." Art (together with myth) therefore "constantly confuses the cells and the classifications of concepts by setting up new translations, metaphors, metonyms; it constantly manifests the desire to shape the given world of the waking human being in ways which are just as multiform, irregular, inconsequential, incoherent, charming and ever-new, as things are in the world of dreams" (translation by Ronald Speirs).

If these are the conditions, the first possibility would be to take refuge in dream as an escape from reality. But Nietzsche himself admits that this dominion of art over life would be deceptive, though supremely enjoyable. Alternatively — and this is the real lesson that posterity has taken from Nietzsche — art can say what it says because it is the Individual himself who accepts whatever definition, since it is unfounded. This fading out of the Individual coincided for Nietzsche with the death of God. This enables some Christians to draw from this proclamation of death a false Dostoyevskian conclusion: if God does not exist, or no longer exists, then all is permissible.

But if there is no heaven or hell, then it is the nonbeliever who realizes it is essential for us to save ourselves on earth through benevolence, understanding, and moral law. Eugenio Lecaldano published a book in 2006[2] that claimed, with ample evidence, that only by leaving God to one side can we lead a truly moral life. I certainly do not intend to establish here whether Lecaldano and the authors he cites are correct; I wish only to point out that there are those who claim that the absence of God does not eliminate the ethical problem — and Cardinal Martini was well aware of this when he established a teaching post in Milan for nonbelievers. That Cardinal Martini did not then become

---

2. Eugenio Lecaldano, *Un'etica senza Dio* (Rome-Bari: Laterza, 2006).

pope may cast doubt on the divine inspiration of the papal conclave, but such matters go beyond my competence. Elie Wiesel reminded us, a couple of weeks ago, that those who imagined they could do what they liked were *not* those who thought God was dead, but those who thought they themselves were God (a common failing among dictators, great and small).

In any event, the idea that there are no facts but only interpretations is certainly not shared by all of contemporary thought, the greater part of which makes these objections to Nietzsche and his followers:

1. If there were no facts but only interpretations, then an interpretation would be an interpretation of what?

2. If interpretations interpret each other, there would still have to have been an object or event in the first place that had spurred us to interpret.

3. If the individual were not definable, we would still have to explain who it is who is talking about it metaphorically, and the problem of saying something true would be shifted from the object to the subject of the knowledge. God might be dead, but not Nietzsche. On what basis do we justify the presence of Nietzsche? By saying he is only a metaphor? But if he is, who says so? And not only that, but even if reality is described using metaphors, in order to be elaborated there have to exist words that have a literal meaning and denote things we understand through experience: I cannot call a table support a "leg" unless I have a nonmetaphorical notion of the human leg, knowing its form and function.

4. And finally, in claiming that there is no longer a criterion for verification between one thing and another, we forget that what is outside us (which Nietzsche calls the terrible forces) every so often opposes our attempts to express that criterion even metaphorically—that, let us say, you cannot cure an inflammation by using the phlogiston theory, whereas you can

with antibiotics; and therefore one medical theory is better than another.

Therefore, an Absolute does not perhaps exist, or if it exists it is neither imaginable nor attainable, but natural forces do exist that support or challenge our interpretations. If I interpret an open door painted in trompe l'oeil as a real door and go to walk straight through it, the fact that it is an impenetrable wall will undermine my interpretation.

There must be a way in which things are or behave — and the evidence is not only that all men are mortal, but also that if I try to pass through a wall, I break my nose. Death and that wall are the only form of Absolute about which we can be in no doubt.

The evidence of that wall, which says no when we want to interpret it as if it were not there, will perhaps be a fairly modest criterion of truth for guardians of the Absolute, but, to quote Keats, "that is all / Ye know on earth, and all ye need to know."

[Lecture given during the Milanesiana festival of literature, music, and cinema, July 9, 2007.]

The Beauty of the Flame

T HE THEME OF THIS YEAR'S Milanesiana festival is the four elements. To speak about all four would be beyond me, so I have chosen to limit myself to fire.

Why? Because, though still essential to our lives, of all the elements it is the one most liable to be forgotten. We breathe air all the time, we use water every day, we continually tread the earth, but our experience of fire is in danger of gradually diminishing. The role once played by fire has slowly been taken over by invisible forms of energy; we have separated our idea of light from that of the flame, and our only experience of fire now is that of gas (which we hardly notice), the matchstick or cigarette lighter (at least for those who still smoke), and the flicker of candles (for those who still go to church).

A lucky few still have a fireplace, and this is where I would like to begin. In the 1970s I bought a house in the country with a fine hearth. For my children, then between ten and twelve, the experience of fire, of burning logs, of flames, was something entirely new, and I realized when the fire was lit they lost all interest in television. The flame was more beautiful and varied than any television program – it told countless stories, it could flare up at any moment, it didn't follow the set patterns of the television show.

Perhaps, among our contemporaries, the person who reflected

most on the poetry, mythology, psychology, and psychoanalysis of fire was Gaston Bachelard, who could hardly avoid encountering fire during his research into archetypes associated with human imagination from earliest times.

The heat of the fire recalls the heat of the sun, which itself is seen as a ball of fire; fire hypnotizes and is therefore the first object and source of wonder; fire reminds us of the first universal injunction (not to touch it), thus becoming an epiphany of law; fire is the first creature that, as it takes life and grows, devours the two pieces of wood that have generated it – and this birth of fire has a strong sexual significance since the seed of the flame is unleashed through friction – and yet, if we want to pursue a psychoanalytical interpretation, we will recall how for Freud the condition for taking control of the fire is renunciation of the pleasure of quenching it with urine, and therefore the renunciation of instinctual life.

Fire is a metaphor for many impulses, from the fire of anger to being inflamed with amorous infatuation; fire is metaphorically present in every discussion about passions, in the same way as it is always linked metaphorically to life through the color that it shares with blood. Fire as heat governs that maceration of food matter that is digestion and shares with the feeding process the fact that, to stay alive, it must be continually fueled.

Fire is ever present as an instrument for every transformation, and fire is called for when something has to be changed: to prevent the fire from dying out requires a care similar to that for a newborn baby; fire immediately highlights the fundamental contradictions in our lives; it is the element that brings life and the element that brings death, destruction, and suffering; it is the symbol of purity and purification but also of filth, since it produces ash as its excrement.

Fire can be a light too strong to look at, like the sun. But properly harnessed, as in the light of a candle, it flickers and casts shadows, accompanying our night vigils, during which a solitary flame takes hold of our imagination, with its rays that spread out into darkness, and the candle symbolizes a source of life and, at the same time, a sun that dies away. Fire is born from matter, to be transformed into an ever lighter and airier substance, from the red or bluish flame at its base to the white flame at its peak, until it vanishes in smoke . . . In that sense the nature of fire is ascendant, it reminds us of transcendence, and yet, perhaps because we learn that it lives at the heart of the earth, from which it bursts forth only when volcanoes erupt, it is a symbol of infernal depth. It is life, but it also dies down and is continually fragile.

And to conclude my consideration of Bachelard I'd like to quote this passage from *Psychoanalysis of Fire* (1964):

> From the notched teeth of the chimney hook there hung the black cauldron. The three-legged cooking pot projected over the hot embers. Puffing up her cheeks to blow into the steel tube, my grandmother would rekindle the sleeping flames. Everything would be cooking at the same time: the potatoes for the pigs, the choice potatoes for the family. For me there would be a fresh egg cooking in the ashes. The intensity of the fire cannot be measured by an hour glass; the egg was ready when a drop of water, perhaps of saliva, evaporated on its shell. I was surprised, then, to learn that Papin watched over his cooking pot using the same methods as my grandmother. Before the egg I had to eat bread soup . . . But on the days when I was on my good behaviour, they would bring out the waffle iron. Rectangular in form it would crush down the fire of thorns burning red as the spikes of gladioli. And soon the *gaufre,* or waffle, would be pressed against my pinafore, warmer to the fingers than to the lips. Yes, then indeed I was eating fire, eating its gold, its odour, and even its crackling while the burning *gaufre* was crunching under my teeth. And it is always like that, through a kind of extra pleasure — like a dessert — that the fire shows itself a friend of man. (translated by Alan C. M. Ross)

Fire is therefore very many things. As well as a physical phenomenon, it becomes a symbol, and like all symbols is ambiguous, polysemous, evoking different meanings according to the circumstances. This evening, therefore, I will not be attempting a psychoanalysis of fire but instead a rough-and-ready semiotic exploration, searching out the various meanings it has acquired for all of us who are warmed by it and sometimes die by it.

FIRE AS A DIVINE ELEMENT

Seeing that our first experience of fire happens indirectly, through the light of the sun, and directly, through the untamable forces of lightning and uncontrollable fires, it was obvious that fire had to be associated from the very beginning with divinity, and in all the primitive religions we find some form of fire cult, from worship of the rising sun to keeping in the inner sanctum of the temple the sacred fire that must never burn out.

In the Bible fire is always an epiphanic image of the divine — Elijah would be taken away on a chariot of fire, the just would triumph in radiant fire ("So let all thine enemies perish, O Lord: but let them that love him be as the sun when he goeth forth in his might," Judges 5:31; "And they that be wise shall shine as the brightness of the firmament; and they that turn many to righteousness as the stars for ever and ever," Daniel 12:3; "And in the time of their visitation they shall shine, and run to and fro like sparks among the stubble," Wisdom 3:7), whereas the fathers of the church spoke of Christ as *lampas, lucifer, lumen, lux, oriens, sol iustitiae, sol novus, stella.*

The first philosophers thought of fire as a cosmic principle. For Heraclitus — according to Aristotle — fire was the *archè*, the origin of all things, and in certain fragments it seems that Heraclitus did actually hold this view. He is thought to have claimed that the universe regenerates itself in every era through fire, that there is a mutual exchange of all things with fire, and of fire with all things, like the exchange of goods for gold and gold for goods. And, according to Diogenes Laertius, he is said to have claimed that everything is formed from fire and returns to fire; that all things, through condensation and

rarefaction, are mutations of fire (which through condensation transforms itself into humidity, humidity consolidates into earth, earth in
turn liquefies into water, and water produces luminous evaporations
that fuel new fire). But alas, we know that Heraclitus was by definition
obscure, that "the Lord whose oracle is at Delphi neither reveals nor
conceals, but gives a sign," and many take the view that the references
to fire were only a metaphor to explain the extreme changeability of
everything. In other words, *panta rei,* everything flows movably and
changeably, and not only (I paraphrase) do we never bathe twice in
the same river, but things never burn twice in the same flame.

We find perhaps the most beautiful identification of fire with the
divine in the work of Plotinus. Fire is a manifestation of the divine because, paradoxically, the One from which everything emanates, and
about which nothing can be said, does not move and is not consumed
in an act of creation. And this primal object can be conceived only as if
it were an irradiation, like a brilliant light encircling the sun and cease-
lessly generated from it, while the sun remains just the same as it was,
unchanging (*Fifth Ennead,* tractate 1, section 6).

And if things are created from an irradiation, nothing can be more
beautiful on earth than fire, which is the very figure of divine irradiation. The beauty of a color, which is something simple, is created
from a form that dominates the obscurity of matter and from the presence in the color of an incorporeal light, which is its formal reason.
For this reason, fire is beautiful in itself more than any other thing,
because of its intangibility of form: of all bodies it is the lightest, to
the point of being almost intangible. It always remains pure because
it does not contain within itself the other elements that make up matter, whereas all other elements contain fire within themselves: they, in
fact, can be heated, whereas fire cannot be cooled. Fire alone, by its
nature, contains colors; other things receive their form and color from
it, and when they distance themselves from the firelight they lose their
beauty.

The pages of Pseudo-Dionysius the Areopagite (fifth to sixth centuries), which influenced the whole of medieval aesthetics, show a strong neoplatonic influence. This can be seen in *Celestial Hierarchy:*

> I believe, then, that fire manifests what is most divine in the celestial minds; for the holy authors often describe the super-essential and formless essence—which has no form at all—with the symbol of fire, since it has many aspects of the divine character, if such can be said, insofar as it can be found in visible things. In fact, the sensitive fire is found, so to speak, in all things and passes through all things without mingling with them, and is separate from everything and at the same time, being all-luminous, remains, as it were, hidden, unknown in its essential nature—until it is placed before a material toward which it can demonstrate its own action—it cannot be taken hold of, nor seen, but it takes hold of everything. (chapter 15)

Medieval perceptions of beauty are dominated by concepts of clarity and luminosity, as well as proportion. Cinema and video games encourage us to think of the Middle Ages as a succession of "dark" centuries, not only metaphorically but also in terms of nocturnal colors and dark shadows. Nothing could be more wrong. People in the Middle Ages certainly lived in dark spaces—forests, castle corridors, small rooms faintly lit by their fireplaces; but apart from the fact that they were people who went to sleep early and were more accustomed to the day than the night (of which the Romantics would be so fond), the Middle Ages was a time of bright hues.

It was a period that identified beauty with light and color (as well as with proportion), and this color was always elementary, a symphony of reds, blues, gold, silver, white, and green, without subtleties and half-tones; the splendor is generated from the overall effect rather than deriving from a light that envelops things from outside or exalts the color beyond the outlines of the figure. In medieval miniatures the light seems to emanate from the objects.

In medieval poetry this sense of radiant color is always present: the grass is green, blood is red, milk pure white, and a pretty woman, in the words of Guido Guinizzelli, has a "a face of snow colored in carmine" (not to forget, later on, Petrarch's "clear, fresh, sweet waters").

Fire animates the visions of mystics, in particular the writings of Hildegard of Bingen. See, for example, *Liber scivias:*

> I saw a dazzling light and in it a human form, the color of sapphire, which was all ablaze with bright gentle fire, and that splendorous light spread throughout the whole bright fire, and this fire was bright with that splendorous light, and that light was dazzling and that fire bright with the whole human form, producing a single glow of matchless virtue and power . . . The flame consists of a splendid clarity, an inherent vigor and a fiery ardor, but the splendid clarity possesses it so that it is resplendent, the inherent vigor so that it endures, and the fiery ardor so that it burns. (book 2, part 2)

Not to forget the visions of brilliant light in Dante's *Paradise* and which have been depicted in their maximum splendor by a nineteenth-century artist, Gustave Doré, who sought (as only he could) to depict those scenes of radiance, those flaming vortexes, those lamps, those suns, that clearness that hides "like an horizon brightening with the dawn" (canto 14, line 69), those white roses, those rubicund flowers that shine out in the third part of *The Divine Comedy*, where even the vision of God appears like an ecstasy of fire:

> Within Its depthless clarity of substance
> I saw the Great Light shine into three circles
> in three clear colours bound in one same space;
> the first seemed to reflect the next like rainbow
> on rainbow, and the third was like a flame
> equally breathed forth by the other two.
> (canto 33, lines 115–20; translated by Mark Musa)

The Middle Ages was dominated by a cosmology of light. Already by the ninth century John Scotus Eriugena said, "This universal manufactory of the world is a vast lamp consisting of many parts like many lights to reveal the pure species of intelligible things and to sense them with the mind's eye, instilling divine grace and the help of reason into the heart of learned followers. It is right then that the theologian calls God the Father of Enlightenment, since all things are from Him, for which and in which He manifests himself and in the light of the lamp of his wisdom he unifies and makes them" (*Commentary on the Celestial Hierarchy*, chapter 1).

In the thirteenth century the cosmology of light put forward by the English churchman Robert Grosseteste built up a picture of the universe formed by a single flow of luminous energy, a source both of beauty and being, making us think of a sort of Big Bang. The astral spheres and natural areas of the elements are created from the single light by gradual rarefaction and condensation, producing the infinite shades of color and the volumes of things. Saint Bonaventure of Bagnoregio (*Commentary on the Book of Sentences*, book 2, distinction 12, chapters 1 and 2) was to record that light is the common nature found in all bodies, whether celestial or terrestrial; light is the substantial form of bodies, and the more they possess it, the more they are a real and worthy part of existence.

HELLFIRE

But while fire moves across the sky and shines down on us, it likewise erupts from the bowels of the earth, bringing death. Thus, from the very earliest times, fire has also been associated with the infernal depths.

In the book of Job (41:19–21), from the mouth of Leviathan "go burning lamps, and sparks of fire leap out . . . His breath kindleth coals, and a flame goeth out of his mouth." In Revelation, when the seventh seal is broken, hail and fire come to devastate the earth, the bottomless pit opens up, and from it emerge smoke and locusts; the four angels, set loose from the river Euphrates where they were bound, move with countless armies of men wearing breastplates of fire. And when the Lamb reappears and reaches the supreme judge on a white cloud, the sun burns the survivors. And, after Armageddon, the beast and the false prophet will be thrown into a lake of burning sulfurous fire.

In the Gospels, sinners are cast into everlasting fire:

> As therefore the tares are gathered and burned in the fire; so shall it be in the end of this world. The Son of man shall send forth his angels, and they shall gather out of his kingdom all things that offend, and them which do iniquity; And shall cast them into a furnace of fire: there shall be wailing and gnashing of teeth. (Matthew 13:40–42)

> Then shall he say also unto them on the left hand, Depart from me, ye cursed, into everlasting fire, prepared for the devil and his angels. (Matthew 25:41)

Curiously, in Dante's inferno there is less fire than we might expect, since the poet contrives to think up a whole range of torments, but we may be satisfied with heretics lying in fiery tombs; men of violence plunged into pools of blood; blasphemers, sodomites, and usurers struck by rains of fire; simoniacs shoved head-first into pits, with flames lapping at their feet; and barrators submerged in boiling pitch.

Hellfire was certainly more prevalent in baroque writings, with descriptions of the torments of hell that exceed the violence of Dante, not least because they are unredeemed by the inspiration of art—like this passage by Saint Alphonsus de Liguori:

> The punishment that most torments the senses of the damned, is the fire of hell . . . Even in this life, the pain of fire is the greatest of all; but there is much difference between our fire and that of hell which, says Saint Augustine, makes ours seem painted . . . Thus the wretched will be surrounded by fire, like wood inside a furnace. The damned will find themselves with an abyss of fire beneath, an abyss above, and an abyss around them. If they touch, see or breathe, they will touch, see or breathe nothing but fire. They

will be in the fire like fish in water. But this fire will not only sur-
round the damned, but will enter even their bowels to torment
them. Their body will become all fire, so that their bowels will
burn within their belly, their heart within their breast, their brains
within their head, their blood within their veins, even their marrow
with their bones: every lost soul will become in himself a furnace of
fire. (*Apparecchio alla morte,* consideration 26)

And Ercole Mattioli, in *Pietà illustrate* (1694), wrote,

Great wonder will it be that a fire alone contains perfectly within
it, according to great theologians, the coldness of ice, the stings
of thorns and iron, the venom of asps, the poisons of vipers, the
cruelty of all wild beasts, the malevolence of all elements and stars
. . . Yet greater wonder, *et supra virtutem ignis,* will be that such
fire, though one specie alone, can make distinction in tormenting
those who sin most, being called by Tertullian *sapiens ignis,* and
by Eusebius of Emesa *ignis arbiter,* since, having to match, according to the greatness and diversity of supplicants, the greatness and
diversity of their sins . . . , the fire, almost as if it were endowed with
reason and full knowledge, to distinguish between sinner and sinner, shall make its rigors felt with more or less severity.

And so we arrive at the last secret of Fatima by Sister Lucia, ex-
shepherdess:

The secret consists of three distinct parts, two of which I am now
going to reveal. The first part is the vision of hell. Our Lady showed
us a great sea of fire, which seemed to be underground. Plunged in
this fire were demons and souls in human form, like transparent
burning embers, all blackened or burnished bronze, floating about
in the conflagration, now raised into the air by the flames that issued from within themselves together with great clouds of smoke,
now falling back on every side like sparks in a huge fire, without
weight or equilibrium, and amid shrieks and groans of pain and
despair, which horrified us and made us tremble with fear. The demons could be distinguished by their terrifying and repulsive like-

ness to frightful and unknown animals, all black and transparent. (Congregation for the Doctrine of the Faith, *The Message of Fatima,* June 26, 2000)

ALCHEMICAL FIRE

Halfway between holy fire and hellfire is fire as an alchemical operator. Fire and crucible seem to be essential in alchemical practice, which seeks to operate on a raw material so as to obtain from it, through a series of manipulations, the philosopher's stone. This is capable of projection, transmuting base metals into gold.

The manipulations of the raw material take place through three stages, distinguished by the color the material gradually assumes: the black work, the white work, and the red work. The black work involves a heating (and therefore the use of fire) and decomposition of the matter, the white work is a process of sublimation or distillation, and the red work is the final stage (red is the color of the sun, which often symbolizes gold, and vice versa). The hermetical furnace, the *athanor,* is an essential instrument, but alembics, vessels, and mortars are also used, each with their symbolic names, such as the philosophical egg, maternal womb, wedding chamber, pelican, sphere, sepulcher, and so forth. The essential substances are sulfur, mercury, and salt. But the procedures are never clear, since the language of alchemists is based on three principles:

1. As the object of the art is highly secret and not to be divulged — the secret of secrets — no expression ever says what it seems to say, no symbolic interpretation will ever be definitive, because the secret will always be elsewhere: "Poor fool! Can you be so naive as to believe we are openly teaching you the greatest and most important of secrets? I assure you that anyone who wants to explain what the Hermetic Philosophers

write according to their ordinary and literal meaning will find himself caught up in the twists and turns of a labyrinth from which he cannot escape, and won't have Ariadne's thread to guide him out of it." (Artefius)

2. When it seems that ordinary substances such as gold, silver, or mercury are being spoken of, other substances are in fact being described — philosopher's gold or mercury — which have nothing at all to do with them.

3. While no description is ever what it seems, everything always relates to the same secret. As the *Turba philosophorum* states, "Know that we are all in agreement, whatever we say . . . One person clarifies what the other has concealed and he who really searches will find everything."

When does fire intervene in the alchemical process? If alchemical fire can be compared with the fire that precedes digestion or gestation, it ought to intervene during the course of the black work, when heat, acting over and against radical, metallic, viscous, oily humidity, produces the *nigredo*. If we can accept a text like the *Dictionnaire mythohermétique* by Dom Pernety (Paris: Delalain, 1787), we read that

when heat acts on these matters, they are changed first into powder, and oily and gluey water, which rises as a vapor to the top of the vase, then descends again in dew or rain, to the bottom, where it becomes almost as an oily black broth. This is why it has been called Sublimation and Volatilization, Ascension and Descension. The water then coagulating more and more, becomes like black tar, which has caused it to be named fetid and stinking earth, also because it emits a musty odor of sepulchers and tombs. ("La clef de l'oeuvre," pp. 155–56)

But statements can also be found in the textbooks to the effect that the terms *distillation, sublimation, calcination,* or *digestion,* or the terms *firing, reverberation, dissolution, descent,* and *coagulation,* are none other than the same "Operation," carried out in a single vessel, in other words, a firing of the substance. Thus, concludes Pernety,

> this Operation must be regarded as unique, but expressed in different terms; and it will be understood that all the following expressions signify the same thing: distil by alembic; separate the soul from the body; burn; calcinate; unite the elements; convert them; change one into the other; corrupt; melt; engender; conceive; bring into the world; exhaust; moisten; wash with fire; beat with the hammer; blacken; putrefy; rubify; dissolve; sublimate; grind; reduce to powder; crush in the mortar; pulverize on marble — and many other similar expressions all mean simply to cook in the same way, until dark red. Care must therefore be taken not to remove the vase from the fire, because if the material cools down, all is lost. ("Règles générales," pp. 202–6)

But what fire is being described, seeing that different writers speak from time to time about fire of Persia, fire of Egypt, fire of the Indies, elementary fire, natural fire, artificial fire, fire of ashes, fire of sand, fire of filings, fire of fusion, fire of flames, fire against nature, Algir fire, Azothic fire, celestial fire, corrosive fire, fire of matter, lion fire, fire of putrefaction, dragon fire, dung fire, and so forth?

Fire heats the furnace throughout, from the beginning to the red work. But is the word *fire* also perhaps a metaphor for the red matter that appears in the alchemical process? And here, in fact, according to Pernety, are some of the names given to the red stone: red gum, red oil, ruby, vitriol, ashes of tartar, red body, fruit, red stone, magnesium, red oil, starry stone, red salt, red sulfur, blood, poppy, red wine, red vitriol, cochineal, and also "fire, fire of nature" ("Signes," pp. 187–89).

Alchemists have therefore always worked with fire, and fire is the basis of alchemical practice. Yet fire itself constitutes one of the most impenetrable mysteries of alchemy. As I have never produced gold, I cannot provide the answer to this problem, and so pass on to another type of fire, another type of alchemy, that of the artist, where fire becomes an instrument of new birth, and artists set themselves up to imitate the gods.

FIRE AS THE ORIGIN OF ART

Plato recounts in *Protagoras* that

once upon a time there were gods, but no mortal creatures . . . and when they were about to bring these creatures to light, they charged Prometheus and Epimetheus to provide and distribute the most appropriate faculties for each race. But Epimetheus asked Prometheus to let him do the distribution himself: "And when I have completed the distribution," he added, "you shall come and see." And so, having thus persuaded him, he started the work of distribution. And to some races he gave strength without speed, while the weaker races he equipped with speed. And to others he gave weapons of defense and attack, while for others, who were defenseless by nature, he devised other faculties to guarantee their safety. To those races that he made small, he gave the capacity to escape using their wings, or to hide underground; whereas to those he made large he gave the possibility of saving themselves with their size. And he distributed all other faculties in this way, so that they balanced each other . . . and when he had provided the various races with the means to avoid mutual destruction, he devised a way for them to defend themselves against the inclemency of the seasons sent by Zeus, covering them with thick hair and leathery skin, sufficient to defend them from coldness and capable of protecting them from hot weather, and such that, when they slept in their lairs, these would serve as natural blankets suitable for each of them. And some he shod with hoofs; others he gave tough skin and no blood. Then he provided different food for the different races: to some he gave the grass of the land, to others the fruits of trees, to others roots. And he allowed some races to devour other races of animals for food; and he provided that the former would have fewer offspring, and that the offspring of the latter would be numerous, to ensure the preservation of the race.

Now Epimetheus, who was not particularly clever, had failed to notice he had used up all the faculties for the animals: but at this point the human race had still not been provided for, and he did not know what to do with it. While he was in this situation of embarrassment, Prometheus came to see the distribution, and realized that whereas all the other creatures were properly provided for, man was naked, barefoot, homeless, and defenseless . . .

So Prometheus, in this embarrassing situation, not knowing what salvation to devise for man, stole technical wisdom and fire from Hephaestus and Athena (since without fire it was impossible to acquire and use that wisdom) and he gave it to man. (sections 320c–321d)

With the conquest of fire, the arts are born — at least in the Greek sense of technical skills — and thus the dominion of man over nature. What a shame that Plato had not read Lévi-Strauss, and had not also told us that the discovery of fire marked the beginning of cooked food; but cooking is, after all, an art and was therefore included under the platonic notion of *techne.*

Benvenuto Cellini gives an excellent description of how much fire has to do with the arts in his *Life,* recounting how he fused his Perseus, covering him in a clay mold and then, with a slow fire, removed the wax from it,

which came out through the many vents that I had made, for the more there are, the better do the molds fill. And when I had finished removing the wax I made a funnel around my Perseus, that is to say around the said mold, of bricks, interlacing one above the other, and I left many spaces through which the fire could the better emerge. Then I began to arrange the wood carefully, and I kept up the fire for two days and two nights continuously; to such purpose that when all the wax had been extracted, and the said mold was afterwards well baked, I immediately began to dig the ditch wherein to bury my mold, with all those skilful methods that this fine art directs us . . .

And holding it very carefully upright, in such a fashion that it hung exactly in the middle of the ditch, I caused it to descend very gently as far as the bottom of the furnace . . .

When I saw it was thoroughly firm, as well as that method of filling it in, together with the placing of those conduit pipes properly in their places . . . I turned to my furnace, which I had made them fill with many lumps of copper and other pieces of bronze. And having piled the one upon the top of the other after the fashion that our profession indicates to us, that is to say raised up, so as to make a way for the flames of the fire, whereby the said metal derives its heat quicker, and by it melts and becomes reduced to liquid, I then happily told them to set light to the said furnace. And laying on those pieces of pinewood, which from the greasiness of that resin that the pine exudes, and from the fact that my little furnace was so well built, it acted so well that . . . the workshop took fire, and we were afraid lest the roof should fall upon us. From the other side toward the kitchen garden the heaven projected upon me so much water and wind that it cooled my furnace. Combatting this for several hours under these perverse conditions, employing so much more effort than my strong vigor of constitution could possibly sustain, there sprang upon me a sudden fever, the greatest that can possibly be imagined in the world, by reason of which I was forced to take to my bed. (book 2, section 75)

And so, after so much planning, accompanied by accidental fire, artificial fire, and bodily fever, his statue took form.

But if fire is a divine element, then man, at the same time, in learning how to make fire, appropriates a power that until then had been reserved for the gods, and so even the fire he lights in the temple is the effect of an act of pride. The Greek civilization immediately gives this connotation of pride to the conquest of fire and it is curious how all the celebrations of Prometheus, not only in Greek tragedy but also later in art, emphasize not so much the gift of fire as the punishment that follows it.

FIRE AS AN EPIPHANIC EXPERIENCE

When the artist accepts and recognizes with pride and with hubris that he resembles the gods, and sees art as a substitute for divine creation, then decadent sensibility opens the way for likening aesthetic experience to fire, and fire to epiphany.

The concept of epiphany (if not the term) first appears with Walter Pater in the conclusion to his essay on the Renaissance. It is no surprise that the famous conclusion opens with a quote from Heraclitus. Reality is a sum of forces and elements that arise and gradually fall away, and only superficial experience makes us see them as solid and fixed in an importunate presence: "But when reflexion begins to act upon those objects they are dissipated under its influence, their cohesive force seems suspended like a trick of magic." We find ourselves among a group of impressions that are unstable, flickering, inconsistent: habit is broken, ordinary life fades away, and from this, beyond this, there remain single moments that can be grasped for an instant and immediately fade away. "Every moment some form grows perfect in hand or face; some tone of the hills or the sea is choicer than the rest; some mood of passion or insight or intellectual excitement is irresistibly real and attractive to us—for that moment only."

To maintain this ecstasy is "success in life": "While all melts under our feet, we may well catch at any exquisite passion, or any contribution to knowledge that seems by a lifted horizon to set the spirit free for a moment, or any stirring of the senses, strange dyes, strange colours, and curious odours, or work of the artist's hands, or the face of one's friend" (Walter Pater, *The Renaissance: Studies in Art and Poetry*, 1873).

All decadent writers feel aesthetic and sensual ecstasy in terms of radiance. But perhaps it was D'Annunzio who first linked aesthetic ecstasy to the idea of fire; we will not be so banal as to associate him only with the rather hackneyed idea that (as Mila di Codro shrills in *The Daughter of Iorio*) "the flame is beautiful." The idea of aesthetic ecstasy as an experience of fire appears in his novel *Il fuoco* (*The Flame*). Before the beauty of Venice, Stelio Effrena has the experience of fire:

> Each moment vibrated through the matter like an unbearable flash of lightning. Everything glittered in a sublime jubilation of light, from the crosses erect on the top of domes swollen by prayer to the delicate salt-crystal droplets hanging beneath the bridges. Just as the look-out on the mast-top shouts aloud of a storm at sea, so the golden angel on the top of the highest tower burst into flame and announced the coming. And so he came! He came seated on a cloud like a chariot of fire, the hem of his purple garments trailing behind him. (translated by Susan Bassnett)

James Joyce, the supreme theorist on epiphany, had read, loved, and was inspired by D'Annunzio's novel. "By an epiphany Stephen meant a sudden spiritual manifestation, whether in the vulgarity of speech or of gesture or in a memorable phrase of the mind itself" (*Stephen Hero*). This experience always appears in Joyce as fiery. In his *Portrait of the Artist as a Young Man,* the word *fire* is repeated fifty-nine times, and *flame* and *flaming* thirty-five times, not to mention other similar words, such as *radiance* or *splendour*. In *Il fuoco,* Foscarina listens to the words of Stelio and feels "attracted to that blazing atmosphere like the hearth of a forge." For Stephen Dedalus aesthetic ecstasy always appears as flashes of splendor and is expressed using metaphors of the sun. The same happens for Stelio Effrena. Let us compare two passages. First, D'Annunzio:

> The boat veered violently. A miracle caught it. The first rays of the sun pierced through the heaving sail, glittered on the bold angels on the bell-towers of San Marco and San Giorgio Maggiore, turned the sphere of the Fortuna to flame, crowned the five mitres on the Basilica with lightning . . . "Hail to the Miracle." A superhuman feeling of power and freedom swelled the young man's heart, as the wind swelled the sail that was transfigured for him. He stood in the crimson splendour of the sail and in the splendour of his own blood.

And then Joyce: "His thinking was a dusk of doubt and self-mistrust, lit up at moments by the lightnings of intuition, but lightnings of so clear a splendour that in those moments the world perished about his feet as if it had been fire-consumed; and thereafter his tongue grew heavy and he met the eyes of others with unanswering eyes, for he felt that the spirit of beauty had folded him round like a mantle."

REGENERATING FIRE

For Heraclitus, as we have seen, the universe regenerates itself through fire in every era. Empedocles was, it seems, on more familiar terms with fire—it was to gain divinity, or to persuade his followers that he was divine, that he threw himself (at least according to some) into Mount Etna. This final purification, this choice of annihilation in fire, has fascinated poets from all periods. Suffice it to recall Hölderlin:

> Have you not seen? They are recurring
> The lovely times of my entire life again today
> And something greater still is yet to come;
> Then upward, son, upward to the very peak
> Of ancient holy Etna, that is where we'll go
> For gods have greater presence on the heights
> With my own eyes this very day I shall survey
> The streams and islands and the sea.
> And may the sunlight, hovering golden over all
> These waters, deign to bless me in departure,
> The splendid youthful light of day, which in
> My youth I loved. Then all about us both
> Eternal stars will scintillate in silence as
> The glowing magma surges from volcanic depths
> And tenderly to all-impelling spirit of the ether will
> Arrive and touch us. Oh, then!
> (*The Death of Empedocles,* translated by
> David Farrell Krell)

Between Heraclitus and Empedocles, then, there is another aspect of fire — fire not only as creator but at the same time as destroyer and regenerator. The Stoics talked about *ekpyrosis* as the great conflagration (or fire and end of the world) through which everything, being derived from fire, returns to fire at the end of its evolutionary cycle. The idea of *ekpyrosis* does not actually suggest that purification through fire can be achieved by human planning and achievement. But certainly behind many sacrifices based on fire there is an idea that, by destroying, fire purifies and regenerates. And thus the sacral nature of death at the stake.

Past centuries are full of burnings at the stake, and not just those of medieval heretics but also witches burned in more recent times, at least up to the eighteenth century. And it is only D'Annunzio's aestheticism that made Mila di Codro say that the flame is beautiful. The fires that have burned so many heretics are terrifying, not least because they followed other tortures. It is enough to quote (from the medieval *Story of Fra Dolcino the Heresiarch*) the description of Fra Dolcino's torture when he and his wife, Margherita, were handed over to the civil authorities for the sentence of the Inquisition to be carried out. While the bells rang the tocsin, they were taken on a cart around the whole city, surrounded by their executioners and followed by armed troops, and in every district their flesh was pierced with red-hot tongs. Margherita was burned first, before Dolcino, whose face flinched not a muscle, nor did he utter any complaint when the tongs ripped into his flesh. Then the cart continued on its way, while the executioners plunged their irons into burning braziers. Dolcino suffered other torments and still he remained silent, except that his shoulders tightened a little when they cut away his nose, and when they tore off his male member he let out a long sigh, like a moan. His last words had the ring of impenitence, and he said that he would rise again on the third day. Then he was burned and his ashes were scattered in the wind.

For inquisitors of every age, race, and religion, fire purifies not only the sins of human beings but also those of books. There are many stories about the burning of books. Sometimes they occur by accident, sometimes through ignorance, but on other occasions, such as the Nazi bonfires of books, they are to purify and to destroy the evidence of a degenerate art. Don Quixote's zealous friends burn his library of books on chivalry for moral reasons and for the sake of his sanity. The library in Elias Canetti's *Auto-da-Fé* burns in a way that reminds us of the sacrifice of Empedocles ("when the flames finally reach him he laughs loudly, as he has never laughed in all his life").

Books condemned to disappearance are burned in Ray Bradbury's *Fahrenheit 451*. My library in the abbey of *The Name of the Rose* is set alight by fate, but the cause is an originating act of censorship.

Fernando Báez, in *A Universal History of the Destruction of Books* (2004), asks for what reasons fire has been the dominant agent in the destruction of books. And he answers:

> Fire is salvation, and for that reason, almost all religions dedicate fires to their respective divinities. This power to conserve life is also a destructive power. When man destroys with fire, he plays God, master of the fire of life and death. And in this way he identifies with a purifying solar cult and with the great myth of destruction that almost always takes place through fire. The reason for using fire is obvious: it reduces the spirit of a work to matter. (translated by Alfred MacAdam)

EKPYROSIS TODAY

Fire is the destroyer in every time of war, from the fabulous and fabled Greek fire of the Byzantines (a military secret if ever there was one, and on this point I'd like to recall Luigi Malerba's fine novel *Il fuoco Greco*) to the chance discovery of gunpowder by Berthold Schwarz, who died as a result, in a personal and punitive *ekpyrosis*. Fire is punishment for traitors in war, and "Fire!" is the command for every firing squad, as if the origin of life is being invoked to hasten the end. But perhaps the fire of war that has most terrified humanity—by which I mean all of humanity, around the globe, conscious for the first time of what was taking place in one part of it—was the explosion of the atomic bomb.

One of the pilots who dropped the bomb on Nagasaki wrote, "All of a sudden the light of a thousand suns lit up the cabin. I was forced to close my eyes for two seconds, despite my sunglasses." In the Bhagavad Gita it was written, "If the radiance of a thousand suns were to burst at once into the sky, that would be the splendor of the mighty one . . . I am become Death, the destroyer of worlds." These verses came to Oppenheimer's mind after the explosion of the first atomic bomb.

With which we come dramatically close to the end of my lecture and—over a more reasonable space of time—to the end of human existence on Earth or the existence of Earth in the cosmos. Because now, as never before, three of the primordial elements are under threat: air, throttled by pollution and by carbon dioxide; water, contaminated on the one hand and increasingly scarce on the other. Only fire is victorious, in the form of a heat that, by parching earth, is upsetting the seasons, and by melting the icecaps, is inviting the seas to invade it. Without realizing it, we are marching toward the first real *ekpyrosis*. While Bush and China reject the Kyoto Protocol, we are marching toward death through fire—and it is of little importance to us whether the universe regenerates after our holocaust, because it will no longer be ours.

The Buddha made this recommendation in his "Fire Sermon":

Monks, all is aflame. What is aflame? The eye is aflame, O monks, forms and colors are aflame, visual awareness is aflame, visual contact is aflame, and whatever sensation arises depending on the contact of the eye with its projections—whether perceived as pleasant, unpleasant, or neutral—that too is aflame. Aflame with what? Aflame with the fire of attachment . . . Aflame, I tell you, because of birth, aging, and death, because of pain, sorrow, anguish, despair. The ear is aflame, sounds are aflame . . . The nose is aflame, aromas are aflame . . . Taste, O monks, is aflame, flavors are aflame . . . Touch, O monks, is aflame . . . The mind, O monks, is aflame . . .

O monks, seeing all thus, the noble disciple who has understood the teachings is serenely disenchanted with the eye, with forms and colors . . . with the ear, with sounds. He is serenely disenchanted with aromas . . . with anything arising depending on the contact of the tongue with its objects, whether perceived as pleasant, unpleasant, or neutral.

But humanity has been unable to relinquish (even in part) its attachment to its own aromas, tastes, sounds, and tactile pleasures — and to relinquish producing fire through friction. Perhaps it should have left the production of fire to the gods, who would have given it to us only once in a while, in the form of a thunderbolt.

[Lecture given during the 2008 Milanesiana festival of literature, music, and cinema, organized around the theme of the four elements — fire, air, earth, and water — on July 7, 2008.]

Treasure Hunting

TREASURE HUNTING IS A fascinating pursuit. It is well worth making a journey, organizing it properly, and following a route that takes in the more interesting treasuries, searching them out also in lesser-known abbeys. There may no longer be any point going to Saint-Denis, on the outskirts of Paris, where in the twelfth century the great Abbot Suger, an avid collector of jewelry, pearls, ivory, gold candelabra, and figured altarpieces, had turned his collection of precious objects into a kind of religion and mystical philosophy. Sadly, the collection of reliquaries and sacred vessels, the robes worn by kings at their coronations, the funeral crowns of Louis XVI and Marie Antoinette, and the panel of the adoration of the shepherds presented by the Sun King have all gone, though some of the finest pieces are still to be found in the Louvre.

A visit to Saint Vitus's Cathedral in Prague, however, should not be missed — here are the skulls of Saint Adalbert and Saint Wenceslas, the sword of Saint Stephen, a fragment of the Cross, the tablecloth from the Last Supper, a tooth of Saint Margaret, a fragment of the tibia of Saint Vitalis, a rib of Saint Sophia, the chin of Saint Eoban, Moses' staff, and Our Lady's robe.

Saint Joseph's engagement ring was listed in the catalog of the fabulous but now dispersed treasury of the duc de Berry, but it is apparently at Notre-Dame in Paris. And on display in the Imperial Treasury in Vienna are a piece of the manger from Bethlehem, Saint Stephen's purse, the lance that struck Jesus' flank, a nail from the Cross, Charlemagne's sword, one of Saint John the Baptist's teeth, a bone from the arm of Saint Ann, the apostles' chains, a piece of Saint John the Evangelist's clothing, and another fragment of the tablecloth from the Last Supper.

But however interested we might be in treasures, those closest to home are the ones we are least likely to know. I reckon, for example, that few people who live in Milan, not to mention tourists, have ever visited the treasury at Milan Cathedral. There you can admire the cover of the Book of the Gospels belonging to Archbishop Aribert (eleventh century), with beautiful cloisonné enamel plaques and gold filigree, inset with precious stones.

Searching out precious stones and their various qualities is one of the favorite pursuits of enthusiasts—it is not just a matter of looking for diamonds, rubies, or emeralds, but also for those so often mentioned in the holy scriptures, such as opal, chrysoprase, beryl, agate, jasper, or sardonyx. If you're clever, you will be able to distinguish between real and false stones. There is a large silver baroque statue of Saint Charles Borromeo in the Milan Cathedral Treasury whose whole breastplate and cross are covered with glistening gems, since those who had commissioned it regarded silver as a poor material. And some, according to the catalog, are real while others are just colored crystal. But leaving aside mercantile considerations, we have to admire above all what the makers of these objects wanted to achieve: an overall effect of amazing richness—not least because most of the precious materials are genuine, and the shop window of the finest Paris jeweler, in comparison to any treasury side-cabinet, is worth little more than a stall in a flea market.

I suggest you then have a look at the larynx of Saint Charles Borromeo, but take a closer look at the Pax of Pope Pius IV, a small shrine with two gold and lapis lazuli columns that frame in gold the Deposition in the Holy Sepulcher. Above it is a golden cross with thirteen diamonds on a disc of banded onyx, while the small pediment is decorated with gold, agate, lapis lazuli, and rubies.

Going back further in time, to the period of Saint Ambrose, there is an embossed silver chest for relics of the apostles, with magnificent bas-reliefs. But the most interesting bas-reliefs are those of the fifth-century *Five-Part Diptych,* an ivory Ravenna-style series of scenes from the life of Christ; at the center is the Mystical Lamb of God in gilded silver with molded glass, a single image in pale colors on a background of ancient ivory.

They are examples of what historical tradition has wrongly accustomed us to describe as lesser arts. They are quite clearly "art," without the adjective, and if there is anything "lesser" (meaning worth less artistically) it is the cathedral itself. If there was a flood, and I was asked whether to save Milan Cathedral or the *Five-Part Diptych,* I would certainly choose the latter, and not because it would be easier to fit inside the ark.

Nonetheless, even considering the crypt (known as the Scurolo) for Saint Charles Borromeo, with the body of the saint in a container of silver and crystal that seems to me more miraculous than its contents, the Cathedral Treasury does not display all that it might. Reading through the *Inventory of the Vestments and Sacred Furnishings of Milan Cathedral,* we realize that the treasury itself is only a tiny part of a collection spread around the various sacristies, which includes splendid vestments, vessels, ivories, sumptuous gold objects, and reliquaries, including several thorns from Christ's Crown, a piece of the Cross, and various fragments of Saint Agnes, Saint Agatha, Saint Catherine, Saint Praxedes, and Saints Simplician, Caius, and Gerontius.

On visiting a treasury, we should not approach the reliquaries with a scientific mind; otherwise there's a risk of losing faith — in the twelfth century, for example, according to legend, the skull of Saint John the Baptist at the age of twelve was kept in a German cathedral. Once, in a monastery on Mount Athos, talking to a monk-librarian, I discovered he had been a student of Roland Barthes in Paris and had taken part in the demonstrations of 1968 — and therefore, knowing him to be a man of culture, I asked whether he believed in the authenticity of the holy relics he kissed devotedly, each morning at dawn, during a magnificent and interminable religious ceremony. He smiled kindly, with a certain malicious complicity, and said that the problem was not one of authenticity but of faith, and that when he kissed the relics he sensed their mystic aroma. In short, it is not the relic that makes faith, but faith that makes the relic.

But not even a nonbeliever can remain immune to the fascination of two phenomena. First of all, the objects themselves, these anonymous yellowing pieces of cartilage, mystically repugnant, pathetic, and mysterious, these scraps of clothing from who knows what period, faded, discolored, frayed, sometimes enclosed in a vial like a mysterious manuscript in a bottle, materials that have often disintegrated, that have become one with the cloth and the metal or bone on which they lie. And secondly, the containers, often incredibly ornate, sometimes made by a devout *bricoleur* from pieces of other reliquaries, in the form of a tower or a small cathedral with pinnacles and domes, and then those baroque reliquaries (the finest are in Vienna), a forest of tiny sculptures, looking like clocks, carillons, or magic boxes. Some of them will remind contemporary art enthusiasts of Joseph Cornell's surrealist boxes and Arman's vitrines filled with ordered objects — secular reliquaries that show, however, the same taste for worn, dusty materials, for manic accumulation — and they require a detailed, analytical study that cannot be done in a simple glance.

Treasure hunting also means knowing not only about the tastes of early medieval patrons but also about Renaissance and baroque collectors, up to the *Wunderkammern* of the German princes: no clear distinction was made between a devotional object, a curiosity, and a work of art. An ivory high relief was precious for its workmanship (today we would say for its artistry) as well as for the value of its material. And a curiosity was recognized, at the same time, as precious, amusing, and marvelous, so that in the duc de Berry's collection, alongside chalices and vessels of great artistic worth, there were also a stuffed elephant, a basilisk, an egg that a priest had found inside another egg, some manna from the desert, a coconut, and the horn of a unicorn.

All lost? No. The horn of a unicorn is to be found in the Imperial Treasury in Vienna, providing proof that unicorns existed, even though the catalog states with positivistic ruthlessness that it is the horn of a narwhal.

But at this point, the visitor, having entered into the spirit of the keen devotee of treasuries, will study with the same interest a horn; a fourth-century agate cup said to be the cup of the Grail; the imperial crown, orb, and scepter (splendors of medieval jewelry); and also — since the Treasury of Vienna has no bounds of time — the imperial four-poster bed in which slept the unfortunate son of Napoleon, the king of Rome, known as the Eaglet (who at this point becomes as legendary as the unicorn and the Grail).

We have to forget what we have read in the art history books, to lose our sense of the difference between curio and masterpiece, to enjoy above all the mass of wonders, the procession of marvels, the epiphany of the incredible. And to dream about the head of Saint John the Baptist at the age of twelve, imagining its reddish veins on an ashen background, the arabesque of crumbling, corroded joints, and the reliquary that has to contain it, of blue enamel like the altar of Verdun and the cushion under it of yellowed satin, covered with withered roses in a glass cabinet, airless for two thousand years, immobilized in a vacuum, before the Baptist could grow up and the executioner was able to chop off his other head. That other, more mature head has a lesser mystical and commercial value since, though it is supposed to be conserved in the Church of San Silvestro in Capite in Rome, an older tradition claims it to be in the cathedral at Amiens and, in any event, the head in Rome has no jaw, which is said to be in the Church of San Lorenzo in Viterbo.

All we have to do is take a map and plot a few possible routes. For example, the True Cross, discovered in Jerusalem by Saint Helena, mother of Constantine, was seized by the Persians in the seventh century and then retrieved by the Byzantine emperor Heraclius. It was carried by the Crusaders in 1187 onto the battlefield at Hattin to ensure their victory over Saladin; but the battle, as we know, ended in their defeat and all trace of the Cross was lost forever. Numerous fragments, however, had been taken over previous centuries and are still conserved in many churches.

The three nails (two for the hands and one for the feet, nailed together) were found still attached to the Cross and were said to have been brought by Helena to her son Constantine. According to legend, one of them was mounted on his battle helmet and another was made into a bit for his horse. The third nail, according to tradition, is to be found in the Church of the Santa Croce in Gerusalemme, in Rome. The Sacred Bit, on the other hand, is in Milan Cathedral, where it is shown to the faithful twice a year. There is no trace of the nail on the helmet — one tradition suggests it is to be found today in the Iron Crown, conserved in Monza Cathedral.

The Crown of Thorns, long kept in Constantinople, was then passed on to King Louis IX of France, who put it in the Sainte-Chapelle, specially built by him in Paris for this purpose. It originally had ten thorns, but over the course of the centuries they were given to churches, sanctuaries, and important people, and all that remains today is the branches woven into the shape of a helmet.

The pillar of the flagellation is in Santa Prassede in Rome; the Sacred Lance belonged to Charlemagne and his descendants, and is now in Vienna; Christ's foreskin was kept and displayed each New Year's Day at Calcata, a small town near Viterbo, until the 1970s, when the priest announced it had been stolen. But Rome, Santiago de Compostela, Chartres, Besançon, Metz, Hildesheim, Charroux, Conques, Langres, Antwerp, Fécamp, and Puy-en-Velay in the Auvergne have all made claims to possess a similar relic.

The blood that poured from Christ's side was, according to tradition, collected by Longinus, the soldier who had pierced him with the lance: he is said to have taken it to Mantua; the ampoule supposed to contain the blood is kept in the city's cathedral. Other blood attributed to Jesus is kept in a cylindrical reliquary that can be seen in the Basilica of the Holy Blood (Heilig-Bloedbasiliek) at Bruges in Belgium.

The Sacred Crib is at Santa Maria Maggiore (Rome), the Sacred Shroud in Turin, the linen napkin used by Christ to wash the feet of the apostles at the Church of Saint John Lateran in Rome, but also at Acqs in Germany – indeed, the latter napkin is said to bear the footprint of Judas.

The swaddling clothes of the infant Jesus are at Aachen; the house of Mary, where the Annunciation took place, was transported through the air by angels from Nazareth to Loreto; many churches hold what is claimed to be the hair of Mary (one hair, for example, is at Messina) or her milk; the sacred girdle of Our Lady is at Prato; Saint Joseph's wedding ring is at Perugia Cathedral; the engagement rings of Joseph and Mary are at Notre-Dame in Paris; Saint Joseph's belt (brought to France by Joinville in 1254) is in the Church of the Feuillants in Paris, and his staff at the Camaldolese church in Florence. There are also fragments of this staff in the churches of Santa Cecilia in Rome, Sant'Anastasia in Rome, and San Domenico and San Giuseppe del Mercato in Bologna. There are fragments of the tomb of Saint Joseph at Santa Maria al Portico and Santa Maria in Campitelli in Rome.

Fragments of the Holy Veil of Our Lady and the cloak of Saint Joseph are to be found at Santa Maria di Licodia, in Sicily, conserved in an artful silver reliquary, made in the seventeenth century. Until the 1970s, this reliquary was carried in procession on the last Saturday of August to mark the festival of the patron saint.

The body of Saint Peter was buried in Rome near where he was martyred, at the Circus of Nero: a basilica was built on the site during the reign of Constantine, and later, the present Saint Peter's Basilica. In 1964, after archaeological excavations, it was announced that the apostle's bones had been found, and today they are beneath the altar.

According to legend, the body of Saint James, son of Zebedee, was transported by the currents to the Atlantic coast of Spain and buried in a place called Campus Stellae. The Sanctuary of Santiago de Compostela stands there today, one of the major pilgrimage destinations, along with Rome and Jerusalem, since the Middle Ages.

The body of Saint Thomas the Apostle is in the Cathedral of Ortona (Chieti), taken there in 1258 from Chios, an island in the Aegean Sea, where it had been brought to safety by Christians after the fall of Edessa in 1146. It had been taken to Edessa by order of the Emperor Alexander Severus in around 230 C.E., from Madras, where Thomas had been martyred in 72 C.E.

One of the thirty pieces of silver for which Judas Iscariot betrayed Christ is in the sacristy of the Collegiate Church at Visso. A body of Saint Bartholomew the Apostle is in Rome (brought to Isola Tiberina by Pius IV); another is at the Church of San Bartolomeo in Benevento. In any event, both bodies ought to be without their skullcaps, since one is conserved in Frankfurt Cathedral and the other at the Monastery of Lüne (Lüneberg). It is not known which body the third skullcap comes from, which is now at the Charterhouse in Cologne. An arm, once again belonging to Saint Bartholomew, is in Canterbury Cathedral, though Pisa boasts possession of a piece of his skin.

The body of Saint Luke the Evangelist is kept in the Church of Santa Giustina in Padua; that of Saint Mark, originally kept at Antioch, was taken to Venice.

What were said to be the remains of the Magi were conserved in Milan in ancient times. They were seized by Frederick Barbarossa in the twelfth century as spoils of war and taken to Cologne, where they remain. Some relics were returned to Milan in the 1950s and are now in the Church of Sant'Eustorgio.

The remains of Saint Nicholas of Bari, otherwise known as Santa Claus, were at Myra, in Asia Minor, until 1087, when they were smuggled away by seamen from Bari and transported to their city.

The body of Saint Ambrose, patron saint of Milan, is buried in the crypt of the basilica dedicated to him, together with the bodies of Saints Gervase and Protase.

In the Basilica of Saint Antony of Padua are the saint's tongue and fingers; the hand of Saint Stephen of Hungary is kept in the basilica at Budapest; two ampoules of the blood of Saint Januarius are in Naples; part of the body of Saint Judith is in Nevers Cathedral, while a fragment of bone is kept in a magnificent rock crystal reliquary in the crypt of the Medici Chapel at San Lorenzo in Florence.

At Misterbianco, in Sicily, the arm of Saint Anthony the Great is displayed every January 17; that of Saint Benedict of Norcia was donated to the monastery of Leno, near Brescia, in the eighth century at the behest of King Desiderius.

The body of Saint Agatha at Catania was divided up, and the goldsmiths of Limoges made reliquaries for the limbs – one for each thigh, one for each arm, and one for each lower leg. One was made in 1628 for her breast. But the ulna and radius of her forearm are at Palermo, in the Royal Chapel. One of Saint Agatha's arm bones is at Messina, in the Monastery of the Santissimo Salvatore, another at Alì, just outside Messina; one of her fingers is at Sant'Agata dei Goti (Benevento); the body of Saint Peter of Verona is in the Portinari Chapel at Sant'Eustorgio, in Milan (devotees bang their heads against his sarcophagus on April 29 to ward off headaches).

The remains of Saint Gregory of Nazianzus are at Saint Peter's in Rome, but a portion was donated by Pope John Paul II to the patriarch of Constantinople in 2004. Relics of Saint Lucidus are at Aquara, near Salerno: they were stolen several times and the head was eventually found by police in a private house in 1999. Relics associated with Saint Pantaleon (the sword that cut off the saint's head, the wheel on which he was tortured, the torch used to burn his flesh, the trunk of an olive tree that sprouted on contact with his body) are to be found in the church named after him at Lanciano, in the Abruzzo.

A rib of Saint Catherine is at Astenet in Belgium; one of her feet is in the Church of Santi Giovanni e Paolo in Venice. A finger and her head (detached from her body in 1381 by order of Pope Urban VI) are in the Basilica of San Domenico in Siena.

A piece of Saint Blaise's tongue is at Carosino, near Taranto, an arm in the cathedral at Ruvo di Puglia, and his skull at Dubrovnik. We can find a tooth of Saint Apollonius in Porto Cathedral, the body of Saint Judas Cyriacus in Ancona Cathedral, the heart of Saint Alfius at Lentini in Sicily, the body of Saint Roch in the high altar of the Church of the Scuola Grande in Venice, part of the shoulder bone and another bone fragment at Scilla, part of an arm bone in the Church of San Rocco at Voghera, near Pavia, another piece of arm bone at the church of the same name in Rome, a tibia and other small parts of the *massa corporis* and what is said to have been his staff in his sanctuary at Montpellier, a phalanx bone in the parish church of Cisterna di Latina, part of his heel in Frigento Cathedral, and several bone fragments in the Basilica Mauriziana and the Church of the Confraternita di San Rocco in Turin.

Relics were venerated in Constantinople but dispersed after the Fourth Crusade, such as Our Lady's mantle (the Maphorion), Christ's sandals, the cloak of Saint John the Baptist, an ampoule of Christ's blood used to sign certain solemn documents, the parapet of the well where Christ met the Samaritan woman, the stone on which Christ's body was laid after his death, Solomon's throne, Moses' rod, the remains of the innocents slaughtered by Herod, a piece of dung dropped by the donkey on which Jesus entered Jerusalem, the icon of the Hodegetria (an image of Mary and child said to have been painted by Saint Luke), other icons considered miraculous since they were not painted by human hand (*acheiropoieta*), and the Mandylion, the cloth imprinted with the face of Christ (originally at Edessa, where it was famed for making the city impregnable when displayed on its walls).

I wouldn't wish to give the impression that the conservation of relics is exclusively a Christian, or indeed Catholic, practice. Pliny tells us about the treasured relics of the Greco-Roman world, such as Orpheus's lyre, Helen's sandal, or the bones of the monster that attacked Andromeda. And by the classical period, the presence of a relic already provided a point of attraction for a city or for a temple, and was therefore a valuable tourist "commodity" as well as a sacred object.

The cult of the relic is to be found in every religion and culture. It depends, on the one hand, upon a sort of impulse that I would describe as mytho-materialistic — so that by touching parts of the body of great men or saints we are able to experience something of their power — and, on the other hand, upon a normal antiquarian taste for the past (so that a collector is prepared to spend money to have not just the first edition of a famous book, but also the book that belonged to an important person).

In this second sense (though perhaps in the first too) there is also a secular cult of the relic — all we have to do is read Christie's auction catalogs to see how a pair of shoes belonging to a famous diva is being offered at prices higher than that of a picture by a Renaissance painter. These kinds of memorabilia can be the actual gloves of Jacqueline Kennedy or those simply worn by Rita Hayworth for the filming of *Gilda*. In that respect, I have seen tourists in Nashville, Tennessee, going to admire Elvis Presley's Cadillac — which by the way wasn't the only one, since he changed them every six months.

The most famous relic of all times is, of course, the Holy Grail, but I wouldn't advise anyone to set out in search of that (or *those*) since past experiences haven't been too encouraging — in any event, it has been scientifically proven that two thousand years aren't long enough.

[An earlier Italian version, titled "Andare per tesori," appeared in *Milano: Meraviglie, miracoli, misteri,* edited by Roberta Cordani (Milan: CELIP, 2011); a second expanded version ("In attesa di una semiotica dei tesori") was published in *Testure: Scritti seriosi e schizzi scherzosi per Omar Calabrese* by Stefano Jacoviello and others (Siena: Protagon, 2009).]

Fermented Delights

MY RELATIONS WITH Piero Camporesi were always very friendly and cordial, marked by a mutual esteem — or at least I hope they were — to the point where I plundered choice quotes from him for my novels *The Name of the Rose* and *The Island of the Day Before* and he asked me to write a preface for the English edition of his book on blood. But we always tended to meet in academic circles — at university course committees, in faculty corridors, or perhaps in the porticoed streets of Bologna — and I never got to know him in any private setting or to visit his library.

So far as I know, Camporesi was a gourmet. He enjoyed good food and I'm told he was a good cook: no surprise for a writer who dedicated so many pages not just to the pains but also the pleasures of the body — to milk, sauces, and dressings. Nor should we expect anything else from someone who once declared (in a newspaper interview in August 1985) that, after having studied Petrarch, the baroque, Alfieri, and Romanticism, his discovery of Pellegrino Artusi toward the end of the 1960s had been devastating.

But my knowledge about Camporesi's passion for food is only bookish; I have dined with him only in the pages of his books.

I am therefore qualified to celebrate Camporesi the gourmet simply as an avid reader of his work. He wrote about squalor, bodily waste, and putrefaction, and at the same time about his lusts and ecstasies. But he did so by delving with his scalpel into the bodies of books, by which I mean into books describing bodies, and—like a latter-day Mondino de Liuzzi—he went about dissecting not corpses stolen from cemeteries, but books unearthed from the musty depths of libraries where they had often languished forgotten, concealing their delights, in the way that the character des Esseintes in Joris-Karl Huysmans's *À rebours* went about rediscovering in neglected early medieval chronicles "the stammering grace, the often exquisite clumsiness of the monks, stirring the poetical leftovers of antiquity into a pious stew . . . verbs of refined sweetness, substantives smelling of incense, and strange adjectives crudely fashioned out of gold in the delightful barbaric style of Gothic jewellery" (translated by Robert Baldrick).

Of course, if Camporesi had wanted literature in which to lick his lips while savoring excessive intemperate and obsolescent words, he could have turned to such classics of linguistic corruption as that Italian forerunner of Joyce, *Hypnerotomachia Poliphili,* or the macaronic macaroni of Teofilo Folengo, or—if he had wanted to gorge himself on modernity—Carlo Emilio Gadda. Instead he went off in search of unknown texts, or books that were familiar in other respects. Having read Camporesi's works we certainly know much more about blood, bread, wine, and chocolate, in the same way that we learn extraordinary things about hunger, worms, buboes and scrofula, fiber, intestines, vomit, greed, as well as fun fairs and carnivals. But I would venture to suggest that these explorations would be fascinating even if the phenomena he writes about had never actually taken place, even if Camporesi had been telling us about bodies and bodily nourishment of aliens from Venus, somewhere too far away to arouse any sense of attraction or disgust. By which I mean that it is fascinating to know that remote centuries were peopled by bands of vagrants, but more fascinating still to discover this purely *flatus vocis,* and to read about fake monks, charlatans, rogues, swindlers, beggars and ragamuffins, lepers and cripples, peddlers, tramps, ballad singers, itinerant clerics, scholar gypsies, cardsharps, jugglers, maimed soldiers, wandering Jews, madmen, fugitives, convicts with docked ears, or sodomites.

It is not pharmaceutics but lexicography or linguistic history that we are most aware of when reading his descriptions of poppy syrups, ointments, unguents, baths, inhalants, powders, tinctures, *spongia somnifera* soaked in opium juices, henbane, hemlock, mandrake . . .

We open *The Anatomy of the Senses* (1994) at the first chapter, "The Cursed Cheese." We know that cheese, though it comes from a pure and sweet liquid, milk, is more appetizing the more it tastes of putrefaction, and reminds us of molds and those body odors we usually try to get rid of with foot baths and bidets—and this is well known not only to the glutton but especially to the gourmet. Yet I doubt whether Camporesi would have been able to write twenty-eight pages on the iniquities of cheese by simply sniffing Gorgonzola and Stilton, or letting the taste of formaggio di fossa, Reblochon, Roquefort, or vacherin linger on his tongue. He had to go off exploring forgotten pages of Campanella's *De sensu rerum et magia* or, worse still, retrieving from the seventeenth century, that most neglected period, *Il mercato delle maraviglie di natura* by Nicolò Serpetro, the *Physica subterranea* by Joachim Becher, *De casei nequitia* by Johann Peter Lotichius, and *Intorno ai latticini* by Paolo Boccone, thus superimposing on the actual aroma of cheese this even ranker and more putrid collage of quotations:

> For many centuries, many people believed in the intrinsic malevolence of cheese, and its "iniquity" could be detected from its smell, which for many was sickening and nauseating, a sure indicator of dying matter. It was a decomposing residue of degenerate and harmful substances, and a terrible corrupter of humours . . . a foul and fetid thing (*res foetida et foeda*), the excremental part of milk, made up of harmful waste, coagulated from the earthy sludge of the white liquid. Lotichius often uses the verb "to copulate" (*coire*) when referring to the coagulation of these inferior parts of the milk. Butter, on the other hand, constituted the best part; it was an elect, pure, and divine delicacy, termed Jupiter's marrow (*Iovis*

medulla). Cheese, however, was variously described as "something foul, rank, filthy, and decaying" or "a shapeless mass, evil-smelling from the dross of milk, from bits of vegetables and refuse, but a source of nourishment, whether curdled or combined." It was suitable only for "labourers and the lower classes." As "something rustic and filthy," it was not worthy of decent people and honoured citizens; it was, in other words, a food for the ragged peasant who was accustomed to eating "bad foods" . . . Lotichius saw those who ate cheese as sordid and degenerate lovers of putrefied substances. Pre-scientific medicine not only agreed with him, but supplied easy arguments to demonstrate the iniquity of cheese, because the humours could only be disturbed and corrupted by fetid and putrid foods. Eating them triggered an uncontrollable proliferation of the worms that, even in normal conditions, "teem in the intestines which are their hiding-place." This was the terrible truth: cheese increased the existing putrefaction in the dark meanders of the intestines and the recesses of the human bowels, generating disgusting little monsters . . . Lotichius argued that the propagation of thousands of vile little animals must occur in human intestines, just as the putrefaction spontaneously created, cow-dung released an abundance of cockroaches, grubs, wasps, and drones, and the dew generated butterflies, ants, locusts, and cicadas. This process was uncontrolled and astounding in that it did not require copulation and the fertilization of eggs. He could not see how the lower abdomen filled with human manure could possibly avoid fermenting the same profusion of perplexing little animals which were a scourge to humanity . . . Why could not the same thing occur, given that "earthworms and tapeworms all draw their origin from phlegmatic, dense, and rough matter." (translated by Allan Cameron)

And similarly his exploration of forgotten writings did not end at *De spiritu ardente ex lacte bubulo* by the eighteenth-century Nicolaus Oseretskowsky, which tells us how the Tartars got drunk on fermented milk. Only Camporesi, among the few devotees who have read *La vita della Venerabile Madre Maria Margherita Alacoque* of 1784, about the saint who first saw the Sacred Heart of Jesus, could have extracted from her biography the shocking information that this mystic saint, though ready for any mortification of the senses, could not overcome her disgust for cheese, to the extent that she was tempted to abandon monastic life so as avoid being forced by her vow of obedience to eat that horrible yet humble food, before succeeding in making the supreme sacrifice. Which prompts Camporesi's comment that "the unbelievable conflict led the saint to the verge of suicidal desperation as her tormented soul struggled over a piece of cheese."

Now, I have to say, the story existed and exists in that saint's biography, but heaven only knows how any human being could have had the idea of searching about among those most saintly pages for some lines on cheese. Perhaps Camporesi never ate cheese (a suggestion I make only out of a love of paradox), but he certainly had a voracious appetite for pages and pages of countless books that had ended up goodness knows where — and this was his heavenly and guilty Camembert.

If this suggestion might appear excessive, see how Camporesi can describe an execrable (or at least execrated) food such as cheese with the same ease that he talks about culinary delights that make our mouths water, or about the practices of penitence that would cause any sensitive soul to feel sick. And when discussing Prince Raimondo di Sangro, rather than going off, like everyone else, on an exploration of his mummified monstrosities and chilling displays of nerves, muscles, and veins laid bare, instead he examines his Arcimboldean fancy for counterfeiting food, so that

> being quite excessively self-indulgent in all things, on certain days [he] ordered an entire dinner to be prepared using nothing but vegetables, on other days nothing but fruit, on yet others nothing but sweet and honeyed dishes, and sometimes dishes all made from milk. He had skilled buffet experts so highly trained in the art of manipulating sweetmeats and dairy products that he could produce marvellous imitations, with milk and honey, of all the dishes the cooks normally make with meat, fish, and many other sorts of

animals. They also knew how to counterfeit every kind of fruit in a thousand different ways. (*Exotic Brew,* 1994, translated by Christopher Woodall)

But likewise, in the same spirit, here he is reading Sebastiano Pauli and his *Prediche quaresimali* (*Lenten Sermons*), making our hair stand on end while he relishes certain pious recommendations when it comes to a peaceful death:

As soon as this well-constituted and well-organized body is closed in its coffin, it changes colour and becomes yellow and sallow, but it is a pallor and sallowness that nauseate and incite fear. It then blackens from the head to the feet, and it is covered by a sombre and dismal colour like spent coal. Then it starts to swell in a strange manner across the face, chest, and stomach, and a fetid and greasy mould starts to grow on this sickening swelling, a filthy indication of imminent corruption. Very soon the yellow and swollen stomach starts to rip here an eruption and there a tear, and out of these there flows a slow lava of decaying material and foulness in which bits of that black and rotting flesh are floating. Here half a maggot-infested eye is carried on a wave, there a cleft lip is putrid and corrupt, and further on there lies a bundle of livid and lacerated bowels. A great quantity of small flies, worms, and other disgusting little animals is generated by this greasy mire, and they swarm and infest the corrupted blood, attach themselves to decomposing flesh, and devour it. One part of these worms rises from the chest, and another from the nostrils, with I don't know what filth and mucus. Still others, covered by putrid matter, enter and leave by the mouth, and the more satiated come and go, and gurgle continuously down in the throat. (*The Anatomy of the Senses*)

Is there a difference between describing a Trimalchion dinner in a land of plenty (bringing to mind Dario Fo, in *Mistero Buffo,* who froths with pleasure over food he is only dreaming about) or taking delight before the horrid spectacle of the damned in the Lenten sermons of Romolo Marchelli and the descriptions in Padre Segneri's sermon on the spectacle of the lower realm of the damned, who endure the greatest punishment by seeing the Almighty laugh at their suffering?

> And yet when they raise their eyes and turn to the great God who lit the fire, they see that He now appears . . . like Nero to them, not because of His injustice but because of His severity, not only does He not wish to console them, or pity them, but what is more *He claps His hands together,* and with incredible pleasure, He laughs at them. Imagine in what frenzy they are driven, and into what a rage! We are burning and God laughs? Oh most cruel God! . . . We let ourselves be deluded by the man who told us that our greatest torment would have been the sight of God's scornful face. God's laughing face, he should have said, God's laughing face. (*The Fear of Hell,* 1990, translated by Lucinda Byatt)

I see no difference between the eagerness with which Camporesi savors, in the pages of Giovan Battista Barpo's *Le delizie e i frutti dell'agricoltura e della villa,* the lists of salted beef and lamb, mutton, pork and veal, and then spring lambs, capons, hens and ducks, and then of parsley roots, which, when boiled, floured, and cooked in oil, are just like lampreys; or pasta made from flour, rosewater, saffron, and sugar, with a little malmsey, cut round, like windowpanes, and stuffed with breadcrumbs, apples, carnation flowers, and ground walnuts, while waiting for Easter to bring kid, veal, lamb, asparagus, and squabs and, over the following months, curd cheeses, fresh ricotta, peas, heads of cabbage, boiled beans floured and fried (*The Anatomy of the Senses*) — between such lists of things dedicated to the palate and other lists dedicated (even though they refer to people) only to the ear — an ear whose eustachian tubes are as voraciously greedy as any throat. Examples of those lists of villains are found in the *Speculum cerretanorum* and other works on villainy: cardsharps, cheats, rascals, villains, wastrels, ne'er-do-wells, tricksters, fraudsters, pimps, fagins, abortionists, sellers of miraculous waters, quacks, *pauperes verecundi,* prayer vendors, fathers begging with their children, fake-saffron vendors, rogues who cheat other rogues, relic sellers, flour beggars, gropers, baptized Jews, fake priests, shivering jimmies, bread beggars, rogues feigning madness from tarantula bites, holy-image bearers, fake miracle-workers, usurers, fake paralytics, dealers, street singers, epileptics, false weepers, charlatans, and so on (*Il libro dei vagabondi*).

Or not very politically correct lists of the defects of women, taken from the pages of *Poetiche dicerie overo vaghissime descrittioni* by Tommaso Caraffa, which might seem to describe the edible virtues of some extremely rare wild animal:

> Do you not know that woman was called the portrait of inconstancy, the model of fragility, the mother of cunning, the symbol of variance, the mistress of malice, the minister of frauds, the inventrix of deception, the friend of simulation and of imperfection itself; since her voice is weak, she is voluble in tongue, tardy in action, fast in anger, steadfast in hatred, quick in envy, readily tired, well-versed in evil, easily prone to lying, like a biting asp nesting in an open field, like dead cinders that conceal a burning ember; a false reef concealed among shallow waters; a prickly thorn covered by lilies and roses; a poisonous snake wrapped in herbs and flowers; a light that fades; a flame that burns out; a glory that falls; a sun eclipsed; a moon that wanes; a star that disappears; a sky that darkens; a shadow that vanishes; and a sea that ruffles. (*I balsami di Venere*, 1989)

If it is still not clear that Camporesi was a gourmet of lists, see the shameless greed with which he gleefully describes the poor and piteous table of the penitent saints — such as Joseph of Copertino, as found in an eighteenth-century *Life*, whose table was furnished with herbs, dried fruits, and cooked broad beans sprinkled only with bitterest powder, and who on Friday fed on a herb that was so bitter and disgusting that even to lick it with the tip of the tongue nauseated him for several days. Or the description in the *Life* of Carlo Girolamo Severoli of Faenza, servant of God, who sprinkled his bread with ashes, which he secretly carried around with him for the purpose, and dipped it into the water used for washing dishes, and sometimes put it to soak in verminous water. Thus, quite rightly,

> such was the manner and number of his self-inflictions and abstinences that his appearance was completely transformed: his countenance was pallid and his bones were barely covered by his bloodless skin, so much had he wasted away; a few meagre hairs sprouted from his chin and his frame was bent and transfigured, so that he had become bare like a skeleton, a living image of penitence. He suffered as a consequence most grievously of languidness, fainting, swooning, and a death-like pallor, so extreme that on journeys he was sometimes obliged to stop and he would sink to the ground to recover some little strength in his flagging limbs; or to relieve the pains of a hernia and other ills, for which he refused to seek any remedy. (*The Incorruptible Flesh*, 1988, translated by Tania Croft-Murray)

If we were to read all of Camporesi's books, one after the other (though they should be savored in small doses), trying to build up a picture of what he is describing, we might become sated and form the suspicion there isn't much difference between an urge to swim in cream and to swim in excrement, so that his work might serve as a Gospel or a Koran for the characters in Ferreri's film *La Grande Bouffe*, at the end of which ingurgitation and evacuation go hand in hand. This would be true if we assumed that Camporesi is talking only of things, rather than realizing that he is talking first and foremost about words—the words Paradise and Inferno, after all, are part of one and the same poem.

Camporesi certainly wanted to be a cultural anthropologist, or historian of everyday life, though he performed this task by probing among long-forgotten works, and in doing so he recounted the vicissitudes of past centuries in relation to the body and food. But not infrequently he highlights parallels between those times and ours—and reflecting on ancient blood rituals and myths he never failed to point out how much blood has been spilled in our own most civilized age, whether it be through holocaust, intifada, genocide, tribal throat-slitting, or massacre, and nor did he ever fail to comment on the perversions of today, from dietary paranoia to mass hedonism, from olfactory decadence to the adulteration of food, as well as the disappearance of the traditional view of hell. He looked back almost nostalgically upon less fastidious and more honest times when you could smell the blood that was spilled, when masochistic mystics kissed leprous ulcers, and excrement was sniffed as part of the sensual panorama of everyday life (I wonder what he would have written about the rubbish piles in Naples).

But this desire to understand the past and the present arose through that form of libido that has been dubbed "librido." Nor could Camporesi savor the aroma of a well-made pie or the stink of a rotting body except through the whiff of paper made from pulped rags, duly watermarked, slightly foxed, and adorned with worm holes, provided it was, as bibliographers would have once said, *de la plus insigne rareté.*

[Lecture given at the international study conference on Piero Camporesi in March 2008 at Forlì. Then published in *Camporesi nel mondo,* edited by E. Casali and M. Soffritti (Bologna: Bononia University Press, 2009).

No Embryos in Paradise

I T IS NOT MY INTENTION in this lecture to support philosophical, theological, and bioethical positions on problems relating to abortion, stem cells, embryos, and the so-called right to life. My approach is purely historical and seeks to examine what Saint Thomas Aquinas thought about such matters. At most, the fact that the church of today thinks differently makes my reconstruction particularly curious.

The debate is extremely old, dating back to Origen, who claimed that God created human souls that had existed from the very beginning. His view was immediately challenged, not least in the light of the words of Genesis (2:7) that "the Lord formed man of the dust of the ground, and breathed into his nostrils the breath of life; and man became a living soul." In the Bible, therefore, God creates the body, and then breathes a soul into it, and this doctrine, which became the church's official doctrine, is called *creationism*. But this position posed problems so far as the transmission of original sin. If the soul is not transmitted by the parents, why are babies not free from original sin, so that they have to be baptized? Thus Tertullian (in *De anima*) claimed that the soul of the parent is "translated" from father to son through his semen. But *traducianism* was immediately judged to be heretical, since it presumed that the soul had a material origin.

The person who found himself in difficulty was Saint Augustine:

he had to reckon with the Pelagians, who denied the transmission of original sin. He therefore supported the creationist doctrine (against bodily traducianism) while admitting, at the same time, a sort of spiritual traducianism. But all commentators take the view that his position is rather convoluted. Augustine was tempted to accept traducianism, but finally, in epistle 190, he admits to being uncertain and observes that the holy scriptures support neither traducianism nor creationism. We can also see how he wavers between the two positions in *De genesi ad litteram*.

Saint Thomas Aquinas was decidedly creationist, and resolved the question of original guilt in a most elegant way. Original sin is transmitted by semen like a natural infection (*Summa Theologica*, second part of part 1, question 81, article 1, reply to objections 1 and 2), but this has nothing to do with the transmission of the rational soul:

> It is said that the child will not carry the iniquity of the father in the sense that he will not be punished for the sin of the father, unless he is a party to the blame. But this is what happens in our case: in fact original sin is transmitted from father to child through procreation, in the same way that actual sin is transmitted by imitation . . . Yet the soul is not transmitted, because the power of the semen is not able to produce a rational soul, nevertheless the semen cooperates as an instrument. Thus, through the power of the semen, human nature is transmitted from parents to children, and the corruption of human nature with it. In fact, he who is born becomes a party to the guilt of his parent; because by force of procreation, he inherits his nature from him.

If the soul is not transmitted with the semen, then when is it introduced into the fetus? Remember that, according to Thomas, plants have a vegetative soul, which in animals is supplanted by the sensitive soul, whereas in human beings these two functions are supplanted by the rational soul, which is what produces intelligent man — and what, moreover, makes a person, insofar as the person was, by ancient tradition, an "individual substance of a rational nature." It is the rational soul that will endure the corruption of the body and will be sent to damnation or to eternal glory – this is what makes man what he is and distinguishes him from an animal or a plant.

Thomas has a very biological view about the formation of the fetus: God introduces the soul only when the fetus acquires, stage by stage, first a vegetative soul and then a sensitive soul. Only at that point, in a body already formed, is the rational soul created (*Summa,* part 1, question 90).

Therefore the embryo has only a sensitive soul (*Summa,* part 1, question 76, article 3):

> The philosopher teaches that the embryo is first animal and then man. But this cannot be so, if the essence of the sensitive soul and the intellective soul are identical: since an animal is so made from its sensitive soul, man however is so constituted by that intellective soul. The essence of the sensitive soul and the intellective soul is therefore not the same . . . We must therefore conclude that in man there exists one soul, which is sensitive, intellective, and vegetative. This can be easily explained if we consider the differences of species and forms. For we observe that the species and forms differ from one another according to various grades of perfection: thus in the order of nature animate beings are more perfect than inanimate beings, animals more than plants; men more than beasts; and in each of these kinds there are various grades. For this reason Aristotle . . . compares the various animals to [geometrical] figures, one of which contains another so that, for example, the pentagon contains and transcends the rectangle. In a similar way, the intellective soul contains virtually all that belongs to the sensitive soul of animals and the vegetative soul of plants. Therefore, in the same way that the surface of the pentagon is not a rectangle because it has one figure different to that of the rectangle, so that the figure of the rectangle being contained in the pentagon would be superfluous, likewise Socrates is not a man by one soul and animal by another, but he is both man and animal by the same soul . . . the embryo has first of all a soul that is merely sensitive, and when eliminated,

it is supplanted by a more perfect soul, which is both sensitive and intellective.

In the *Summa* (part 1, question 118, article 1, reply to objection 4) it is said that the sensitive soul is transmitted with the semen:

> In perfect animals, generated by coitus, the active force, according to the Philosopher, is in the semen of the male: but the fetal matter is provided by the female. This vegetative soul exists in this material from the very beginning, not at a later instance but in the initial act, like the sensitive soul exists in one who sleeps. But when it begins to attract nourishment, then it actually operates. This matter is therefore transmuted by the power enclosed in the semen of the male, until it becomes the sensitive soul: not in the sense that the power present in the semen passes to become the sensitive soul; because in such a case, the generator and the generated would be the same thing; and the process would be more like nourishment and growth than generation, as the Philosopher observes. But when, by the power of the active principle in the semen, the sensitive soul is produced in the principal structure of the generated being, then the sensitive soul of the offspring begins to work toward the perfection of its own body, through the acts of nutrition and development. The active power of the semen ceases to exist as soon as the semen is dissolved and the spirit enclosed within it has vanished. Nor is there anything strange in this fact, because this force is not a principal agent, but instrumental; and the movement of the instrument ceases once the effect is produced in the being.

And in the *Summa* (part 1, question 118, article 2, reply) Thomas denies that the power of the semen can produce the intellective element, and therefore that a soul exists at the moment of conception. Since the intellective soul is an immaterial substance, it cannot be caused through procreation, but only through creation by God. Anyone admitting that the intellective soul is transmitted by semen would also have to admit that it does not exist alone and, as a result, that it is corrupted upon the corruption of the body.

In the same question (*ad secundum*) Thomas also denies that to the vegetative soul, present at the beginning, there is added another, namely, the sensitive soul; and after this another still, that is, the intellective soul. In this way man would have three souls, so that one would be in the power of another. And he denies that the same soul, which at the beginning was merely vegetative, then develops, by action of the power of the semen, until it also becomes sensitive; and finally develops until it becomes an intellective soul, not just by the active power of the semen, but through the power of a superior agent, namely God, who would come from outside to illuminate it:

> But this does not hold. First, because no substantial form is susceptible of more or less; but the addition of greater perfection changes the species, just as the addition of unity changes the species of number. Now it is not possible for the same identical form to belong to different species. Secondly, because it would follow from this that the generation of an animal would be a continuous movement, proceeding from the imperfect to the perfect, as happens in alteration. Thirdly, because the generation of a man or an animal would no longer be generation in the strict sense, because their subject would already be taking place. For if the vegetative soul is in the matter of offspring from the beginning, and is subsequently gradually brought to a state of perfection, this would involve an addition of further perfection without destruction of the preceding perfection. And this is contrary to the concept of generation in the strict sense. Fourthly, because that which is caused by God is either something subsistent: and thus it must needs be essentially distinct from the preexisting form, which was nonsubsistent; and we shall then come back to the opinion of those who held the existence of several souls in the body. Or else it would not be subsistent, but a perfection of the preexisting soul: and then the intellective soul would perish with the body: and this is unacceptable . . . We must therefore say that, when a more perfect form supervenes, the previous form is corrupted, since the generation of one being always implies the corruption of another being, both in men and in animals: and this occurs in such a way that the subsequent form has all the

perfections of the previous form, and something more. In this way, through various generations and corruptions, we arrive at the ultimate substantial form, both in man as well as in other animals. And this can also be seen in animals generated from putrefaction. We must conclude therefore that the intellective soul is created by God at the end of human generation, with the disappearance of the preexisting forms, and that this soul is both sensitive and nutritive.

The rational soul, at the moment in which it is created, therefore *formats,* so to speak, the two souls — vegetative and sensitive — and recharges them as an integral part of the rational soul.

In the *Summa contra Gentiles* (book 2, part 89, reply to argument 11) it is repeated that there is an order, a grading in the generative process, "due to intermediate forms in which the fetus is equipped from the beginning until its final form."[1]

At what point in the formation of the fetus is it infused with that intellective soul that makes it a human person in all respects? Traditional doctrine was very cautious on this point, and it was generally said to be forty days. Thomas says only that the soul is created when the body of the fetus is ready to receive it.

In the *Summa* (part 3, question 33, article 2) Thomas asks whether Christ's soul was created at the same time as his body. Note that, since Christ's conception did not take place through the transfer of semen but through the grace of the Holy Spirit, it should not be surprising if in such a case God had created the fetus and the rational soul at the same time. But even Christ, as Man and God, must follow human laws: "The beginning of the infusion of the soul may be considered in two ways. First, in regard to the disposition of the body. In this sense the soul of Christ, like the soul of other men, was infused when his

---

1. "In generatione animalis et hominis in quibus est forma perfectissima, sunt plurimae formae et generationes intermediae, et per consequens corruptiones, quia generatio unius est corruptio alterius. Anima igitur vegetabilis, quae primo inest, cum embryo vivit vita plantae, corrumpitur, et succedit anima perfectior, quae est nutritiva et sensitiva simul, et tunc embryo vivit vita animalis; hac autem corrupta, succedit anima rationalis ab extrinseco immissa, licet praecedentes fuerint virtute seminis."

body was formed. Secondly, in relation to time alone. And thus, because Christ's body was perfectly formed in a shorter space of time than that of other men, so he also received his soul before them."

But the problem here is not so much when a fetus becomes a human being, but whether the embryo is already a human being. And Thomas is very clear on this point, as we have seen. And even though the Supplement to the *Summa* is not written by him but probably by his disciple Reginald of Piperno, it is interesting to read question 80, article 4. The problem is whether, upon the resurrection of bodies, all that has contributed to the growth of these bodies is resurrected. Several apparently grotesque questions arise from this. Food is transformed into substance of a human nature; humans eat the flesh of oxen: therefore, if what was the substance of a human nature is resurrected, will the flesh of oxen also be resurrected? It is impossible for one and the same thing to be resurrected in different men. And yet it is possible for something to have belonged in substance to different men, as in the case of the cannibal who eats human flesh, which is transformed into his own substance. Who then is resurrected? The eater or the one who is eaten?

Question 80 is answered in a complex and tortuous manner and seems not to side with any of the various opinions. But what interests us is that at the end of the discussion it is said that natural beings are what they are, not in terms of matter, but in their form. Therefore if the matter that first had the form of beef is then resurrected in man in the form of human flesh, it will certainly not do so as the flesh of an ox but as that of a human being. Otherwise it would mean that the mud from which Adam's body was created would also be resurrected. As for the question of cannibalism, according to one view, the flesh eaten never truly becomes part of the human nature of the person eating it, but remains that of the person who has been eaten. Such flesh will therefore be resurrected in the latter and not in the former.

But the specific point that interests us is that, according to this question, embryos will not take part in the resurrection of the flesh unless they have first been animated by the rational soul.

Now it would be infantile to ask Thomas to absolve those who carry out an abortion within a given period of time, and probably he didn't even think of the moral implications of his reasoning, which today we would describe as being purely scientific. It is curious, however, that the church, which is always quoting the teachings of Thomas Aquinas, has decided on this point to distance itself tacitly from his position.

Something similar has happened with the theory of evolution, with which the church came to terms a long time ago—it was sufficient to interpret the six days of the creation figuratively, as the fathers of the church have always done, and in this way there are no biblical objections to an evolutionary view. Indeed, the book of Genesis is an extremely Darwinian text because it tells us that the creation took place in stages from the least complex to the most complex, from mineral to vegetable, animal, and human.

In the beginning God created the heaven and the earth . . . And God said, Let there be light: and there was light. And God saw the light, that it was good: and God divided the light from the darkness. And God called the light Day, and the darkness he called Night . . . And God made the firmament, and divided the waters which were under the firmament from the waters which were above the firmament . . . And God said, Let the waters under the heaven be gathered together unto one place, and let the dry land appear: and it was so. And God called the dry land Earth; and the gathering together of the waters called he Seas . . . And God said, Let the earth bring forth grass, the herb yielding seed, and the fruit tree yielding fruit after his kind . . . And God made two great lights; the greater light to rule the day, and the lesser light to rule the night: he made the stars also . . . And God said, Let the waters bring forth abundantly the moving creature that hath life, and fowl that may fly above the earth in the open firmament of heaven. And God created great whales, and every living creature that moveth, which the waters brought forth abundantly . . . And God said, Let the earth bring forth the living creature after his kind, cattle, and creeping thing, and beast of the earth after his kind . . . And God said, Let us make man in our image, after our likeness . . . And the Lord God formed man *of* the dust of the ground, and breathed into his nostrils the breath of life; and man became a living soul. (Genesis 1:1–27 and 2:7)

The choice of a battle against evolution and in defense of life, back as far as the embryo, seems rather more in line with the positions of Protestant fundamentalism.

But, as I have said, this lecture was not intended to enter into present disputes but only to explain the thinking of Thomas Aquinas, with which the church of Rome can do as it pleases. I therefore propose to stop here, leaving these documents for the consideration of my listeners.

[Lecture given on November 25, 2008, in Bologna, at the Scuola Superiore di Studi Umanistici, during a conference on the ethics of research, later published in the proceedings: *Etica della ricerca medica e identità culturale europea,* edited by Francesco Galofaro (Bologna: CLUEB, 2009).]

Hugo, Hélas!: The Poetics of Excess

DISCUSSIONS ABOUT Victor Hugo usually start with a comment by Gide who, when asked who was the greatest French poet, replied, "*Hugo, hélas!*" ("Hugo, alas!").[1] Anyone wanting to hit harder might go on to quote Cocteau: "Victor Hugo was a madman who believed he was Victor Hugo."[2]

Gide's lament meant many things, but now tends to be read as meaning that Hugo (and perhaps, in particular, Hugo the narrator) is a great writer despite his innumerable defects, his bombast, his sometimes insufferable rhetoric. Cocteau's quip, however, is not quite correct: Victor Hugo was not a madman who believed he was Victor Hugo—Victor Hugo simply believed he was God, or at least his official interpreter.

In Hugo there is always an excess in the description of earthly events, and an indomitable desire to see them always from God's point of view. The taste for excess leads him to descriptions that become interminable lists, to the creation of characters whose psychological workings are always regarded as unsustainable, rough-hewn,

---

1. For the story of this reply and the justifications that followed it, see *Hugo, Hélas!* by André Gide, edited by Claude Martin (Paris: Éditions Fata Morgana, 2002).

2. Jean Cocteau, *Le mystère laïc,* in *Oeuvres complètes,* vol. 10 (Lausanne: Maguerat, 1946), p. 21.

but whose passions are taken to such levels of paroxysm as to become memorable, a sign of the forces that move history. His desire to be God enables him to see the great forces that move human history, above and beyond the events in which his heroes are involved, and if it is not God then it is Fate, a Destiny that is sometimes presented as providence and sometimes as an almost Hegelian plan that dominates and directs the desires of individuals.

The taste for excess explains why one could mistake Hugo for the Almighty, a personality who, by definition, is larger than life, who convulses the abyss to create heaven and earth, unleashes universal floods, plunges sinners into the fiery bowels of Gehenna, and so forth (a little moderation, please!), and also justifies the plaintive lament from Gide, who evidently identified art with Apollonian poise and not with Dionysian frenzy.

I am perfectly aware of my passion for Hugo. Elsewhere I have praised his sublime excess: and excess can turn even bad writing and banality into a Wagnerian tempest. To explain the fascination of a film like *Casablanca,* I have noted[3] that while a single cliché is kitsch, shamelessly letting fly a hundred clichés makes an epic; and I have noted how the *Count of Monte Cristo* might be badly written (unlike other novels by Dumas, such as *The Three Musketeers*) and may be rambling and verbose, but it is precisely because of these defects, taken beyond reasonable limits, that it reaches that Kantian vision of the sublime, and justifies the hold it has had, and still has, on millions of readers.[4]

But returning to Hugo, let us look at an area typical of Romantic excess, the representation of ugliness and evil.

From the time of Achilles to the dawn of Romanticism, the hero was always handsome, while from Thersites up until more or less the same period, the villain was always ugly, hideous, grotesque, or

3. Umberto Eco, "Casablanca: Cult Movies and Intertextual Collage", in *Faith in Fakes* (London: Vintage, 1998), pp. 197–211.

4. "Elogio del Montecristo," in *Sugli specchi e altri saggi* (Milan: Bompiani, 1985), pp. 147–58.

absurd. And when a hero is made from a villain, he becomes hand-some, as with Milton's Satan.

But by the time we reach the gothic novel, the picture is reversed: not only does the hero appear unsettling and fearsome, but the anti-hero also, in his darkness, becomes if not appealing at least interesting.

Byron says of his Giaour that the glare beneath his dusky cowl was "dark and unearthly," and his eye and his bitter smile aroused fear and guilt. And Ann Radcliffe, describing another dark spirit in *The Ital-ian; or, The Confessional of the Black Penitents,* tells us that his ap-pearance was striking, his limbs large and uncouth, and as he stalked away, wrapped in the black habit of his order, his features expressed something terrible and almost superhuman, while his cowl, casting a shadow over the livid paleness of his face, gave a sense of horror to his large melancholy eyes . . .

The figure of William Beckford's Vathek was pleasing and majes-tic, but when angry, one of his eyes became so terrible that no per-son could bear to behold it, and the wretch upon whom it was fixed fell instantly backward and sometimes died. For Stevenson, Hyde was pale and dwarfish, he gave an impression of deformity without any nameable malformation, he had a displeasing smile, behaved himself with a disturbing mixture of timidity and boldness, and spoke with a husky, whispering, and somewhat broken voice, which inspired dis-gust, loathing, and fear.

Of Heathcliff, Emily Brontë writes that his forehead was shaded with a heavy cloud, his eyes were basilisks, and his lips seemed sealed in an expression of unspeakable sadness. And here is how Eugène Sue describes the Schoolmaster in *Les mystères de Paris:* his face scored in all directions with deep, livid scars; his lips swollen by the corro-sive action of vitriol; the cartilage of his nose cut; his nostrils replaced by two shapeless holes; his head was disproportionately large; he had long arms and short, stubby hands, with hairy fingers, and bow legs and restless, mobile eyes, flashing like those of a wild beast.

But Hugo too is excessive in his descriptions of ugliness, for rea-sons set out in his famous preface to *Cromwell,* where he theorizes comprehensively on the revolution of beauty, which, in the Romantic period, is transformed into its opposite – into ugliness and deformity, or at least into the grotesque.

Modern ingenuity – he says – transforms giants into dwarfs; from Cyclopes gnomes are made. Contact with deformity has given modern sublimity something greater, more sublime than ancient beauty.

The grotesque is the other face of the sublime, as shadow is to light. Grotesqueness is the richest resource nature can offer art. The universal beauty that antiquity solemnly gave to everything was not without its monotony, and this impression can produce tedium through repetition. Beauty is only of one kind; there are a thousand kinds of ugliness. It is difficult to compare one sublime with another, and we need to take a rest from everything, even from beauty. The salamander makes the Ondine more attractive; the gnome makes Sisyphus more handsome.

But Hugo is more radical when he is creating than when he is theorizing. Deformity is not only a form of evil that contrasts with beauty and goodness; it is, in itself, an atrocious and unsought modesty, as if God had wanted to conceal from others, under the guise of external ugliness, an inner beauty that is destined nonetheless to be lost. Hugo softens the irredeemable ugliness of the spider and the nettle ("I love the spider and the nettle / because they hate us. / O passer-by, forgive / that obscure plant, / that poor animal, / for their ugliness and their sting. / Have pity on evil!").

Quasimodo, the hunchback of Notre-Dame, has a tetrahedral nose and a horseshoe mouth; his left eye is obstructed by a red, bushy brow, while his right disappears under an enormous wart; his straggling teeth are broken here and there like the battlements of a fortress; a tooth protrudes from his callused lip like the tusk of an elephant . . . He has a huge head, bristling with red hair; between his shoulders an enormous hump; large feet, monstrous hands, legs so strangely aligned that they could touch each other only at the knees and, viewed from the front, resembled the crescents of two scythes joined by the handles . . .

To contrast this repellent aspect, Hugo gives Quasimodo a sensitive soul and a great capacity to love. But he reaches the highest point with the figure of Gwynplaine, the Man Who Laughs.

Gwynplaine is not only the ugliest of all and, due to his ugliness, the unhappiest; he is also the most pure-spirited of all, capable of infinite love. And — paradox of Romantic ugliness — monstrous as he is, and precisely because he is monstrous, he stirs the desires of the most beautiful woman in London.

For those who have forgotten the story, let us summarize it. The scion of a noble family, kidnapped as a child in a political feud, Gwynplaine is transformed by *comprachicos* into a grotesque mask, his features surgically disfigured, and he is condemned to an eternal smile.

Nature had been prodigal of her kindness to Gwynplaine. She had bestowed on him a mouth opening to his ears, ears folding over to his eyes, a shapeless nose to support the spectacles of the grimace maker, and a face that no one could look upon without laughing . . .

But was it nature? Had she not been assisted? Two slits for eyes, a hiatus for a mouth, a snub protuberance with two holes for nostrils, a flattened face, all having for the result an appearance of laughter; it is certain that nature never produces such perfection single-handed . . .

Such a face could never have been created by chance; it must have resulted from intention . . . Had Gwynplaine when a child been so worthy of attention that his face had been subjected to transmutation? Why not? Needed there a greater motive than the speculation of his future exhibition? According to all appearance, industrious manipulators of children had worked upon his face. It seemed evident that a mysterious and probably occult science, which was to surgery what alchemy was to chemistry, had chiseled his flesh, evidently at a very tender age, and manufactured his countenance with premeditation. That science, clever with the knife, skilled in obtusions and ligatures, had enlarged the mouth, cut away the lips, laid bare the gums, distended the ears, cut the cartilages, displaced the eyelids and the cheeks, enlarged the zygomatic muscle, pressed the scars and cicatrices to a level, turned back the skin over the lesions whilst the face was thus stretched, from all which resulted that powerful and profound piece of sculpture, the mask, Gwynplaine. (part 2, book 2, chapter 1)

With this mask, Gwynplaine becomes an acrobat, highly popular with audiences. Since childhood he has been in love with Dea, a blind girl who performs with him. Gwynplaine had eyes for only one woman in the whole world – that blind creature. Dea idolized Gwynplaine. She would touch him and say, "How beautiful you are."

Until two things happen. Lady Josiane, the queen's sister, adored by all the gentlemen of the court for her beauty, sees Gwynplaine at the theater, sends him a letter: "You are hideous, I am beautiful. You are a player; I am a duchess. I am the highest, you are the lowest. I desire you! I love you! Come!"

Gwynplaine grapples between his feelings of excitement and desire, and his love for Dea. Then something happens. He thinks he has been arrested. He is questioned, and brought face to face with a bandit who is dying; in short, all of a sudden he has been recognized as Lord Fermain Clancharlie, baron of Clancharlie and Hunkerville, marquis of Corleone in Sicily, and an English peer, who had been kidnapped and disfigured at a tender age in a family feud.

We move onward by leaps and bounds, as Gwynplaine suddenly finds himself propelled from the gutter to the stars, hardly realizing what is going on, except that at a certain point he finds himself, extravagantly dressed, in the room of a palace that, he is told, is his.

It seems to him like an enchanted palace, and already the series of marvels he discovers there (alone in the resplendent desert), the succession of halls and chambers, is bewildering not only to him but to the reader. It is no coincidence that the title of the chapter is "The Resemblance of a Palace to a Wood," and the description of what seems like the Louvre or the Hermitage takes up five or six pages (depending on the edition). Gwynplaine wanders, dazed, from room to room until he reaches an alcove where, on the bed, beside a tub of water made ready for a virginal bath, he sees a naked woman.

Not literally naked, Hugo tells us. She is clothed. But the description of this clothed woman, especially if we see her through the eyes of Gwynplaine, who has never seen a naked woman, certainly represents one of the heights of erotic literature.

At the center of this web, where one might expect a spider, Gwynplaine saw a formidable object — a woman naked.

Not literally naked. She was dressed. And dressed from head to foot. The dress was a long chemise, so long that it floated over her feet, like the dresses of angels in holy pictures, but so fine that it seemed liquid. From here, the appearance of female nudity, more treacherous and dangerous than real nudity . . . The silver tissue, transparent as glass, was a curtain. It was fastened only at the ceiling, could be lifted aside . . . On that bed, which was silver like the bath and the canopy, lay the woman. She was asleep . . .

Between her nudity and his gaze there were two obstacles, her chemise and the silver veil, two transparencies. The room, more an alcove than a room, was lit with a sort of discretion from the light reflected from the bathroom. The woman may have had no modesty, but the lighting did. The bed had neither columns nor canopy, so that the woman, when she opened her eyes, could see herself a thousand times naked in the mirrors above her. Gwynplaine saw only the woman. He recognized her. She was the duchess. Again he saw her, and saw her terrible. A woman naked is a woman armed . . . That immodesty was merged in splendor. That creature lay naked with the same calm of one with the divine right of cynicism. She had the security of an Olympian who knew that she was daughter of the depths, and might say to the ocean, "Father!" And she exposed herself, unattainable and proud, to everything that should pass — to looks, to desires, to ravings, to dreams; as proud in her languor, on her boudoir couch, as Venus in the immensity of foam. (part 2, book 7, chapter 3)

And so Josiane awakens, recognizes Gwynplaine, and begins a furious seduction, which the poor man can no longer resist, except that she brings him to the peak of desire but does not yield. She erupts into a series of fantasies, more stimulating than her own nudity, in which she reveals herself as a virgin (as she still is) and a prostitute, anxious to enjoy not only the pleasures of the teratology that Gwynplaine promises her, but also the thrill of defying the world and the court, a prospect that intoxicates her. She is a Venus awaiting the double orgasm of private possession and public exhibition of her Vulcan:

> "I feel degraded in your presence, and oh, what happiness that is! How insipid it is to be a grandee! I am noble; what can be more tiresome? Disgrace is a comfort. I am so satiated with respect that I long for contempt.
>
> "I love you, not only because you are deformed, but because you are low. I love monsters, and I love mountebanks. A lover despised, mocked, grotesque, hideous, exposed to laughter on that pillory called a theater, has for me an extraordinary attraction. It is tasting the fruit of hell. An infamous lover, how exquisite! To taste the apple, not of Paradise, but of hell — such is my temptation. It is for that I hunger and thirst. I am that Eve, the Eve of the depths. Probably you are, unknown to yourself, a devil. I am in love with a nightmare. You are a moving puppet, of which the strings are pulled by a specter. You are the incarnation of infernal mirth . . . Gwynplaine, I am the throne; you are the footstool. Let us join on the same level. Oh, how happy I am in my fall! I wish all the world could know how abject I am become. It would bow down all the lower. The more man abhors, the more does he cringe. It is human nature. Hostile, but reptile; dragon, but worm. Oh, I am as depraved as are the gods! . . . Now, you are not ugly; you are deformed. Ugliness is mean, deformity is grand. Ugliness is the devil's grin behind beauty; deformity is the reverse of sublimity.
>
> "I love you!" she cried. And she bit him with a kiss. (part 2, book 7, chapter 4)

Just as Gwynplaine is about to yield, a message arrives from the queen, telling her sister that the Man Who Laughs has been recognized as the rightful Lord Clancharlie and that he is to be her husband. Josiane comments, "Be it so." She gets up, gives him her hand (moving from familiar to formal address), saying "Get out" to the man she had so wildly sought to seduce, and adds: "Since you are my husband, get out . . . You have no right to be here; this place is for my lover."

Gwynplaine is excessive in his disfigurement; Josiane is excessive in her initial sadomasochism, excessive in her reaction. There is another reversal in the situation, which has already been reversed through a normal recognition device (you are not an acrobat but a lord) and added to by a double change of fortune (you were a wretch, now you are not only a lord but desired by the most beautiful woman in the realm, whom you too now desire with all your confused and disturbed soul)—and this would be enough as comedy, if not as tragedy. The reversal, however, is not into tragedy (at least not for the moment: Gwynplaine will kill himself only at the end), but into a grotesque farce. The reader is exhausted and, all of a sudden, understands the threads of Destiny as well as the weave of gallant society of that century. Hugo has no shame: compared to him, Josiane is as prim as a saint.

And now we come to the other reversal of fortune. Gwynplaine—who, after the episode with Josiane, had already begun to understand the laws and powers and customs that she represents—enters the House of Lords and is greeted with suspicion and curiosity. He does nothing to make himself accepted; indeed, at the first vote he stands up and makes a passionate appeal in support of the people, and against the aristocracy who are exploiting them. It is a passage worthy of Marx's *Das Kapital*, but when spoken with a face that laughs even when it is expressing scorn, passion, pain, and love for the truth, it stirs not scorn but hilarity. The sitting ends in fun and laughter, Gwynplaine understands that this cannot be his world, and after a desperate search, returns to Dea. She, alas, suffering more from the loss of her lover than from the illness that has afflicted her for some time, dies happily in his arms. Gwynplaine does not hold back. Divided between two worlds—one that disowns him and the other that has gone—he kills himself. Thus, in Gwynplaine, the quintessential

Romantic hero, we find a synthesis of all the elements of the Romantic novel: purest passion, the temptation and fascination of sin, the rapid reversals of fortune with his passage from the depths of poverty to the magnificence of the court, his titanic rebellion against the world of injustice, his heroic testimony to truth, even at the cost of losing everything, the death of his lover from consumption, a destiny crowned by his own suicide. But everything highly exaggerated.

The Hunchback of Notre-Dame, though an early work, shows all the signs of a poetics of excess. In the opening chapters, to create the idea of public celebration and the participation of the aristocracy as well as members of the bourgeoisie and the populace, to create the impression of *grouillement* (to use Hugo's word), of a teeming mass, the reader has to digest a vast series of names of characters who may be historical but are completely unfamiliar and therefore meaningless. Heaven help anyone who tries to identify them, or to find out anything about them. It is like watching a procession — perhaps a July 14 parade in Paris or Trooping the Colour in London — where we cannot identify the various regiments from their uniforms and know nothing about their history, but are struck by the immensity of the parade, and woe betide us if we see only half of it, since we will lose the charm and majesty of the event. Hugo never says to us, "There was a crowd." He puts us right there in the middle of it, as if he is presenting each of its members to us one by one. We can shake a few hands, pretend to recognize someone we ought to know, and then return home with the feeling of experiencing its immensity.

The same can be said about Gringoire's Dantesque visit to the Court of Miracles, among villains, vagrants, beggars, defrocked priests, young delinquents, whores, gypsies, *narquois, coquillarts, hubins, sabouilleux,* false cripples, cutpurses, scoundrels, and so on. We don't need to recognize them all: it is the descriptions of them that create the effect; we have to feel the place teeming with criminals and wretches to understand this turbulent festering swamp population who, many chapters later, will attack the cathedral like an immense colony of termites, sewer rats, cockroaches, locusts — the protagonist is not one person but the mass. In short, we have to learn to read through the inventories, lists, catalogs like a flow of music. And then we become absorbed into the book.

And we arrive at the point where the poetics of excess is apparent through the technique of the catalog and the list. Hugo uses this technique on countless occasions but perhaps it is used most continuously, most completely and convincingly in *Ninety-three*.

Though we might be able to spot and list many shortcomings in this book—above all, the rhetorical incontinence—as we thrust the knife deeper in the wound, they begin to appear splendid to us. It would be like a devotee of Bach and his disembodied, almost cerebral compositions, saying that Beethoven creates more noise in comparison with those fine pieces for the well-tempered clavier: but to what purpose? Can we resist the power of the Fifth or the Ninth?

We can avoid indulging in a Pantagruelian feast, but once we have accepted the rules of the game, there is no point remembering the dietitian's advice or longing for the delicate sensations of nouvelle cuisine. If we have the stomach to join the orgy, it will be an unforgettable experience. Otherwise it is better to leave straightaway and lull ourselves to sleep reading a few aphorisms by an eighteenth-century gentleman. Hugo is not for the faint-hearted. Yet while the battle of *Hernani* is later than Sturm und Drang, the shadow of that storm and that assault still illuminates the last Romantic in 1874, the date of the novel's publication (though not of its gestation).

To understand just how *Ninety-three* is fueled by excess, let us look at the story, which, all in all, is very simple, though heavily melodramatic, and in the hands of an Italian opera librettist could have produced the equivalent, perhaps, of *Tosca* or *Il trovatore* (by which I mean their plots, without the music that allows us to take the verses more seriously).

It is the annus horribilis of the Revolution. The Vendée is in revolt. An old aristocrat with a glorious military past, the marquis de Lantenac comes ashore to take command of the peasant masses, who emerge like devils from mysterious forests and shoot while they recite the rosary. The Revolution, in the form of the Convention, has set its men against him. First there is Gauvain (Lantenac's nephew), a young aristocrat turned republican, a man of feminine beauty fired with warlike fervor, but an angelic utopian who still hopes that the conflict can be settled in a spirit of compassion and respect for the enemy. Then we meet Cimourdain, a man we'd call a political adviser today. He is a former priest, as ruthless as Lantenac, who is convinced that social and political regeneration will happen only through a bloodbath, and that every hero pardoned today will become the enemy who will kill us tomorrow. Cimourdain, moreover—melodrama does have its demands—was Gauvain's tutor when he was a child and loves him like a son. Hugo never allows us to think of a passion different from that of a man (first celibate through faith and later through revolutionary vocation) who is consecrated to spiritual fatherhood—but who knows? Cimourdain's passion is ferocious, complete, and carnally mystical.

In this struggle between Revolution and Reaction, Lantenac and Gauvain try to kill each other, attacking and retreating in a whirl of endless massacres. Yet this story of multiple horrors opens when a hungry widow and her three children are discovered by the men of a republican battalion, who decide to adopt the children one radiant day in May when "les oiseaux gazouillaient au-dessus des baïonnettes." The children will later be captured by Lantenac, who shoots the mother and takes the little ones (now republican mascots) as hostages. The mother survives the execution and wanders about, desperately looking for them, while the republicans fight to free the three innocent captives, who are held prisoner in the dark medieval tower where Lantenac is then besieged by Gauvain. After fierce resistance, Lantenac manages to escape from the siege along a secret passage, but his followers have set fire to the tower and the children are about to perish. The desperate mother reappears, and Lantenac (who undergoes a sort of transfiguration and is transformed from Satan into a salvific Lucifer) reenters the tower and allows himself to be captured by his enemies in order to rescue the children and bring them to safety.

While waiting for the trial that Cimourdain has organized on the spot, arranging for the guillotine to be brought there, Gauvain asks himself whether a man who has redeemed his errors through an act of generosity has to be sent to death. He enters the prisoner's cell where, in a long monologue, Lantenac reaffirms the rights of the throne and the altar. In the end Gauvain lets Lantenac escape, and waits in the cell in his place. When Cimourdain discovers what he has done, he has no choice but to put Gauvain on trial and, with his casting vote, to decide his death — the death of the only person he has ever loved.

The recurring theme of the three children to some extent accompanies the troubled story of Gauvain, who, through his kindness and compassion, will face the punishment that awaits him, and both of the themes cast a ray of hope on that future that can only be brought about through human sacrifice. It is to no avail that the whole army shouts out for their commander to be reprieved. Cimourdain knows the suffering of deepest love but has dedicated his life to duty, to the law, and he is guardian of that revolutionary purity that is identified with terror — or rather, with the Terror. Yet at the moment Gauvain's head rolls into the basket, Cimourdain fires his pistol into his own heart, "and those two souls, tragic sisters, took flight together, the shadow of the one blending with the light of the other."

Is that it? Did Hugo simply want to reduce us to tears? Of course not, and the first observation has to be made in narrative rather than political terms. It is now part of the *koinè*, the common language of every scholar of narrative structures (and I will avoid making learned reference to secondary theoretical notions), that in a story the actors of course take part in the action, but the actors are the embodiment of the *actants*, which might be described as the narrative roles through which the actors can pass, perhaps changing their function in the plot structure. For instance, in a novel like *I promessi sposi* (*The Betrothed*), the forces of evil or human weakness can act against the forces of a providence that controls everyone's destinies, and one and the same actor, such as L'Innominato, can suddenly change from the role of Opponent to that of Auxiliary. And — compared to actors chained to an unchangeable actant role, such as Don Rodrigo on the one hand and Fra Cristoforo on the other—this explains the ambiguity of Don Abbondio, "a vessel of fragile earthenware, obliged to journey in company with many vessels of iron," who constantly moves from one role to another, and this is why we feel, in the end, that his bewilderment is forgivable.

When Hugo, in his old age, wrote this novel, which he had been pondering for some time (he had mentioned it in the preface to *The Man Who Laughs,* several years earlier), the political and ideological position of his youth had drastically changed. Although as a young man he had expressed legitimist ideas and had supported the Vendée, he later regarded 1793 as a cloud in the blue sky of 1789 and moved toward liberal, then socialist principles and then, after Louis Napoleon's coup d'état, toward socialist, democratic, and republican principles. In his 1841 admission speech to the Académie française, he paid tribute to the Convention, which "smashed the throne and saved the country, . . . which committed acts and outrages that we might detest and condemn, but which we must admire." Though he did not understand the Paris Commune, after the Restoration he fought for an amnesty for the communards. In short, the gestation and publication of *Ninety-three* coincide with the completion of his movement toward an increasingly radical position. To understand the Commune, Hugo must justify even the Terror. He had fought for a long time against the death penalty but—mindful of the great reactionary lesson of an author he knew well, Joseph de Maistre—he knew that redemption and purification also occur through the horrors of human sacrifice.

His reference to de Maistre appears in book 1, chapter 4, of *Les misérables,* in that scene where Monsignor Myriel contemplates the guillotine:

> He who sees it shivers with the most mysterious of shivers . . . The scaffold is a vision . . . It seems as though it were a being, possessed of I know not what sombre initiative; one would say that this piece

of carpenter's work saw, that this machine heard, that this mechanism understood, that this wood, this iron, and these cords were possessed of will . . . The scaffold is the accomplice of the executioner; it devours, it eats flesh, it drinks blood . . . a spectre which seems to live with a horrible vitality composed of all the death which it has inflicted. (translated by Isabel F. Hapgood)

But in *Ninety-three* the guillotine, even though it will kill the Revolution's purest hero, passes from the side of death to that of life and, in any event, stands as a symbol for the future against the darkest symbols of the past. It is now erected in front of La Tourgue, the stronghold where Lantenac is besieged. Fifteen hundred years of feudal sin are condensed in it—a hard knot to untie. The guillotine stands before it with the purity of a blade that will slice through that knot—it was not created out of nothing, it has been drenched by the blood spilled over fifteen centuries on that same land, and it rises up from the ground, an unknown vindicator, and says to the tower, "I am thy daughter." And the tower realizes that its end is near. This exchange is not new for Hugo: it is reminiscent of Frollo in *The Hunchback of Notre-Dame,* when he compares the printed book to the towers and gargoyles of the cathedral: "Ceci tuera cela." Though the guillotine is still a monster, in *Ninety-three* it takes the side of the future.

What is a ferocious, death-giving monster that promises a better life? An oxymoron. Victor Brombert has observed how many oxymorons populate this novel: rapacious angel, intimate discord, colossal sweetness, odiously obliging and terrible serenity, venerable innocents, frightening wretches, hell in the midst of dawn, and Lantenac himself, who at one point shifts from being an infernal Satan to a celestial Lucifer.[5] The oxymoron is "a rhetorical microcosm that affirms the substantially antithetical nature of the world," though Brombert

---

5. Victor Brombert, *Victor Hugo and the Visionary Novel* (Cambridge, MA: Harvard University Press, 1984).

emphasizes that the antitheses are ultimately resolved into a higher order. *Ninety-three* tells the story of a virtuous crime, a healing act of
violence whose deep purposes must be understood for its events to
be justified. *Ninety-three* is not the story of what a few men did, but
the story of what history forced those men to do, irrespective of their
wishes, often undermined by contradictions. And the idea of a purpose to the story justifies even that force — the Vendée — which osten-
sibly seeks to move against it.

This takes us back to defining the relationship between the novel's
minor actors and the actants. Each individual and each object, from
Marat to the guillotine, represent not themselves but the great forces
that are the actual protagonists of the novel. Hugo presents himself
here as the authorized interpreter of divine will, and seeks to justify
each story he tells from the point of view of God.

Whatever Hugo's God might be, he is always present in his narrative to explain the bloody enigmas of history. Perhaps Hugo would
never have written that everything real is rational, but he would have
agreed that everything ideal is rational. In any event, there is always a
Hegelian tone in acknowledging that history marches toward its own
ends, over the heads of the actors condemned to embody its purposes.
Just think of the Beethovenian description of the Battle of Waterloo in
Les misérables. Unlike Stendhal, who describes the battle through the
eyes of Fabrizio, who is in the midst of it and doesn't understand what
is going on, Hugo describes the battle through the eyes of God — he
watches it from above. He knows that if Napoleon had known there
was a cliff beyond the crest of the Mont-Saint-Jean plateau (but his
guide had failed to tell him about it), Milhaud's cuirassiers would not
have been destroyed by the English army; that if the shepherd boy
who was Bülow's guide had suggested a different route, the Prussian
army would not have arrived in time to decide the fate of the battle.
But what does it matter, and what is the importance of the miscalcu-
lations of Napoleon (actor), the folly of Grouchy (actor) — who could
have returned but didn't — or the ruses, if such they were, of the actor

Wellington, seeing that Hugo describes Waterloo as a first-rate victory by a second-rate leader?

> This vertigo, this terror, this downfall into ruin of the loftiest bravery which ever astounded history,—is that causeless? No. The shadow of an enormous right hand is projected athwart Waterloo . . . The disappearance of the great man was necessary to the advent of the great century. Someone, a person to whom one replies not, took the responsibility on himself. The panic of heroes can be explained. In the battle of Waterloo there is something more than a cloud, there is something of the meteor. God has passed by. (volume 2, book 1, chapter 13)

And God also passes through the Vendée and the Convention, gradually putting on the actorial guise of wild, ferocious peasants, of aristocrats converted to *égalité,* of heroes gloomy and nocturnal like Cimourdain, or radiant like Gauvain. Hugo sees the Vendée rationally, as a mistake. But since this mistake was deliberate and kept under control by a providential (or fatal) plan, he is fascinated by the Vendée, and turns it into an epic. He is skeptical, sarcastic, petty in describing the men who populate the Convention, but he sees them as giants, or rather, he gives us a gigantic picture of the Convention.

This is why he isn't worried that his actors are psychologically rigid and bound up in their destiny. He isn't worried that the cold frenzies of Lantenac, the harshness of Cimourdain, or the hot passionate sweetness of his Homeric Gauvain (Achilles? Hector?) are improbable. Hugo wants us to feel through them the Great Forces at play.

He wants to tell us a story about excess, and about excess that is so inexplicable that it can only be described through oxymorons. What style do you use to talk about one excess, about many excesses? An excessive style. That is exactly the style that Hugo adopts.

We have seen in *The Man Who Laughs* that one of the manifestations of excess is the vertiginous reversal in events and points of view. It is difficult to explain this technique, of which Hugo is the master. He knows that the rules of tragedy require what the French call a *coup de théâtre*. In classical tragedy, one is generally more than enough: Oedipus discovers he has killed his father and slept with his mother — what more do you want? End of the tragic action, and catharsis — if you're able to swallow it.

But for Hugo this is not enough (doesn't he believe he is Victor Hugo, after all?). Let us see what happens in *Ninety-three*. The corvette Claymore is trying to break through the republican naval blockade along the Brittany coast to bring ashore Lantenac, the future head of the Vendée revolt. It looks like a freighter from the outside but is armed with thirty guns. And the drama begins — Hugo, lest we fail to realize its magnitude, announces that "nothing more terrible could have happened." A twenty-four-pounder cannon breaks loose. In a ship that plunges and pitches at the mercy of a rough sea, a cannon rolling from port to starboard is worse than enemy fire. It hurtles about, like one of its cannonballs, crashing into the walls, opening up leaks. No one can stop it. And the ship is destined to sink. It is a supernatural beast, Hugo warns us, fearing that we haven't yet understood, and to avoid any misunderstanding, he describes the catastrophic event for five pages. Until one brave gunner, playing with the iron beast like a matador with a bull, takes up the challenge, throws himself before it, risking his life, dodges it, provokes it, attacks it once again, and is about to be crushed by it when Lantenac throws a bale of counterfeit banknotes between its wheels, stopping it for a moment, allowing the sailor to plunge an iron bar between the spokes of its hind wheels, to lift up the monster, turn it over, and restore it to its mineral immobility. The crew rejoices. The sailor thanks Lantenac for having saved his life. Shortly afterward, before the whole crew, Lantenac commends him for his courage and, taking a cross of Saint-Louis from an officer, pins it on his chest.

Then he orders him to be shot.

He has been brave, but he was also the gunner in charge of that cannon, and he should have prevented it from breaking loose. The man, with the medal on his chest, offers himself up to the firing squad.

Is this reversal enough? No. With the ship now damaged, Lantenac will reach the coast in a small boat rowed by a sailor. Halfway there, the sailor reveals he is the brother of the executed man and declares he will kill Lantenac, who then stands up before this avenger and makes a speech that carries on for five pages. He explains what duty means, reminds him that their duty is to save France, to save God; he convinces him that he, Lantenac, has acted in accordance with justice, while if the sailor yields to the desire for revenge, he will be committing the greatest injustice ("You take my life from the King, and you give your eternity to the devil!"). The sailor, overcome, asks him for forgiveness. Lantenac grants it, and from that moment, Halmalo, the failed avenger, will become the servant of his brother's executioner, in the name of the Vendée.

Enough of this excessive series of reversals. Let us turn to the other, and principal, force for excess, the Endless List. Having described the leader, he has to give an idea of the army that awaits him. Hugo wants to build up a picture, village by village, castle by castle, region by region, of every aspect of the uprising in support of the monarchy. He could, rather flatly, have reproduced a map of those towns, marking out the main centers of revolt. But he would have ended up reducing to a regional dimension an event he wanted to portray as cosmic. Instead, with remarkable narrative inventiveness, he devises a messenger reminiscent of a Pico della Mirandola. Halmalo cannot read, which suits Lantenac very well — a man who reads is a hindrance. It is enough that he has a good memory. And he gives him his instructions, which I will set out only in part, because this time the list covers eight pages.

> "Good. Listen, Halmalo. You must go to the right and I to the left. I shall go in the direction of Fougères, and you must go towards Bazouges. Keep your bag, which gives you the appearance of a peasant. Conceal your weapons. Cut a stick for yourself in the hedges. Creep through the rye, which is high . . . Keep a distance from those you meet. Avoid the roads and the bridges. Do not enter Pontorson . . . You know the woods?"

"Everywhere."

"All over the country?"

"From Noirmoutiers to Laval."

"You know their names too?"

"I know the woods, I know their names, I know all of them."

"You will not forget anything?"

"Nothing."

"Good. Now, pay attention. How many leagues can you walk a day?"

"Ten, fifteen, eighteen, twenty, if necessary."

"It will be necessary. Don't lose a word of what I am going to tell you. You must go to the woods of Saint-Aubin."

"Near Lamballe?"

"Yes. On the edge of the ravine between Saint-Rieul and Plédéliac there is a great chestnut-tree. You must stop there. You will see nobody . . . You must make a call. Do you know how to make this call?" . . .

He handed the green silk bow to Halmalo.

"Here is my badge of command. Take it. It is important that nobody should know my name at present. But this bow will be enough. The fleur-de-lis was embroidered by Madame Royal, in the Temple prison . . . Listen carefully to this. This is the order: 'Rise in revolt. No quarter.' Then on the edge of the woods of Saint-Aubin give the call. You must give it three times. The third time you will see a man come out of the ground . . . This man is Planchenault, also called Coeur-de-Roi. Show him this knot. He will understand. Then go, whatever way you can, to the woods of Astillé; you will find there a knock-kneed man surnamed Mousqueton, and who shows pity to nobody. You will tell him that I love him and that he is to stir up his parishes. You will then go to the woods of Couesbon, which is one league from Ploërmel. Make the call of the owl; a man will come, out of a hole; it will be M. Thuault, seneschal of Ploërmel, who has belonged to what is called the Constitution Assembly, but on the good side. Tell him to arm the castle of Couesbon, belonging to the marquis de Guer, a refugee . . . Then go to Saint-Guen-les-Toits, and speak to Jean Chouan, who is, in my eyes, the real chief. Then go to the woods of Ville-Anglose, where you will see Guitter, called Saint-Martin. Tell him to have an eye for a certain Courmesnil, son-in-law of old Goupil de Préfeln, and who leads the Jacobins of Argentan. Remember all this well. I write nothing because nothing must be written . . . Then go to the woods of Rougefeu, where Miélette is, who leaps ravines, balancing himself on a long pole."

I jump ahead three whole pages:

"Go to Saint-M'Hervé. There you will see Gaulier, called Grand-Pierre. Go to the district of Parné, where the men blacken their faces . . . Go to the camp of La Vache Noire, which is on a height, in the midst of the wood of La Charnie, then to the camp of L'Avoine, then to Champ Vert, then to Champ des Fourmis. Go to the Grand-Bordage, also called the Haut-du-Pré, which is inhabited by a widow whose daughter is married to Treton, called the Englishman. The Grand-Bordage is in the parish of Queslaines. You must go to Épineux-le-Chevreuil, Sillé-le-Guillaume, Parannes, and all the men in every wood . . ."

And so on to the final exchange:

"Forget nothing."
"Have no fear."
"Start now. God be with you. Go."
"I will do all you have told me. I will go. I will speak the word. I will obey. I will command." (book 3, chapter 2)

It is, of course, impossible for Halmalo to remember everything, and the reader is fully aware of it — one line later, we have already forgotten the names on the previous line. The list is tedious, but it has to be read, and reread. It is like music. Pure sound, it could be an index of names at the back of an atlas, but this frenzy of cataloging makes the Vendée into an infinity.

The technique of the list is an ancient one. The catalog becomes useful when something has to appear so immense and confused that a definition or description would be insufficient to show its complexity, especially to give the feeling of a space and all it contains. The list or catalog does not fill up a space (which in itself would be neutral) with significant phenomena, associations, facts, details that catch the eye. It brings together objects or people, or places. It is a hypotyposis, which creates a description through an excess of *flatus vocis,* as if the ear had given the eye part of the impossible task of memorizing everything it hears, or as if the imagination was striving to construct a place in which to put all the things named. The list is a Braille hypotyposis.

Nothing is inessential in the list that Halmalo is pretending (I hope) to remember: altogether it represents the very enormousness of the counterrevolution, its extension throughout the land, into the hedgerows, villages, woods, and parishes. Hugo knows every ploy, as well as being aware (as perhaps Homer also was) that readers would never read the whole list (or that those listening to the ancient bard would have listened in the same way that people listen to the recital of the rosary, yielding to its pure captivating incantation). Hugo, I am sure, knew that his reader would have skipped these pages, as Manzoni did when, contrary to every rule of narrative, he leaves us in suspense with Don Abbondio faced by two villains, and then gives us four pages about local laws and edicts (four in the 1840 edition, but almost six in the 1827 edition). The reader skips over these pages (or might perhaps look at them on a second or third reading), but we cannot ignore the fact that the list is there before our eyes, forcing us to jump ahead as the suspense is unbearable — it is its unbearableness that amplifies its power. Returning to Hugo, the insurrection is so enormous that we, while reading it, cannot remember all the main characters, or even just their leaders. It is the compunction of this prolonged reading that makes us feel the sublimity of the Vendée.

The Royalist revolt is sublime, as must be the picture of the Convention, the very essence of the Revolution. We reach the third book, titled "The Convention." The first three chapters describe the hall, and already in these first seven pages the abundance of description leaves the reader dazed and deprived of all feeling of space. But it then continues — for another fifteen pages — with the list of the members of the Convention, more or less as follows:

> On the right, the Gironde, a legion of thinkers; on the left the Mountain, a group of athletes. On one side, Buissot, who received the keys of the Bastille; Barbaroux, whom the Marseilles troops obeyed; Kervélegan, who had the battalion of Brest garrisoned in the Faubourg Saint-Marceau, under his hand; Gersonné, who established the supremacy of representatives over generals . . . Sillery, the humpback of the Right, as Couthon was the cripple of the Left. Lause-Duperret, who when called a "rascal" by a journalist, invited him to dine with him, saying: "I know that rascal means simply a man who does not think as we do"; Rabaut-Saint-Étienne, who commenced his Almanac of 1790 with these words: "The revolution is ended" . . . Vigée, who had the title of grenadier in the second battalion of Mayenne-et-Loire, who, when threatened by the public tribunes, cried out: "I ask that at the first murmur of the public tribunes, we withdraw and march to Versailles, sword in hand!"; Buzot, destined to die of hunger; Valazé, victim of his own dagger; Condorcet, who was to die at Bourg-la-Reine, changed to Bourg-Égalité, denounced by the Horace he carried in his pocket; Pétion, whose fate was to be worshiped by the multitude in 1792, and devoured by the wolves in 1793; twenty others beside, Pontécoulant, Marboz, Lidon, Saint-Martin, Dussaulx, the translator of Juvenal, who took part in the campaign of Hanover; Boilleau, Bertrand, Lesterp-Beauvais, Lesage, Gomaire, Gardien, Mainvielle, Duplantier, Lacaze, Antiboul, and at their head a Barnave called Vergniaud . . .

And so on, for fifteen pages, like the litany of a black mass, Antonie-Louis-Léon Florelle de Saint-Just, Merlin de Thionville, Merkin de Douai, Billaud-Varenne, Fabre d'Églantine, Fréron-Thersite, Osselin, Garan-Coulon, Javogues, Camboulas, Collot, d'Herbois, Goupilleau, Laurent Lecointre, Léonard Bourdoin, Bourbotte, Levasseur de la Sarthe, Reverchon, Bernard de Saintres, Charles Richard, Châteauneuf-Randon, Lavicomterie, Le Peletier de Saint-Fargeau, almost as if Hugo realized that anyone reading this mad catalog would have lost the identity of the actors in order to become aware of the titanic dimensions of the only actant he was interested in — the Revolution itself, with its glories and its miseries.

Yet it seems that Hugo (was it due to weakness, shyness, excessive excess?) is worried that the reader (even though he presumably skips ahead) will not fully grasp the dimensions of the monster he wishes to portray and so — using an entirely new technique in the history of the list, and in any case different from the description of the Vendée — the author's moralizing voice continually intervenes at the beginning, at the end, in the list itself:

> Here is the Convention.
>
> The attention must be fixed on this summit.
>
> Never did anything higher appear on man's horizon.
>
> There is Mt. Himalaya, and there is the Convention . . .
>
> The Convention is the first avatar of the people . . .
>
> The effect of all this was intense, savage, regular. Savage correctness; this is a suggestion of the whole Revolution . . .
>
> Nothing was more deformed, nor more sublime. A pile of heroes, a herd of cowards. Wild beasts on a mountain, reptiles in a marsh . . . A gathering of Titans . . .
>
> Tragedies knotted by giants and untied by dwarfs . . .
>
> Minds, a prey to the wind. But this wind a miraculous wind . . .
>
> Such was this boundless Convention; an entrenched camp of the human race attacked by all the powers of darkness at once, the night fires of a besieged army of ideas, the immense bivouac of minds on the edge of a precipice. Nothing in history can be compared to this gathering, both senate and populace, conclave and street crossing, areopagus and public square, tribunal and the accused.
>
> The Convention always yielded to the wind; but the wind came from the mouth of the people and was the breath of God . . .
>
> It is impossible not to give attention to this great procession of shades. (section 2, book 3, chapter 1)

Unbearable? Unbearable. Bombastic? Much worse. Sublime? Sublime. See how I am being swept away by my author and have even begun to speak like him: but when bombast bursts its banks, breaks down the wall of the sound of excessive excess, a hint of poetry begins to form. *Hélas.*

Authors (unless they are writing with no interest in money and no hope of immortality, for a readership of seamstresses, traveling salesmen, or lovers of pornography whose tastes at that specific time and in one given country are well-known) never write for their own specific kind of reader but try to construct a Model Reader—in other words, the kind of reader who, having accepted from the beginning the rules of the textual game on offer, will become the ideal reader of that book, even a thousand years later. What kind of Model Reader is Hugo thinking of? I think he had two kinds in mind. The first was someone reading in 1874, eighty years after the fateful year of 1793—someone who still knew many of the names of the Convention. It would be like someone in Italy today reading a book about the 1920s, who would not be taken completely by surprise at the sight of names like Mussolini, D'Annunzio, Marinetti, Facta, Corridoni, Matteotti, Papini, Boccioni, Carrà, Italo Balbo, or Turati. The second kind is the future reader (or perhaps even the foreign reader of Hugo's time), who—with the exception of a few names like Robespierre, Danton, and Marat—would have been bewildered in the face of so many unfamiliar names; but at the same time, he would have the impression of listening to endless tittle-tattle about the village he is visiting for the first time and where he gradually learns to separate himself from the crowd of contradictory figures, to sniff the atmosphere, to become accustomed little by little to moving about in that crowded arena where he imagines that each unknown face is a mask hiding a story of bloodshed and is, ultimately, one of the many masks of history.

As I have said, Hugo is not interested in the psychology of his wooden or marmoreal characters. He is interested in the antonomasia to which they relate or, if you like, their symbolic value. The same applies for things: for the forests of the Vendée, or for La Tourgue, the immense Tour Gauvain in which Lantenac is besieged by Gauvain, both men attached to the ancestral fortress that both will try to destroy, one laying siege from outside and the other besieged within, each threatening a final holocaust. Much has been written about the symbolic value of this tower, not least because another innocent symbolic gesture takes place in it — the destruction of a book by the three children.

The children are hostages of Lantenac, who threatens to blow them up if the republicans try to set them free. They are locked in the library of the besieged tower and have nothing better to do than destroy, transforming a magnificent book about Saint Bartholomew into a pile of paper fragments — and there are those who see in their gesture the reenactment, in reverse, of the night of Saint Bartholomew, carried out to the shame of the monarchy of the time, and therefore perhaps a revenge of history, a childish antistrophe of that work of annihilating the past that is being carried out elsewhere by the guillotine. What is more, the title of the chapter that narrates this story is "The Massacre of Saint Bartholomew" — Hugo was always worried his readers weren't quaking quite enough.

But this gesture, due to its excess, can also be seen as symbolic. The children's games are described in every detail for fifteen pages, and it is thanks to this excess that Hugo warns us that we are not dealing even here with an individual story but with the tragedy of an actant — Innocence — which is at least benevolent if not redemptive. He could obviously have resolved everything in a sudden epiphany. That he was capable of doing so can be seen in the last lines of book 3, chapter 6 — little Georgette picks up handfuls of the book assigned to that sacred *sparagmos,* throws them from the window, sees them being scattered in the breeze, and says, "*Papillons*" — and the ingenuous massacre ends with these butterflies disappearing into thin air. But Hugo could not weave this very brief epiphany into the plot of so many other excesses at the risk of it going unnoticed. If excess is to exist, even the most dazzling numinous apparitions (contrary to every mystical tradition) have to last for a very long time. In *Ninety-three*, even charm must appear murky, like a froth of white-hot lava, waters spilling forth, inundations of affections and of effects. It is pointless asking Wagner to reduce his entire *Ring* to the size of a Chopin scherzo.

So as not to allow our author to take over, let us move on finally to the end. After a truly epic battle (what a great screenwriter Hugo would have made!), Gauvain finally captures Lantenac. The duel is over. Cimourdain has no hesitation and — even before the trial — gives orders for the guillotine to be set up. Killing Lantenac would mean killing the Vendée, and killing the Vendée would mean saving France.

But Lantenac, as I revealed at the beginning, has voluntarily given himself up to save the three children who were in danger of being burned to death in the library to which he alone had the key. In the face of this gesture of generosity, Gauvain does not have the heart to send the man to his death, and saves him. Hugo uses other rhetorical devices to compare two worlds, first in the dialogue between Lantenac and Gauvain, and then in the dialogue between Cimourdain and Gauvain, who at that point awaits his death. In Lantenac's first invective against Gauvain (before realizing he was going to save him), he expresses all the arrogance of the *ci-devant* before the representative of those who have guillotined the king. In the confrontation between Cimourdain and Gauvain a deep gulf appears between the high priest of vengeance and the apostle of hope. I would like man to be made according to Euclid, says Cimourdain, and Gauvain replies that he would like man to be made according to Homer. The whole novel suggests to us (in stylistic terms) that Hugo would have taken Homer's part, which is why he fails to make us loathe his Homeric Vendée, but in ideological terms this Homer has tried to tell us that to build the future it is necessary to follow the straight line of the guillotine.

This is the story told in the novel, the story of Hugo's stylistic choices, the story of one interpretation (my own — and others are possible). What can we say? That historians have identified many anachronisms and unacceptable liberties in this book? Does that matter? Hugo wasn't interested in writing history; he wanted us to feel the panting breath, the often fetid roar of history. Did he want to deceive us, like Marx, who claimed that Hugo was more interested in the moral conflicts of individual people than in understanding the class struggle?[6] If anything, it was the opposite, and he said so. Hugo carves his psychological portraits with a hatchet to make us feel the forces in conflict—and if it wasn't class conflict that he was thinking about, it was certainly (as Lukács recognized) the ideals of a "revolutionary democracy that point the way ahead"—though Lukács then tempered his judgment with the stern warning that "the real human and historical conflicts of the aristocrat and the priest who sided with the Revolution become, for each of them, artificial conflicts of duty in the context of this abstract humanism."[7] Heavens above, it has even been suggested that Hugo was not interested in class but in the People and in God. It was typical of Lukács's mental rigidity that he failed to understand that Hugo could not be Lenin (if anything, Lenin was a Cimourdain who doesn't kill himself) and that indeed the tragic and Romantic magic of *Ninety-three* lies in the interplay between the reasons of history and those of various moral individuals, measuring the constant divide between politics and utopia.

But I believe there is no better book for understanding the underlying motives of the Revolution and of its enemy, the Vendée, which is an ideological force even today for so many nostalgics of *la France profonde.* To tell the story of two excesses, Hugo (faithful to his poetics) could choose only the technique of excess, taken from excess. Only by accepting this convention is it possible to understand the Convention, becoming the Model Reader that Hugo had hoped to reach—made not with flimsy cardboard cutouts but with an *opus in-*

---

6. Karl Marx, *The Eighteenth Brumaire of Louis Bonaparte,* translated by Eden and Cedar Paul (1926).

7. Georg Lukács, *The Historical Novel*, translated by Hannah and Stanley Mitchell (1962).

certum of rough-hewn boulders. If we enter into the spirit that animates this novel, we may come out dry-eyed but with our minds in tumult. *Hélas!*

[Previously unpublished in this form, this essay summarizes various articles and lectures.]

Censorship and Silence

THOSE OF YOU who are younger may think that *veline* are pretty girls who dance about on television shows, and that a *casino* is a chaotic mess.[1] Anyone of my generation knows that the word *casino* used to mean "brothel" and only later, by connotation, did it come to mean "somewhere chaotic," so that it lost its initial meaning, and today anyone, perhaps even a bishop, uses it to indicate disorder. Likewise, once upon a time a bordello was a brothel, but my grandmother, a woman of the most upright morals, used to say, "Don't make a bordello," meaning "Don't make too much racket"; the word had completely lost its original meaning. The younger ones among you may not know that, during the Fascist regime, *veline* were sheets of paper that the government department responsible for controlling culture (called the Ministry of Popular Culture, shortened to MinCul-Pop—they didn't have sufficient sense of humor to avoid such an ambiguous-sounding name) sent to the newspapers. These sheets of thin copy paper told the newspapers what they had to keep quiet about and what they had to print. The *velina*, in journalistic jargon,

---

1. *Translator's note:* The word *casino* in Italian is in effect two words, with two pronunciations—a *casinò*, with the accent on the final syllable, is the same as the English casino, or gambling house; but here we are concerned with the other word *casino*, pronounced, confusingly, with the stress on the penultimate syllable in exactly the same way as the English word.

therefore came to symbolize censorship, the inducement to conceal, to make information disappear.[2]

The *veline* that we know today—the television showgirls—are, however, the exact opposite: they are, as we all know, the celebration of outward appearance, visibility, indeed of fame achieved through pure visibility, where appearance signifies excellence—even that kind of appearance that would once have been considered unseemly.

We find ourselves with two forms of *velina,* which I would like to compare with two forms of censorship. The first is censorship through silence; the second is censorship through noise; I use the word *velina,* therefore, as a symbol of the television event, the show, entertainment, news coverage, and so on.

Fascism had understood (as dictators generally do) that deviant behavior is encouraged by the fact that the media give it coverage. For example, the *veline* used to say "Don't write about suicide" because the mere mention of suicide might inspire someone to commit suicide a few days later. This is absolutely correct—we shouldn't assume all that went through the minds of the Fascist hierarchy was wrong—and it is quite true that we know about events of national significance that have occurred only because the media have talked about them. For example, the student protests of 1977 and 1989: they were short-lived events that sought to repeat the protests of 1968 only because the newspapers had begun saying "1968 is about to return." Anyone involved in those events knows perfectly well that they were created by the press, in the same way that the press generates revenge attacks, suicides, classroom shootings—news about one school shooting pro-

---

2. Now that we have established what *veline* originally were, I can explain how the word came to take on its present meaning. When Antonio Ricci started the television entertainment show *Striscia la notizia* in the 1990s, he wanted some girls, usually appearing on roller-skates, to bring messages for the two presenters, and he called them *veline.* But the choice is very significant; it means that when Ricci created *Striscia la notizia,* the fact that he could make a joke out of the word *veline* indicated there was still an audience that remembered and knew what the *veline* sent out by the MinCulPop were. If no one knows this today, it is another reflection that can be made on "noise," on the superimposition of information: in the space of two decades one notion is canceled out because it has been taken over by the obsessive use of another.

vokes other school shootings, and a great many Romanians have probably been encouraged to rape old ladies because the newspapers told
them it is the exclusive speciality of immigrants and is extremely easy
to commit: all you have to do is loiter in any pedestrian passage, near a
railway station, and so forth.

If the old-style *velina* used to say, "To avoid causing behavior considered to be deviant, don't talk about it," the *velina* culture of today
says, "To avoid talking about deviant behavior, talk a great deal about
other things." I have always taken the view that if, by some chance, I
discovered that tomorrow's newspapers were going to take up some
wrong I had committed that would cause me serious harm, the first
thing I'd do would be plant a bomb outside the local police headquar-
ters or railway station. The next day the newspaper front pages would
be full of it and my personal misdemeanor would end up as a small inside story. And who knows how many real bombs have been planted
to make other front-page stories disappear. The example of the bomb
is sonically appropriate, as it is an example of a great noise that si-
lences everything else.

Noise becomes a cover. I would say that the ideology of this censorship through noise can be expressed, with apologies to Wittgenstein,
by saying, "Whereof one cannot speak, thereof one must talk a great
deal." The flagship *TG1* news program on Italian state television, for
example, is a master of this technique, full of news items about calves
born with two heads and bags snatched by petty thieves — in other
words, the sort of minor stories papers used to put low on an inside
page — which now serve to fill up three-quarters of an hour of information, to ensure we don't notice other news stories they ought to have
covered have not been covered. Several months ago, the press controlled by Berlusconi, in order to undermine the authority of a magistrate
who criticized the premier, followed him for days, reporting that he
sat smoking on a bench, went to the barber, and wore turquoise socks.
To make a noise, you don't have to invent stories. All you have to do is
report a story that is real but irrelevant, yet creates a hint of suspicion
by the simple fact that it has been reported. It is true and irrelevant

that the magistrate wears turquoise socks, but the fact it has been reported creates a suggestion of something not quite confessed, leaving a mark, an impression. Nothing is more difficult to dispose of than an irrelevant but true story.

The error made by *La Repubblica* in its campaign against Berlusconi was to give too much coverage to a relevant story (the party at Noemi's house).[3] If, instead, it had reported something like this—"Berlusconi went into Piazza Navona yesterday morning, met his cousin, and they had a beer together . . . how curious"—it would have triggered such a series of insinuations, suspicions, and embarrassments that the premier would have resigned long ago. In short, a fact that is too relevant can be challenged, whereas an accusation that is not an accusation cannot be challenged.

At the age of ten I was stopped in the doorway of a bar by a lady who said, "I'll give you one lira if you write a letter for me—I've hurt my hand." Being a decent child I replied that I didn't want any money and would do it simply as a favor, but the lady insisted on buying me an ice cream. I wrote the letter for her and explained what had happened when I got home. "Good Lord," said my mother, "they've made you write an anonymous letter. Heaven knows what will happen to us when they find out!" "Look," I explained, "there's nothing terrible in that letter." In fact, it was addressed to a wealthy businessman, whom I also knew (he had a shop in the city center) and it said, "It has come to our attention that you intend to ask for the hand of Signorina X in marriage. We wish to inform you that Signorina X is from a respectable and prosperous family and is highly regarded throughout the city." Now, you don't usually see an anonymous letter that praises the subject of the letter rather than damning her. But what was the purpose of that anonymous letter? Since the lady who recruited me clearly had no grounds for saying anything else, she wanted at least to create unease. The recipient would have wondered, "Why should they send

---

3. *Translator's note:* Silvio Berlusconi appeared as guest at a girl's eighteenth-birthday party in April 2009, prompting his wife to file for divorce.

me such a letter? What does 'highly regarded throughout the city' actually mean?" I believe the wealthy businessman would have decided in the end to postpone the idea of marriage for fear of setting up home with someone so gossiped about.

This form of noise doesn't even require that the transmitted messages be of any particular interest, since one message adds to another, and together they create noise. Noise can sometimes take the form of superfluous excess. A few months ago there was a fine article by Berselli in *L'Espresso* magazine, saying, Do you realize that advertising no longer has any effect on us? No one can prove that one soap powder is better than another (in fact they are all the same), so for the past fifty years the only method anyone has come up with shows us housewives who refuse the offer of two packets in exchange for their own brand, or grandmothers who tell us that this recalcitrant stain will disappear if we use the right powder. Soap companies therefore carry out an intensive and relentless campaign, consisting of the same message, which everyone knows by heart, so that it becomes proverbial: "Omo washes whiter than white," and so on. Its purpose is twofold: partly to repeat the brand name (in certain cases it becomes a successful strategy: if I have to go into a supermarket and ask for soap powder, I will ask for Tide or Omo because I have known these names for the past fifty years), and partly to prevent anyone from realizing that no epideictic discussion can be made about soap powder—either for or against. And the same happens with other forms of advertising: Berselli observes that in every mobile phone advert, none of us actually understand what the characters are saying. But there's no need to understand what they say—it is the great noise that sells cell phones. I think it is most probable that companies have jointly agreed to stop promoting their own particular brands and to carry out general publicity, to spread the mobile telephone culture. If you buy Nokia instead of Samsung, you will be persuaded by other factors, but not by advertising. In fact the main function of the publicity noise is to remind you of the advertising sketch, not the product. Try to think of the most pleasant, the most enjoyable piece of advertising—some are even quite funny—and to remember which product it relates to. It is very rare that you manage to remember the name of the product to which that advertisement refers: the child who mispronounces "Simmenthal," or perhaps "No Martini, no party" or "Ramazzotti is always good for you." In all other cases the noise compensates for the fact that there is no way to demonstrate the excellence of the product.

The Internet, of course, generates, with no intention to censor, the greatest noise that yields no information. Or rather: first, you receive information, but you don't know whether it is reliable; second, you try searching for information on the Internet: only we academics and researchers, after ten minutes' work, can begin to select the information we want. Most other users are stuck on blogs, or on a porn site, and so forth, without surfing too far, because surfing isn't going to help them find reliable information.

Looking further at cases of noise that do not presuppose any intention to censure, but nevertheless tend toward censorship, we should also mention the newspaper with sixty-four pages. Sixty-four pages are too many to give real prominence to the most essential information. Here again, some of you will say, "But I buy a newspaper to find the news that interests me." Certainly, but those who do that are an elite who know how to deal with information—and there must be some good explanation for the frightening drop in the number of newspapers being sold and read. Young people no longer read newspapers. It is easier to find the *La Repubblica* or *Corriere della Sera* sites on the Internet—there, at least, it is all on one screen—or to read the free sheets at the train station, where the news is set out on two pages.

Therefore, as a result of noise, we have a deliberate censorship—this is what is happening in the world of television, in creating political scandals, and so forth—and we have an involuntary but fatal censorship whereby, for reasons that are entirely legitimate in themselves (such as advertising revenue, product sales, and so forth), an excess of information is transformed into noise. This (and here I am moving from communications to ethics) has also created a psychology and morality of noise. Look at that idiot walking along the street, wearing his iPod headphones; he cannot spend an hour on the train reading a newspaper or looking at the countryside, but has to go straight to his mobile phone during the first part of the journey to say "I've just left" and on the second part of the journey to say "I'm just arriving." There are people now who cannot live away from noise. And it is for this reason that restaurants, already noisy places, offer extra noise from a television screen — sometimes two — and music; and if you ask for them to be switched off, people stare at you as if you're mad. This great need for noise is like a drug; it is a way to avoid focusing on what is really important. *Redi in interiorem hominem:* yes, in the end, the example of Saint Augustine could still provide a good ideal for the world of politics and television.

It is in silence alone that the only truly powerful means of information becomes effective — word of mouth. All people, even when they are oppressed by the most censorious tyrants, have been able to find out all that is going on in the world through popular word of mouth. Publishers know that books do not become bestsellers through publicity or reviews but by what the French call *bouche à oreille* and the Italians call *passaparola* — books achieve success through word of mouth. In losing the condition of silence, we lose the possibility of hearing what other people are saying, which is the only basic and reliable means of communication.

And that is why, in conclusion, I would say that one of the ethical problems we face today is how to return to silence. And one of the semiotic problems we might consider is the closer study of the function of silence in various aspects of communication, to examine a semiotics of silence: it may be a semiotics of reticence, a semiotics of silence in theater, a semiotics of silence in politics, a semiotics of silence in political debate — in other words, the long pause, silence as creation of suspense, silence as threat, silence as agreement, silence as denial, silence in music. Look how many subjects there are to study concerning the semiotics of silence. I invite you to consider, therefore, not words but silence.

[Lecture given during the conference of the Associazione Italiana di Semiotica, 2009.]

Imaginary Astronomies

I WOULD LIKE TO MAKE it clear straightaway that in talking about imaginary geographies and astronomies I will not be dealing with astrology. The history of astrology has continually crossed paths with that of astronomy, but the imaginary astronomies and geographies I will be talking about have all now been recognized as entirely imaginary or false, whereas businessmen and heads of state still turn to astrologers for guidance. Therefore astrology is not a science, whether exact or otherwise, but a religion (or a superstition — superstitions being other people's religions), and as such cannot be demonstrated as true or false. It is only a question of faith, and in questions of faith it is always better not to get involved, if only out of respect for those who believe.

The imaginary geographies and astronomies I will be discussing were created by people of good faith who explored the sky and the earth as they saw them — and though they were wrong, we cannot doubt their good intentions. Yet those who are still involved in astrology today know perfectly well they are describing a sky that is different from that explored and defined by astronomy, and still they continue to behave as though their conception of the sky were true. There can be no sympathy for astrologers' bad faith. They are not people who are deceived; they are deceivers. End of argument.

As a child I dreamed over atlases. I imagined journeys and adventures in exotic lands, or I thought of myself as a Persian conqueror traveling far into the steppes of central Asia, then descending toward the seas of the Sonda to build an empire stretching from Ecbatana to the island of Sakhalin. This is perhaps why as an adult I decided to visit all those places whose names had caught my imagination, like Samarkand or Timbuktu, the Alamo or the river Amazon, and all I am missing now are Mompracem[1] and Casablanca.

My astronomical exploits have been more difficult, and always practiced vicariously. A friend of mine, a Czechoslovak exile who stayed at my house in the country during the 1970s and '80s, built telescopes and explored the sky at night from the terrace, calling me out when he found anything of interest. I came to the conclusion that only I and Rudolf II of Prague had had the privilege of lodging a Bohemian astronomer permanently under our roof, but then the Berlin Wall came down and my Bohemian astronomer returned to Bohemia.

I have found consolation in my collection of antique books—I call it the *Bibliotheca semiologica curiosa, lunatica, magica, et pneumat-*

---

1. *Translator's note:* An imaginary island in Emilio Salgari's novels.

ica — and it consists entirely of books that describe falsities. It includes the works of Ptolemy but not those of Galileo, and though as a child I dreamed up my journeys over the classic modern-day atlas, I now prefer to do it over maps of Ptolemaic origin.

Is this representation of the known world of that time an imaginary one? We need to distinguish between the various meanings of the word *imaginary*. Some astronomies have imagined a world based on pure speculation and mystical impulses — they tell us not what the visible cosmos looks like but what the invisible and spiritual forces are that pervade it. Other astronomies, though based on observation and experience, have nonetheless conceived explanations that we regard today as wrong. Look at the explanation that Athanasius Kircher gives for sunspots, in his *Mundus subterraneus* of 1665, as being puffs of steam from the surface of the star. Ingenuous, but ingenious. And to remain with Kircher, this is how he applied the principles of physics and mathematical calculus, in his *Turris Babel* of 1679, to show that it

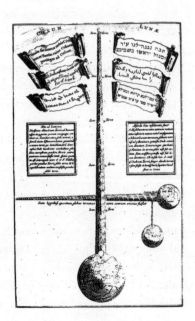

was impossible for the Tower of Babel to rise up to heaven. Beyond a certain height, having reached the same weight as the globe itself, the tower would have caused Earth's axis to rotate 45 degrees.

THE SHAPE OF THE EARTH

Anaximenes, in the sixth century B.C.E., spoke of a terrestrial rectangle made of earth and water, framed by the ocean, which sailed around on a sort of cushion of compressed air.

It was fairly realistic for the ancients to believe the Earth was flat. For Homer it was a disc surrounded by ocean and covered by the canopy of the heavens, and it was a flat disc for Thales and for Hecataeus of Miletus. It seemed less realistic to think it was spherical, as Pythagoras did, for mystical and mathematical reasons. The Pythagoreans had elaborated a complex planetary system in which the Earth was not even at the center of the universe. The sun was also at the edge of it, and all the planetary spheres rotated around a central fire. Each rotating sphere, moreover, produced a sound from a range of musical notes, and to establish an exact correspondence between sounds and astronomical phenomena, a nonexistent planet, the Antichthon (Counter-Earth), was also introduced. In their mathematical and musical zeal (and in their scorn of sensory experience), the Pythagoreans had not considered that if each planet produced a sound from this range of notes, their planetary music would have produced a repugnant dissonance, as if a cat had suddenly jumped onto the keys of a piano. But we still find this idea more than a thousand years later in Boethius—and let us not forget that Copernicus was also inspired by mathematical-aesthetic principles.

Subsequent demonstrations of the Earth's roundness, though, were based on empirical observations. Ptolemy, of course, knew that Earth was round; otherwise he wouldn't have been able to divide it into 360 degrees of longitude. But Parmenides, Eudoxus, Plato, Aristotle, Euclid, and Archimedes had already understood this. And Eratosthenes knew it in the third century B.C.E., when he had calculated fairly accurately the length of Earth's meridian, calculating the different inclination of the sun, at midday on the summer solstice, when it reflected into the bottom of the wells of Alexandria and Syene (now Aswan).

But—so far as the Earth being flat—I must digress for a moment to say that there is not only a history of imaginary astronomy, but also an imaginary history of astronomy, which still survives today in many scientific circles, not to mention in popular opinion. Try an experiment. Ask any reasonably intelligent person what Christopher Columbus wanted to demonstrate when he decided to reach the East by way of the West, and what the learned men of Salamanca persistently denied. The answer, in most cases, will be that Columbus thought the Earth was round, while the learned men of Salamanca believed it was flat and that after a short distance the three caravels would fall off the edge into the cosmic abyss.

Nineteenth-century secular thought, irritated by the fact that the church had not accepted the heliocentric theory of the universe, attributed to Christian thought (both patristic and scholastic) the idea that the Earth was flat. This idea gained force during the campaign by supporters of Darwin against all forms of fundamentalism. They wanted to show that since the church was wrong about the Earth's being round, it could be wrong about the origin of species. They therefore took advantage of the fact that the fourth-century Christian writer Lactantius (in his *Divinae institutiones*) had contested the pagan theories about the roundness of the Earth by arguing that the Bible describes the universe on the model of the tabernacle. It must therefore be rectangular in form, not least because Lactantius could not accept the existence of the Antipodes, where people would have to walk around upside-down.

Then it was discovered that a sixth-century Byzantine geographer, Cosmas Indicopleustes, in his *Topografia Christiana,* thinking once more of the biblical tabernacle, had claimed the cosmos was rectangular, with an arch over the flat floor of the Earth.

The curved vault remained hidden from our eyes by the *stereoma,*

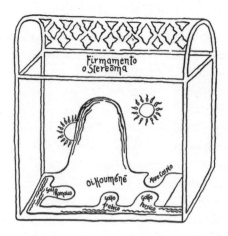

in other words, by the veil of the firmament. Beneath this was the *ec-umene,* namely, all the land on which we live, which sits on the ocean and slopes imperceptibly and continually upward to the northwest. Here there is a mountain so high that it is lost to our view and its peak disappears among the clouds. The sun, moved by angels—who also control earthquakes, and the rains and all other atmospheric phe-nomena—passes in the morning from the east toward the meridian, in front of the mountain, lighting up the world, and in the evening it reaches the west and disappears behind the mountain. The reverse cycle is followed by the moon and by the stars.

Cosmas also shows us the Earth as if we were looking at it from above. There is the frame of the ocean, beyond which are the lands where Noah lived before the flood. Farthest east from these lands, sep-arated from the ocean by regions inhabited by monstrous beings, is the earthly paradise. The Euphrates, Tigris, and Ganges spring from paradise. They pass under the ocean and flow out into the Persian Gulf. The Nile takes a more tortuous route via the antediluvian lands, it enters the ocean, continues its course into the low northern re-gions—more accurately, into the land of Egypt—and flows out into the Golfo Romaico, the Hellespont.

As Jeffrey Burton Russell has shown in his *Inventing the Flat Earth*

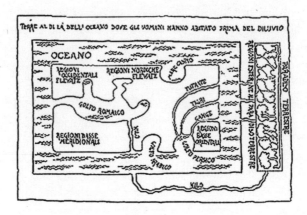

(1991), many influential books on the history of astronomy still studied at school claim that Cosmas's theory became the prevailing view throughout the Middle Ages. They also claim the medieval church taught that the Earth was a flat disc, with Jerusalem at the center, and that the works of Ptolemy remained unknown throughout the Middle Ages. The fact is, Cosmas's text — written in Greek, a language the medieval Christian had forgotten — became known in the Western world only in 1706 and was published in English in 1897. No medieval writer knew of it.

A first-year pupil at a secondary school can easily work out that if Dante enters the funnel of hell and leaves from the other side, seeing unknown stars from the slopes of Mount Purgatory, this means he knew perfectly well that the Earth was round. But Origen, Saint Ambrose, Albertus the Great, Thomas Aquinas, Roger Bacon, and John of Holywood (to mention just a few) were all of the same view. The point of dispute at the time of Columbus was that the calculations made by the learned men of Salamanca were more accurate than his. They claimed that the Earth, which was certainly round, was larger than our Genoese voyager imagined, and it was therefore pure folly to try to circumnavigate it. Columbus, however, a fine navigator but a useless astronomer, thought the Earth was smaller than it was. Neither he nor the learned men of Salamanca, of course, suspected the existence of another continent between Europe and Asia. Though they were right, the doctors of Salamanca were wrong; and Columbus, though wrong, faithfully pursued his error and was right—through serendipity.

How did the idea develop that in the Middle Ages people thought the Earth was a flat disc? In the seventh century, Isidore of Seville (though hardly a model of scientific accuracy) calculated the equator to be eighty thousand rods long. Therefore, he thought the Earth was round. But among Isidore's manuscripts is a diagram that influenced many representations of our planet, the so-called T-O map.

The upper part represents Asia—at the top because, according to legend, earthly paradise was to be found in Asia. The horizontal bar represents the Black Sea on one side and the Nile on the other, and the vertical bar is the Mediterranean, so that the quarter circle on the left represents Europe and that on the right, Africa. All around it is the great circle of the ocean.

The impression that the Earth was seen as a circle is given by the maps illustrating the *Commentary on the Apocalypse* by Beatus of Liébana. This text, written in the eighth century but illustrated by Mo-

zarabic illuminators in later centuries, was to have a major influence on the art of the Romanesque abbeys and Gothic cathedrals — and its model is to be found in countless other illuminated manuscripts.

How was it possible for people who thought the Earth was round to draw maps showing it to be flat? The first explanation is that we do the same ourselves. Criticizing the flatness of these maps would be like criticizing the flatness of our modern-day atlas. It was a naive and conventional form of cartographic projection.

It could be pointed out that over the same centuries the Arabs had produced more accurate maps, though they had the bad habit of representing north at the bottom and south at the top. But we have to bear in mind other considerations. The first is suggested by Saint Augustine, who was well aware of the debate begun by Lactantius about the cosmos in the shape of a tabernacle, but was at the same time aware of the views of the ancients on the roundness of the globe. Augustine's conclusion is that we should not place too much emphasis on the biblical description of the tabernacle because, as we know, the holy scriptures often speak through metaphor, and perhaps the Earth is round. But since knowledge about whether it is spherical or not doesn't help us to save our souls, we can ignore the question.

This doesn't mean, as has often been suggested, that there was no medieval astronomy. We need only cite the story of Gerbert d'Aurillac, the tenth-century pope Sylvester II, who in order to obtain a copy of Lucan's *Pharsalia* promised an armillary sphere in exchange; not realizing that the *Pharsalia* had been left incomplete on Lucan's death, upon receiving an incomplete manuscript he gave only half of the armillary sphere in exchange. This indicates the great attention given to classical culture during the early Middle Ages, but it also indicates the interest in astronomy at the time. Ptolemy's *Almagest* and Aristotle's *De caelo* were translated during the twelfth and thirteenth centuries. As we all know, astronomy was one of the subjects of the quadrivium taught in medieval schools, and in the eighth century John of Holywood's *Tractatus de sphaera mundi,* based on Ptolemy, was to be the undisputed authority for centuries to come.

Yet it is also true that geographical and astronomical notions had long been confused by the ideas of authors such as Pliny or Solinus, for whom astronomy was certainly not of uppermost concern. The picture of the Ptolemaic cosmos, formed perhaps indirectly through other sources, was theologically most credible. Each element of the world, as Aristotle taught, had to remain in its proper natural place, from which it could be moved only by violence and not by nature. The natural place for the earthly element was the center of the world, whereas water and air had to remain in an intermediate position, and fire was at the edge. It was a reasonable and a reassuring picture, and this idea of the universe enabled Dante to imagine his journey into the three realms of the afterlife. And if this representation did not take account of all celestial phenomena, Ptolemy himself contrived to introduce adjustments and corrections, such as the theory of epicycles and deferents, according to which, in order to explain various astronomical phenomena such as accelerations, positions, retrograde motions, and the variations in distances of various planets, it was supposed that each planet rotates around the Earth along a larger circle, called the deferent, but also moves in a small circle, or epicycle, around a point C of its own deferent.

Lastly, the Middle Ages was a period of great travel, but with the roads in disrepair, great forests to pass through, and stretches of sea to be crossed at the mercy of buccaneers, there was no possibility of drawing adequate maps. They were purely indicative, like the instructions in the *Pilgrim's Guide* at Santiago de Compostela, which said, more or less, "If you want to get from Rome to Jerusalem, head southward and ask along the way." Now, try thinking of the rail maps you find with train timetables. No one could deduce the exact shape of Italy from that series of junctions, each perfectly clear in itself when you have to take a train from Milan to Livorno (and realize that you have to change at Genoa). The exact shape of Italy is of no interest to anyone traveling to that station.

The Romans built a series of roads that linked every city in the known world, but this is how those roads were represented in the map

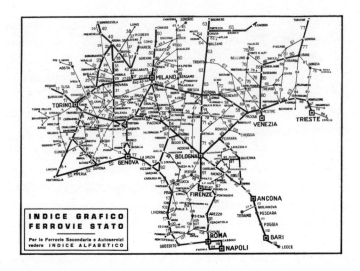

known as the *Tabula Peutingeriana*, named after the man who had rediscovered it in the fifteenth century. The upper part represents Europe, with Africa below, but we are in exactly the same situation as the
railway map. From this map we can see the roads, our points of departure and arrival, but have absolutely no idea about the shape of Europe, or the Mediterranean, or Africa—and the Romans certainly had
a much clearer notion of geography than this. They were not interested in the shape of the continents, but rather in whether, for example, there was a road that would take them from Marseille to Genoa.

Then again, medieval journeys were imaginary. The Middle Ages
produced encyclopedias, *Imagines mundi*, whose authors tried as
far as possible to satisfy the taste for wonder, writing about far-off, inaccessible lands, and these books are all written by people who had
never seen the places they are describing—the force of tradition at
that time was more important than experience. A map did not seek to
represent the form of the Earth but to list cities and peoples along the
way.

Once again, symbolic representation was more important than em-

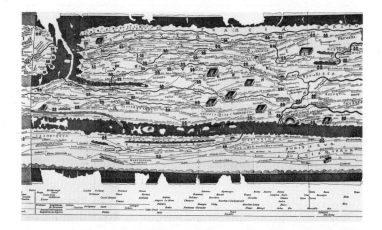

pirical representation. In many maps, the illuminator was most concerned about placing Jerusalem at the center of the Earth, rather than
showing how to get there. Yet most maps of that period represent Italy
and the Mediterranean fairly accurately.

One last consideration. Medieval maps did not have a scientific
purpose but instead responded to the audience's need for wonder, in
rather the same way that popular magazines today show us that flying saucers exist and we are told on television that the pyramids were
built by an extraterrestrial civilization. The creators of these maps
looked up at the sky with the naked eye to see comets, which the imagination immediately transformed into something that (today) would
confirm the existence of UFOs. On many fifteenth- and sixteenth-century maps with a reasonably accurate cartographic layout, mysterious
monsters are depicted in the lands where they are supposed to live,
and are reproduced on the map in a not entirely mythical fashion.

So let us not be too critical of medieval maps. It is with them that
Marco Polo arrived in China, the Crusaders in Jerusalem, and perhaps
the Irish or the Vikings in America.

A short aside—is it really true, as legend suggests, that the Vikings
reached America? We all know that the real revolution in medieval

navigation came with the invention of the stern-mounted hinged rudder. On Greek and Roman ships, as well as those of the Vikings and even those of William the Conqueror who landed on the English coast in 1066, the rudder consisted of two rear side-oars, operated in such a way as to set the intended direction of the boat. The system, apart from being fairly exhausting to use, made it practically impossible to maneuver large wooden vessels. Above all, it was impossible to sail against the wind; to do so, it was necessary to tack — to move the rudder so that each side of the boat faced alternately into the wind, first one side and then the other. Sailors therefore had to limit themselves to navigating close to shore, following the coastlines so that they could take shelter when the wind was unfavorable.

The Vikings (and the same was true for the Irish monks) could never, therefore, have sailed from Spain to Central America, as Columbus would later do. But the picture changes if we imagine they

first took a route from Iceland to Greenland, and from there to the Canadian coast. Looking at a map, we can easily see how skilled mariners
in longships could succeed (with who knows how many shipwrecks
along the way) in reaching the far north of the American continent
and perhaps the coast of Labrador.

THE SHAPE OF THE SKY

But let us leave the Earth and look at the sky. Aristarchus of Samos had
advanced a heliocentric theory between the fourth and third centuries
B.C.E., as Copernicus recorded. Plutarch tells us that Aristarchus was
accused of impiety precisely because he had put the Earth in movement so as to explain, through earthly rotation, astronomical phenomena that could not otherwise be accounted for. Plutarch did not agree
with this theory and Ptolemy later judged it "ridiculous." Aristarchus
was way ahead of his time, and perhaps he reached his conclusion for
the wrong reasons. There again, the history of astronomy is curious.
A great materialist such as Epicurus developed an idea that survived
for so long that it was still being discussed by Gassendi in the seventeenth century, as well as appearing in Lucretius's *De rerum natura*.
He suggested that the sun, the moon, and the stars (for many very serious reasons) can be neither larger nor smaller than how they appear
to our senses. So Epicurus judged the sun to have a diameter of about
thirty centimeters.

Copernicus's *De revolutionibus orbium coelestium* was published
in 1543. We imagine the world was suddenly turned upside-down and
we talk about the Copernican revolution. But Galileo's *Dialogo sopra
i due massimi sistemi* was published in 1632 (eighty-nine years later)
and we know what opposition this met. There again, the astronomies of both Copernicus and Galileo were imaginary, since they were
wrong about the nature of planetary orbits.

But the most rigorous of imaginary astronomies was that of Tycho
Brahe, a great astronomer and Kepler's teacher, who admitted that

planets rotate around the sun—otherwise many astronomical phenomena could not be explained—but claimed that the sun and planets rotate around the Earth, which remains immobile at the center of the universe.

Brahe's theory was taken seriously, for example, by the Jesuits and especially by Athanasius Kircher. Kircher was a cultured man and could no longer accept the Ptolemaic system. In an illustration of solar systems in his *Iter extaticum coeleste* (1660 edition), alongside the Platonic system and the Egyptian system he shows us the Copernican system, explaining it accurately, but adding this note: *quem deinde secuti sunt pene omnes Mathematici Acatholici et nonnulli ex Catholicis, quibus nimirum ingenium et calamus prurit ad nova venditanda.* This was later accepted by almost all non-Catholic and some Catholic mathematicians, namely those who evidently had a craving to peddle new ideas in their writings. Not being of that accursed breed, Kircher thus prefers Brahe.

There were, however, very strong arguments against the idea of an Earth that moves around the sun. In his *Utriusque cosmi historia* of 1617, Robert Fludd uses mechanical arguments to show that if you have to turn a wheel, like that of the celestial wheel, it is easier to make it turn by exercising a force around the circumference—the point among the spheres where the primum mobile was—than by acting on the center, where the foolish Copernicans would place the sun and every generating force of life and motion. Alessandro Tassoni, in his *Dieci libri di pensieri diversi* of 1627, lists a range of reasons why the movement of the Earth seemed inconceivable. I will quote two of them.

Argument of the Eclipse. By removing the Earth from the center of the universe, it has to be placed either below or above the moon. If we place it below, there will never be an eclipse of the sun since the moon, being above the sun and above the Earth, will never come between the Earth and the sun. If we place it above, there will never be an eclipse of the moon, since the Earth will never be able to come between it and the sun. And what is more, astronomy could no longer

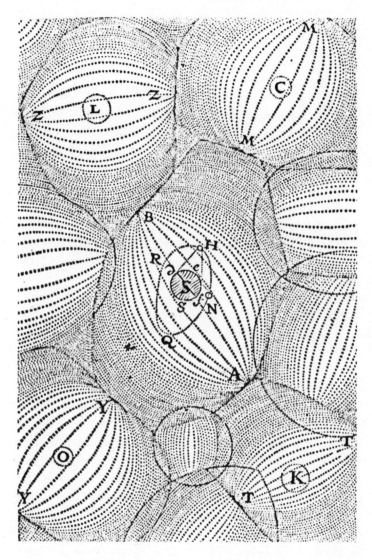

predict eclipses, since it bases its calculations on the movements of the sun, and if the sun does not move, such calculations would be in vain.

Argument of the Birds. If the Earth moves, birds flying westward

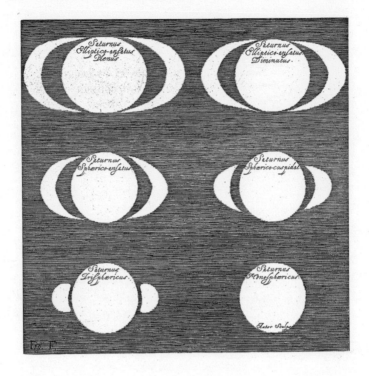

would never be able to keep up with its rotation and would never go forward.

Descartes, who favored Galileo's hypothesis but never had the courage to publish his opinions about it, had developed quite an interesting theory involving vortexes, or *tourbillons,* in *Principia philosophiae* (1644). He imagined that the heavens were liquid matter, like a sea, swirling about, forming eddies or whirlpools. These vortexes carry planets with them, and the Earth is carried in a vortex around the sun. But it is the vortex that moves. The Earth remains immobile in the vortex that carries it. Descartes was shrewd in setting out these astonishing explanations—a way of getting out of the impasse between the geocentric and heliocentric arguments—as a mere hypothesis, without having to dispute the truth recognized by the church.

As Apollinaire said, *Pitié, pitié pour nous qui combattons aux fron-*

tières de l'illimité et de l'avenir, pitié pour nos péchés, pitié pour nos erreurs . . . These were times when the astronomer could still commit many serious mistakes, as happened to Galileo when, through his telescope, he discovered the rings of Saturn but could not work out what they were.

First of all he declares he has seen not one single star but three joined together in a straight line parallel to the equinoctial, and represents what he has seen as three small circles. In his later writing he suggests that Saturn may appear in the shape of an olive, and finally he no longer describes three bodies or an olive, but "two semi-ellipses with two very dark little triangles in the middle of the said figures" and draws Saturn to look very much like Mickey Mouse.

Only later would Huygens describe a ring.

AN INFINITY OF WORLDS

Roaming among worlds constructed by the imagination, the imaginary astronomy of our forebears, shaded with hints of the occult, was able to create a revolutionary idea: that of the plurality of worlds. It was an idea already present among the ancient atomists — in Democritus, Leucippus, Epicurus, and Lucretius. As Hippolytus tells us in his *Philosophumena,* if atoms are in continuous movement in the void, they cannot but produce infinite worlds, each different from the other; and some have neither sun nor moon, for others the stars appear larger than they do for us, and from others many more stars are seen. For Epicurus, it was a hypothesis that, since it could not be contradicted, had to be taken as true until shown to be false. In the words of

Lucretius (*De rerum natura,* book II, lines 1050–51), "Nulla est finis: uti docui, res ipsaque per se / vociferatur, et elucet natura profundi" ("There is no limit; I have shown this, the facts speak for themselves, and the nature of the void is evident"). And he continues: "Thus it is increasingly necessary you recognize that other congregations of material bodies exist elsewhere in the universe, like this of our world, which the ether encircles in eager embrace" (lines 1064–66).

Both the void and the plurality of worlds were disputed by Aristotle and, as well as Aristotle, by great scholars such as Thomas Aquinas and Roger Bacon. But when it came to the debate over the *infinita potentia Dei,* suspicions about the plurality of worlds would be expressed by William of Ockham, Buridan, Nicole Oresme, and others. Nicholas of Cusa spoke about an infinity of worlds in the fifteenth century, and Giordano Bruno in the sixteenth century.

The deadly poison contained in this hypothesis would emerge more clearly when it gained support from the new epicureans, the seventeenth-century freethinkers. The idea of visiting other worlds, of finding other inhabitants there, was a far more dangerous heresy than the notion of heliocentricity. The infinity of worlds casts doubt on the uniqueness of redemption: Adam's sin and Christ's passion are either just minor episodes relevant to our world but not to other divine creatures, or else Golgotha would have to be repeated an infinite number of times on endless planets, removing the sublime uniqueness of the sacrifice of the Son of Man.

As Fontenelle would recall in his *Entretiens sur la pluralité des mondes* (1686), the suggestion was already there in the Cartesian theory of vortexes, because if every star sweeps its planets into a vortex, and the star is swept away by a larger vortex, it was possible to imagine in the sky an infinity of vortexes carrying an infinity of planetary systems.

The idea of the plurality of worlds heralded the beginning of modern science fiction in the seventeenth century, from the travels of Cyrano di Bergerac in the empires of the sun and of the moon, to Francis Godwin's *The Man in the Moone* and John Wilkins's *Discov-*

ery of a World in the Moone. As to methods for takeoff, we have not yet reached Jules Verne. Cyrano, the first time, attaches to his body a great number of ampoules filled with dewdrops, and the heat of the sun, attracting the dewdrops, makes him rise. On a second occasion he uses a machine driven by firecrackers. Godwin, however, proposes an airplane *ante litteram* propelled by birds.

SCIENCE FICTION

Modern science fiction, from Verne to the twenty-first century, opens up another chapter of imaginary astronomies, in which theories of astronomy and scientific cosmology are taken to the extreme. My old pupil Renato Giovannoli has written a fascinating book on science in science fiction,[2] in which he examines not only all the (often highly convincing) pseudoscientific theories developed in stories about the future, but also shows how science in science fiction consists of a fairly uniform body of ideas and topoi that return from narrator to narrator, with subsequent improvements and developments. These include Verne's cannons loaded with nitroglycerin and Wells's antigravitational rooms; time travel and the various techniques for space navigation; traveling while in a state of hibernation; the spaceship as a small, ecologically self-sufficient world, with hydroponic gardening systems; and the infinite variations on the Langevin paradox, whereby the astronaut returns from a voyage in space at the speed of light, only to find himself ten years younger than his twin brother. Robert A. Heinlein, for example, in *Time for the Stars,* wrote a story involving twins who communicate telepathically during the journey, but Tullio Regge, in his *Cronache dell'universo,* noted that if telepathic messages arrive instantly, the answer from the brother in space ought to arrive before the question.

Another recurring theme is that of hyperspace, which Heinlein, in

---

2. Renato Giovannoli, *Scienza della fantascienza* (Milan: Bompiani, 1991).

Starman Jones, describes using a scarf as a model: "Here's Mars . . . Here's Jupiter. To go from Mars to Jupiter you have to go from here to here . . . But suppose I fold [the scarf] so that Mars is on top of Jupiter? What's to prevent us just stepping across?" So science fiction has been off in search of abnormal parts of the universe where space can fold back on itself. It has also used scientific hypotheses, such as Einstein-Rosen bridges, black holes, and space-time wormholes. Kurt Vonnegut, in *The Sirens of Titan,* theorized about "chrono-synclastic infundibula," tunnels in hyperspace, while others have invented tachyons, particles that move faster than light.[3]

All the problems of time travel have been discussed — with and without the time traveler meeting his own double (including the famous grandfather paradox, whereby if we go back in time and kill our grandfather before he gets married, perhaps we would disappear at that moment) — using also the concepts developed by scientists, such as Hans Reichenbach in *The Direction of Time,* in relation to closed causal chains whereby, at least in the subatomic world, A causes B, B causes C, and C causes A. Philip K. Dick, in *Counter-Clock World,* theorized about entropic inversion. The first part of Fredric Brown's short story "The End" makes the supposition that time is a field and that the character Professor Jones has found a machine that reverses it. Jones presses the button, and the second part consists of the same words as the first, but in reverse order.

And finally, using the ancient theory of the infinity of worlds, writers have imagined parallel universes, so that Fredric Brown, in his novel *What Mad Universe,* reminds us that an infinite number of universes can exist at the same time: "There is, for example, a universe in which this exact scene is being repeated, except that you — or the equivalent of you — are wearing brown shoes instead of black ones . . . There are an infinite number of permutations on that variation, such as one in which you have a slight scratch on your left forefinger, and one in which you have purple horns . . ." But on the logic of possible

---

3. According to a recent hypothesis, yet to be proved, tachyons could exist — as neutrinos.

worlds, philosophers such as D. K. Lewis, in *Counterfactuals* (1973), has also stated, "I emphatically do not identify possible worlds in any way with respectable linguistic entities; I take them to be respectable entities in their own right. When I profess realism about possible worlds, I mean to be taken literally . . . Our actual world is only one world among others . . . You believe in our actual world already. I ask you to believe in more things of that kind."

How much separates science fiction from the science that preceded it or will come after it? Given that science fiction writers certainly read the work of scientists, how many scientists have nourished their imaginations reading science fiction? How many imaginary astronomies of science fiction are, or will remain, imaginary?

I have found a text by Thomas Aquinas (*In primum sententiarum,* distinction 8, article 1.2) in which he distinguishes two types of morphological relationship between cause and effect: cause can resemble effect, as a person resembles his portrait, or cause can be different from effect, as happens with fire that causes smoke; and in this second category of causes Aquinas includes the sun, which produces heat but is itself cold. We may laugh, since he reached this model from his theory of celestial spheres, but if one day cold fusion is taken seriously, might we have to reconsider this idea of Aquinas with more respect?

THE COLD SUN AND THE HOLLOW EARTH

Speaking of the cold sun, certain kinds of geo-astronomy have gone beyond the bounds of imagination into the realms of insanity, and yet seem to have influenced some very serious, though scarcely laudable, ideas and decisions.

In 1925, the theory of an Austrian pseudoscientist, Hanns Hörbiger, which was called the WEL, the *Welteislehre* or world ice theory, began to circulate within Nazi circles.[4] This theory was to enjoy the

---

4. Hans Hörbiger, *Glazial-Kosmogonie* (Leipzig: Kaiserslautern Hermann Kaysers, 1913).

support of men like Rosenberg and Himmler. But when Hitler rose to power Hörbiger was taken seriously even by some members of the scientific community, including people like Lenard, who had discovered x-rays with Röntgen.

According to Hörbiger, the cosmos was the theater of an eternal struggle between ice and fire, which produces not an evolution but an alternation of cycles, or epochs. An enormous hot body, millions of times larger than the sun, had once collided with an immense accumulation of cosmic ice. The mass of ice had penetrated into this incandescent body and, after having worked within it as a vapor for hundreds of millions of years, had made the whole thing explode. Various fragments were propelled into frozen space as well as into an intermediate zone, where they established the solar system. The moon, Mars, Jupiter, and Saturn are blocks of ice, and the Milky Way is a circle of ice — traditional astronomy purports that the Milky Way is made up of stars, but trick photography creates this illusion. Sunspots are produced by blocks of ice that break off from Jupiter.

The power of the original explosion is now diminishing and each planet does not revolve elliptically, as official science erroneously believes, but is (imperceptibly) spiraling toward the planet that most attracts it. At the end of the cycle in which we are living, the moon will move closer and closer to Earth, gradually raising the level of the oceans, submerging the tropics, and leaving only the highest mountains above water. The cosmic rays will become more powerful and will produce genetic mutations. In the end our own satellite will explode and be transformed into a ring of ice, water, and gas, which will then precipitate onto Earth. As the result of a complex series of events caused by the influence of Mars, Earth will also become a globe of ice and in the end will be reabsorbed by the sun. There will then be a new explosion and a new beginning. In the same way, the Earth in the past has already had, and then reabsorbed, three other satellites.

This cosmogony obviously presupposed a sort of eternal return, which harked back to ancient myths and epics. What Nazis today call "knowledge of tradition" was once again contrasted with the "false knowledge" of liberal and Jewish science. A glacial cosmogony, moreover, seemed very Nordic and Aryan. Pauwels and Bergier, in their *Le matin des magiciens*,[5] attribute this great belief in the frozen origins of the cosmos to the faith, encouraged by Hitler, that their troops would cope very well in frozen Russia. But the authors also suggest that the need to test how cosmic ice would react had also delayed experiments on the V-1 flying bombs. Someone writing under the name of Elmar Brugg[6] published a book in 1938 in which he paid tribute to Hörbiger as the twentieth-century Copernicus, claiming that the world ice theory explained the profound links between earthly events and cosmic forces and concluding that the silence on the part of democratic-Jewish science to Hörbiger's ideas was a typical case of the conspiracy of mediocrity.

The fact that the Nazi party was surrounded by followers of magical, hermetic, and neo-Templaristic practices, such as the disciples of the Thule Gesellschaft founded by Rudolf von Sebottendorff, has already been amply studied.[7]

Another theory was taken seriously in Nazi circles: that the Earth is hollow and that we do not live outside, on the convex external crust, but inside, on the concave internal surface. This theory was first proposed in the early nineteenth century by a certain Captain John Cleves Symmes of Ohio, who wrote to various scientific societies, "To all the World: I declare that the earth is hollow and habitable within; containing a number of solid concentric spheres, one within the other, and that it is open at the poles twelve or sixteen degrees." The wooden model of his universe can be seen today at the Academy of Natural Sciences in Philadelphia.

The theory was taken up again fifty years later by Cyrus Reed

5. Louis Pauwels and Jacques Bergier, *Le matin des magiciens* (Paris: Gallimard, 1960). The book was translated into English in 1963.

6. In fact, it was Rudolf Elmayer-Vestenbrugg, in *Die Welteislehre nach Hanns Hörbiger* (Leipzig: Koehler Amelang, 1938).

7. For example, René Alleau, *Hitler et les sociétés secrètes* (Paris: Grasset, 1969), or Giorgio Galli, *Hitler e il nazismo magico* (Milan: Rizzoli, 1989).

Teed, who declared that what we believe to be the sky is a mass of gas that fills the interior of the globe with areas of brilliant light. The sun, the moon, and the stars were not, he said, celestial globes but visual effects caused by various phenomena.

After the First World War the theory was introduced into Germany by Peter Bender, and then by Karl Neupert, who founded the movement based on the *Hohlweltlehre,* the hollow earth theory. According to some sources,[8] the theory was taken seriously among members of the German hierarchy, and in certain parts of the German navy it was believed that the hollow earth theory made it possible to fix the positions of English ships more accurately because, if infrared rays were used, the curvature of the Earth would not have obscured observation. It is even said that some of the V-1 firings were wrong because the trajectory was calculated on the basis of a concave and not a convex land surface. If this is true, then the historical and providential utility of insane astronomies is perfectly apparent.

IMAGINARY GEOGRAPHY AND TRUE HISTORY

During the second half of the twelfth century, a letter reached the West telling how in the Far East, beyond the regions occupied by the Muslims, beyond those lands that the Crusaders had tried to take from the dominion of the infidels but had nonetheless returned to their dominion, there flourished a Christian kingdom, governed by the legendary Prester John, or Presbyter Johannes, *re potentia et virtute dei et domini nostri Iesu Christi.* The letter began as follows:

> Hear and believe: I, Presbyter Johannes, the Lord of Lords, surpass all under heaven in virtue, in riches, and in power; seventy-two kings pay us tribute . . . In the three Indies our Magnificence

---

8. For example, Gerard Kuiper, of the Mount Palomar Observatory, in an article that appeared in *Popular Astronomy* in 1946, and Willy Ley, who had worked on the V-1 in Germany, in his article "Pseudoscience in Naziland," in *Astounding Science Fiction* vol. 39 (1947).

rules, and our lands extend beyond India, where rests the body of the holy apostle Thomas; they reach toward the sunrise over the wastes, and extend toward deserted Babylon near the Tower of Babel . . . In our domains live elephants, dromedaries, camels, hippopotami, crocodiles, metagallinari, cametennus, tinsirete, panthers, onagers, red and white lions, white bears and blackbirds, mute cicadas, griffins, tigers, jackals, hyenas, wild oxen, centaurs, wild men, horned men, fauns, satyrs and women of the same species, pygmies, men with dogs' heads, giants forty cubits tall, monocles, cyclopes, a bird called phoenix, and almost every kind of animal that lives beneath the vault of the heavens . . . In one of our provinces the river known as Indus flows. This river, whose source is in Paradise, winds its way along various branches through the entire province and in it are found natural stones, emeralds, sapphires, garnets, topazes, chrysolite, onyx, beryl, amethyst, sardonyx, and many other precious stones.

And so it went on, listing other wonders. Translated and paraphrased many times during the following centuries, up to the seventeenth century, and in various languages and versions, the letter was to be highly influential in the expansion of the Christian West toward the East. The idea that a Christian kingdom might exist beyond the Muslim lands justified all enterprises in expansion and exploration. Giovanni da Pian del Carpine, William of Rubruck, and Marco Polo all mentioned Prester John. Toward the middle of the fourteenth century, Prester John's kingdom moved from a vague Orient toward Ethiopia when Portuguese mariners began their African campaign. Attempts to contact him were made in the fifteenth century by Henry IV of England, by the duc de Berry, and by Pope Eugene IV. In Bologna, at the time of the coronation of Emperor Charles V, there were still discussions about Prester John as a possible ally for the recapture of the Holy Sepulcher.

How did Prester John's letter come into being, and what was its purpose? Perhaps it was a piece of anti-Byzantine propaganda, produced in the scriptoria of Frederick I, but the problem is not so much

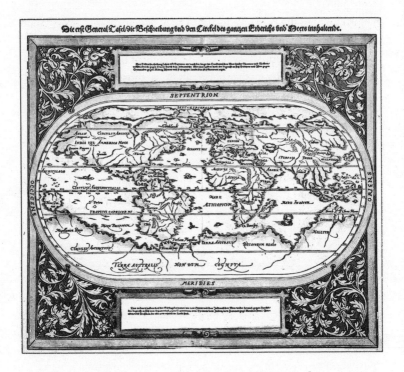

its origin as the way it was received. Through geographical fantasy a political project gradually gained strength. In other words, the specter evoked by some scribe inclined to forgery (a highly respectable literary genre at the time) was used as an excuse for expanding the Christian world toward Africa and Asia, a friendly gesture in supporting the white man's burden.

And thus we have a case of imaginary geography that has produced real history. And it is not the only case. I would like to finish with the sixteenth-century *Typus orbis terrarum* by Ortelius.

Ortelius had already portrayed the American continent with remarkable precision, but he still thought, like many before and after, that Terra Australis, an immense cap covering the southern part of the planet, existed. It was in search of this hypothetical austral land that indefatigable mariners like Mendaña, Bougainville, Tasman, and

Cook explored the Pacific. Thanks to an imaginary map, the real Australia, Tasmania, and New Zealand were eventually discovered.

Spare a thought, then, for those who fought at the frontiers of infinity and the future. Remember the greatness of those imaginary geographies and astronomies, and those errors that often bore fruit.

[Revised version of two lectures, one given in 2001 at a conference of astronomers and the other in 2002 at a conference of geographers.]

Living by Proverbs

N o COPY IN THE NUC. And not only that: not mentioned in
Brunet or Graesse; not to be found, despite its subject, in the
bibliographies on occultism (Caillet, Ferguson, Duveen, Verginelli-
Rota, Biblioteca Mágica, Rosenthal, Dorbon, Guaita, and so on), so
that it is difficult to obtain information about this anonymous pamphlet, which, apart from bearing no date, was published in one of the
usual phantom cities (Philadelphia, printed by Secundus More), with
a very appealing title: *On the New Utoppia* [sic] *or de Insula Perdita,
wherein a most Ingenious Legislatore had created the Republik of Happiness following the Principle by which Proverbes are the Wisdom of
Mankind*, 8vo (2) 33; 45 (6) (1 white).

The book is divided into two parts: the first sets out the basic principles on which the Republic of Happiness was founded; the second
lists its disadvantages and the misfortunes that followed the constitution of that state, and the reasons why this utopia failed after only a
few years.

The fundamental utopian principle from which the Legislator
started was that proverbs are not only the wisdom of humanity, but
that the voice of the people is the voice of God; the perfect state must
therefore be based on this single wisdom; all other moral, social, political, or religious ideologies and designs having previously failed be-

cause intellectual hubris had distanced them from ancient wisdom (*learn from the past, believe in the future, and live for the present*).

A few months after this Republic of Happiness had been established, it was quickly realized how the utopian principle complicated daily life. Difficulties arose at once when it came to hunting and obtaining basic supplies, since people followed the principle that *those with no dog must hunt with a cat* (with poor results). They had originally restricted themselves to fishing, but the fishermen used to take excessive quantities of stimulants, convinced that *those who sleep don't catch any fish*, so that they were worn out in body and spirit and ended their careers at an early age. Agriculture was in continual crisis, since it was said that *when the pear is ripe it falls by itself*. It was impossible to make or sell cooking pans due to a deep-rooted mistrust of coppersmiths, given, as we know, that *it's the devil who makes the pots* (so the coppersmiths tried to make and sell just the lids, for which there was a complete lack of demand since no one was buying any pans).

Traveling by road was difficult: assuming that *he who leaves the old road for the new knows what he's left but not what he'll find*, U-turns were prohibited (*there's no going back to where you began*) as well as junctions (*he who follows every path will discover many dangers*). In any event, all vehicles were banned (*slow and steady wins the race*) and people were generally discouraged not only from traveling but also from industry, since *he who dreams much needs little* (which also encouraged the use of drugs). Even the postal services were abolished, since *those who want something serve themselves; those who don't send someone else*. It was difficult to protect property: *a dog that barks doesn't bite*, so they were muzzled to stop them from barking and the muzzles were so restrictive that burglars could come and go as they pleased.

A misinterpreted principle of cooperation had established that for a well-dressed salad *you want a miser for the vinegar, a wise man for the salt, and a spendthrift for the oil* (it was well-known that *oil, vinegar, salt, and pepper make even an old boot taste better*): so that every time they wanted to do any cooking (since *it is easy to play with fire using someone else's hand*) they had to work with someone they con-sidered suitable (or whoever applied for the job). It wasn't difficult to find a spendthrift to make the dressing—*a born idiot is the source of perpetual amusement*—but it was difficult finding a miser, since no one wished to be described as such and, what is more, a miser is also stingy with his own time (and *a miser, like a pig, is excellent after he's dead*). In the end, they usually gave up dressing salad since, after all, *hunger is the best sauce.*

Social life was reduced to the exchange of a few monosyllables, given that *silence is golden,* it often *speaks louder than words, one word is enough to the wise, a closed mouth catches no flies, give every man your ear but few your voice,* and *man is weakened by the words he speaks and strengthened by those he doesn't (better safe than sorry).* What is more, it was well known that *when the wine is poured, the wit is gone,* that *wine brings out joy but also secrets,* that *drink and bad luck follow the same path,* so that convivial gatherings were therefore avoided—and on the rare occasions they took place, they ended in fu-rious violence, since *he who strikes first strikes twice.* Gambling was also impossible, as a result of a misunderstood principle of coopera-tion, since *he who trusts in chance takes a blind man as his guide,* and it was difficult to find a blind man for every player—and then it was enough for someone with one eye to arrive for the game to end in his favor, since *in the land of the blind, the one-eyed man is king.* Games involving skill, such as archery, were forbidden since, sooner or later, *the arrow strikes back at he who shoots it.*

It was difficult to run any kind of shop: difficult for confection-ers, since *you get what you deserve,* and they were continual victims of their customers' custard-pie humor. Negotiations degenerated into unpleasant arguments since, it being true that *it's the rudest one who does the buying,* when a customer entered the shop asking how such rubbish could possibly be on sale, the angry shopkeeper would reply, "You're the rubbish, and that whore your mother!" thus provoking what has been called the Zidane syndrome. Finally, as we know, *there's*

always a time to pay and a time to die, and shopkeepers were being ruined by their customers' habitual failure to honor their debts.

In any event, little work was done, because *for every saint a feast,*
so that there were 365 feast days a year (though *when the feast is over,
the saint's forgotten*) with continual celebration, and *at table you grow
young* (and of course, *on Saint Martin's Day the must turns to wine*).
Due to this excessive veneration of the saints, at carnival time, when
anything goes, joking was limited to the confines of the barracks,
bringing disorder among the entire army. Indeed, starting off from the
conviction that *I can protect myself from my enemies, but may God protect me from my friends,* the armed forces were then disbanded.

Religious life was fraught with difficulties: first of all, it was difficult to recognize priests because *clothes don't make the man,* and these
clerics were always traveling around in disguise. Secondly, bearing in
mind that *God speaks to those who stay silent,* prayer was discouraged.

The administration of justice was a real headache. A criminal conviction was almost unheard of, since *confession is halfway to forgiveness,* and in any event it could not be made public, since as they say,
judge the sin but not the sinner. It was far too expensive to go to law-
yers since *good advice is beyond all price,* and judges were reluctant to
call witnesses to trial, claiming that *the more you listen the less you understand* (and the few to be summoned were terminally ill, as it was
thought that *those leaving hospital or the graveyard are always more
sincere*). Crimes committed against other members of the family could
not be punished (*everyone is king in their own home*) and industrial
injuries could not be investigated as it was taken for granted that *the
higher you climb the farther you fall* (suddenly and at great speed).
There was plea-bargaining for the more serious crimes, and convicts
could avoid the death penalty by having their tongue cut out (*a still
tongue makes a wise head,* and *a raw deal is better than none at all*).
Sometimes there were beheadings followed by barbarous attempts to
organize races between those executed (*those who lose their heads have
strong legs*), with results that were obviously disappointing. What is

more, it was very hard to convict robbers, who, believing that *courtesy is the key that opens every door,* rather than arriving armed, managed to take money and possessions through simple persuasion and then used the defense that the victims had willingly handed over their property. Generally speaking, however, there was a reluctance to inflict any penalty, since *those who fear not the sermon heed not the punishment.*

At a certain point it was recognized that *he who lives by the sword dies by the sword,* and the law of retaliation was established and carried out in public. This method brought effective results for crimes such as murder but caused some embarrassing situations in the carrying out of public punishments for the offense of sodomy, and the practice was soon abandoned.

Desertion was not a crime, since *he who fights and runs away lives to fight another day,* though strangely enough it was a crime to use invisible ink, given that *only fools can't read their own writing.* Pictures of the dead could no longer be shown on tombs: since *all those you think are dead keep cropping up when you least expect them,* therefore those who really are dead are better not seen at all. Finally, the judges enjoyed the worst possible reputation by reason of the so-called First Principle of the Bandana: *the wrongdoer always blames his accuser* (according to the Second Principle *the petty thief ends up in prison while the big-time crook ends up in power*).

In a republic based on such blatant injustice, the position of women was tragic: popular wisdom had never treated them kindly, establishing that *when it comes to fire, women, and sea, there is little to joke about; keep your wife well away from your priest, your best friend, and your brother-in-law; a crying woman and a sweating horse are more false than Judas; woman is a fickle thing; there's no point in locking your doors when women fall in love; women know more than the devil; a woman is first sweet as honey, then bitter as gall; there's no peace in the chicken coop when the hen crows and the rooster stays silent; woman is woe.*

Every single day, wives were condemned to hear complaints about their husband's mother, since it was thought that *the best way to get through to the mother-in-law is through her daughter-in-law.* When they had the misfortune to marry a loving husband, they would be subjected to continual ill-treatment since *those who love hard, fight hard (all is fair in love and war)*, and spinsters couldn't even hope to find an older, less fiery husband since *men after the age of fifty-nine leave the women and take to wine.*

This basic misogyny made sexual relationships generally difficult: indeed, it was known that *wine, women, and tobacco are the undoing of all men — better alone than in bad company —* and there was a general mistrust of amorous behavior, since *warm caresses are the sure sign of a guilty conscience.* Conversely, adultery was commonly practiced — *best make love with the woman next door; you'll save on travel and see her more.* As *the New Year brings new life,* it was thought that children should all be born in January and therefore conceived in early April. But since *Christmas is for family and Easter for friends,* all conceptions were adulterous, so that the Republic of Happiness consisted almost entirely of illegitimate children.

These sexual difficulties were not even compensated by onanistic practices or the sale of pornography, since (though it is true that *a contented mind is a perpetual feast*) *to look and not to touch is one hell of a task.* Cases of homosexuality were not infrequent, since it was thought that *birds of a feather flock together* (why not? *beauty is in the eye of the beholder*).

Nor was it felt that many problems could be resolved by doctors, in relation to whom there was the greatest distrust. It was thought, above all, that *anxiety was worse than the ailment,* that *no doctor can cure fear,* that *doctors' mistakes end up in the graveyard,* that *the dentist gets fat with other people's teeth,* and finally, that *not all that's bad is harmful,* and *where there's life there's hope* (at worst they resorted to euthanasia, since *desperate ills require drastic remedies*). *An apple a day keeps the doctor away,* and *shaving makes you feel good for a day, a wife makes you feel good for a month, and a pig makes you feel good for a year,* so people used to kill a pig rather than go to the doctor. *The heart cannot be commanded,* so there wasn't much work for cardiologists; ear, nose, and throat specialists were notorious for *cutting off the nose to spite the face,* and veterinary surgeons did not enjoy a particularly fine reputation as they were always *looking a gift horse in the mouth* and would treat only the most expensive stallions. Doctors preferred to avoid visiting the hospitals, thinking that *those who walk with the lame man end up limping.*

The last consolation for these unfortunate people would have been games and entertainments. But any sports competition was always decided before it began (*when you have them by the balls, their hearts and minds will follow*). Since *a good horseman is never without his lance,* horseracing was practically impossible, given the way that the lance impeded the jockey. Traditional mud wrestling was hardly worth it, since *when you fight with mud, win or lose, the mud will continue to stick.*

The only game that was actually played involved a sort of tall greasy fairground pole, at the top of which a chicken bone was placed (*nothing ventured nothing gained*).

But do not imagine that citizens, due to the lack of sporting and sexual activity, would take solace in education. First of all, they were mistrustful of schooling, since *experience is more important than learning,* and they were mistrustful of logic, since *ifs and buts don't make history.* The teachers were terrible, since *those who can, do, and those who can't, teach* (nor were the pupils aware of it — *he who asks the question makes no mistakes*). The study of mathematics was reduced to a minimum, since children got only as far as learning that *two's company but three's a crowd.* Advanced math was worse still, since there was a taboo against squaring the circle (*those who are born round cannot die square*). The brighter students were at a disadvantage (*those who speak first know least*) and quickly fell ill — *a little knowledge is a dangerous thing.* So they decided *it is better to be a live ass than a dead doctor.*

Once they had completed their studies, students could not present a curriculum vitae when applying for a job, fearing that *pride comes before a fall.* This tended to lead to unemployment or underemployment (*learn an art and keep it apart*). There again, *he who at twenty doesn't have it, at thirty doesn't do it,* and by forty has lost what little he had.

Technological skills were minimal: recycling systems were forbidden (*water that has passed the mill can no longer turn the wheel*) and only very slow traditional methods were followed (*the seas fill up drop by drop, while the horse lives the grass grows,* and *haste makes waste*).

In short, it is clear that the people of the Republic of Happiness were most unhappy, so that they gradually abandoned the island and its Legislator, who had to recognize that his utopia had failed. *Better late than never.* As the anonymous author of this pamphlet wisely states, in criticizing the excessive trust in proverbs, *old wisdom does not nourish the hungry man, between saying and doing many a pair of shoes is worn out,* and *you can have too much of a good thing.* The Legislator thought that *one thing would lead to another,* but *we recognize the tree by its fruit,* and *sooner or later the comb finds all the knots.* If *all's well that ends well,* and *slow and steady wins the race,* conversely, *all that's bad ends badly,* and *he who makes his bed must lie on it,* since *he who is born miserable dies disconsolate* and *he who sows when the wind blows, harvests only confusion. All good things come to an end.*

It would have been better to know from the very start that *there's woodworm in every plank* and *two sides to every coin.* But *there's no point crying over spilled milk,* and *so long as you have your own teeth, there's no telling what the future holds.*

And this is also true for our anonymous author of long ago. *Let the dead bury the dead.* And I have described only what I have read, so *don't shoot the messenger.*

[A spurious review that appeared in *Almanacco del bibliofilo — Viaggi nel tempo: Alla ricerca di nuove isole dell'utopia,* edited by Mario Scognamiglio (Milan: Rovello, 2007)].

I Am Edmond Dantès!

S OME UNFORTUNATES HAVE been initiated into literature reading someone like, say, Robbe-Grillet. You can read Robbe-Grillet only after you have understood the age-old narrative structures he violates. To enjoy the lexical inventions and distortions of Gadda, you need to know the rules of Italian and be familiar with the fine Tuscan of *Pinocchio*.

I remember that when I was a child, I found myself in continual competition with a friend from an educated family who read Ariosto, and I spent what little money I had on a copy of Tasso from a second-hand bookstall to keep up with him. I dipped into it from time to time, but was secretly reading *The Three Musketeers*. The boy's mother, visiting our house one evening, spotted the incriminating book in the kitchen (future men of letters did their reading in the kitchen, propped against a kitchen cupboard, with our mothers shouting at us that we would ruin our eyes and ought at least go outside and get some fresh air). She was scandalized: "But how can you read trash like this?" That same lady, it should be said, told my mother that her idol was Wodehouse, whom I also used to read, and with great enjoyment but – one lightweight author against another – why was Wodehouse more noble than Dumas?

A century-old sentence hung over the serialized novel, and its de-mise was threatened not only by the Riancey Amendment of 1850, which imposed a punishing tax on newspapers that published these feuilletons, but also by the general opinion among God-fearing people that feuilletons were the ruin of families — they corrupted the young, drove adults to communism, and undermined the throne and the altar. See, for example, the two-volume *Études critiques sur le feuilleton ro-man,* almost a thousand pages that Alfred Nettement devoted in 1845 to this devilish literature.

And yet it is only through the serialized novel that, from early child-hood, we learn about classic narrative devices. Here they appear in their purest form, often brazenly, but with an overwhelming mytho-poeic energy.

And so I would like to consider not a particular book, but a par-ticular genre (the feuilleton) and a specific device: anagnorisis, or recognition.

If it were necessary to remind you, as I have just done, that the feuilleton makes use of timeless narrative devices, then we would cite Aristotle (*Poetics,* section 1452 a–b). Anagnorisis is the "change from ignorance to knowledge," and in particular the recognition of one per-son by another, as when a character unexpectedly discovers (by an-other person's revealing it, or by discovering a necklace or a scar) that someone else is his father or son or worse still, as when Oedipus real-izes that Jocasta, the woman he has married, is his mother.

One reacts to anagnorisis either with a simple willingness to play the narrator's game or in accordance with the rules of narrative. In the second case, some think the effect is in danger of being lost, but that is not correct — and to prove this I will make a few observations about narrative before turning swiftly to look at the miracles of anagnorisis at first hand.

A *double* anagnorisis must take not only the character but also the reader unawares. This surprise may have been prepared through hints and suspicions or it may arrive quite unexpectedly even for the reader, and the way these subtle, almost imperceptible clues or sudden *coups de théâtre* are handled depends on the skill of the narrator. A *simple* anagnorisis, on the other hand, occurs when a character is taken completely by surprise at a certain revelation, but the reader already knows what is going on. Typical of this category is the multiple unmasking of Monte Cristo to his enemies, which the reader has been eagerly awaiting since halfway through the book.

In a double anagnorisis, the reader identifies with the character, sharing his joy and suffering as well as his surprises. But in simple anagnorisis the reader projects his own frustrations or hopes of revenge onto the character, whose secret he already knows or can guess, and anticipates the turn of events. In other words, the reader would like to deal with his enemies, his boss, or the woman who has walked out on him in the same way that Monte Cristo does. "You used to despise me? Well then, now I shall tell you who I really am!" And he licks his lips, waiting for the final moment to arrive.

A useful element for the successful outcome of an anagnorisis is disguise: by removing his mask, the person disguised increases the other characters' surprise; and the reader either shares that surprise or, having seen through the disguise, enjoys the surprise of the unsuspecting characters.

For the two types of anagnorisis there are then two sorts of degeneration—when the recognition is *redundant* or *pointless*. Revelation is, in fact, a currency to be spent thriftily and should provide the *clou* to a respectable plot. The case of Monte Cristo, who reveals his identity many times and, in turn, gradually learns of the plot in which he has been victim, is a rare and masterly case of revelation that, though used numerous times, is no less satisfying for it. In the popular feuilleton, however, since revelation "sells well," it is repeated to the point of excess, thus losing all dramatic power and acquiring a purely consoling function, in the sense that it provides a drug that the reader comes to depend on and cannot do without. The overuse of this device reaches extreme proportions when the revelation is obviously completely pointless in terms of plot development, and the novel becomes stuffed with it purely for publicity purposes, so that it can be promoted as the ideal serial novel and worth every penny. A patent example of pointless moments of anagnorisis, one after the other, is Ponson du Terrail's *Le forgeron de la Cour-Dieu*. Note that the pointless anagnorises in the following list are those marked with an asterisk (and, as you will see, they are in the majority). This is the story: *Dom Jérôme reveals who he is to Jeanne; Dom Jérôme reveals who he is to Mazures; *the comtesse des Mazures, from Valognes's description, recognizes Jeanne as the sister of Aurore; *from the portrait in the small box left to her by her mother, Aurore recognizes Jeanne as her sister; Aurore, while reading her mother's letter, recognizes old Benjamin as Fritz; *Lucien learns from Aurore that Jeanne is her sister (and that his mother killed their mother); *Raoul de la Maurelière realizes that César is the son of Blaisot and that his temptress is the comtesse des Mazures; *Lucien, after wounding Maurelière in a duel, discovers under his shirt a medallion with the portrait of Gretchen; *the gypsy girl realizes from a medallion found in Polyte's hand that Aurore is free; *Bibi recognizes Jeanne and Aurore as being the aristocrats described by the gypsy girl; *Paul (alias the chevalier des Mazures), having seen the medallion of Gretchen that Bibi shows him (after having received it from the gypsy girl who received it from Polyte), recognizes that the aristocrat he should be arresting is his daughter Aurore; *Bibi reveals to Paul that his daughter has been arrested in place of Jeanne; Bibi, who has escaped, learns that the girl saved from the guillotine is Aurore; Bibi discovers that his fellow stagecoach passenger is Dagobert; *Dagobert learns from Bibi that Aurore and Jeanne are in Paris and that Aurore is in prison; Polyte recognizes Dagobert as the man at the Tuileries who saved his life; *Dagobert recognizes the gypsy girl who had once foretold his fortune; *Dagobert's doctor realizes that the German doctor who arrives unexpectedly — sent by the Masques Rouges — is his old master and he recognizes him to be his pupil and Polyte to be the young man whom he had just saved on the road; years later, Polyte recognizes a stranger who comes up to talk to him as Bibi; both recognize the gypsy girl, and Zoe to be her assistant; Benedict comes across and recognizes Bibi; *Paul (who has been mad for years) regains his sanity and recognizes Benedict and Bibi; the old hermit is recognized as Dom Jérôme; *the chevalier des Mazures learns from Dom Jérôme that his daughter is alive; *the gypsy girl discovers that her manservant is none other than Bibi; *the republican (lured into a trap) realizes that an attractive German lady was the young girl whose parents he had sent to the guillotine (her identity was revealed to the reader two pages earlier); *the gypsy girl (condemned by the gypsies) recognizes Lucien, Dagobert, Aurore, and Jeanne as those who have trapped and ruined her.

It does not matter whether those who have (fortunately) not read *Le forgeron de la Cour-Dieu* have managed to make head or tail of this torrent of anagnorisis involving characters they know nothing about. It is all the better for them to remain in a state of confusion, since this novel, in comparison to feuilleton classics, is like a film that, to attract a *Last Tango in Paris* audience, offers its spectators 120 minutes of uninterrupted rear penetration between a hundred patients in a psychiatric hospital. Which is exactly what Sade did in *The 120 Days of Sodom,* pushing down the accelerator pedal for hundreds of pages, whereas Dante limited himself to writing "he kissed my mouth, trembling all over."

Ponson du Terrail's recognitions are pointless, apart from being exaggeratedly redundant, because the reader already knows all about his characters. But for the benefit of readers who are easy to please, a touch of sadism is brought into play. The characters in the novel play the part of village idiots — they are the last to understand what the readers and the other characters in the story have understood perfectly well.

Village-idiot anagnorisis is divided into anagnorisis of *real idiots* and *falsely accused idiots.* We have a real idiot when the elements of plot, details, facts, confidential information, and unambiguous signs all point toward the anagnorisis, and the character alone remains ignorant; in other words, the plot has provided both him and the reader with the means of resolving the enigma, and the fact that he has failed to do so is inexplicable. The perfect example of the real idiot, used critically by authors, is the detective story in which the policeman offers a sharp contrast to the detective (who gains knowledge at the same rate that the reader does). But there are cases in which the idiot is falsely accused because the events themselves are of no help to him, and what makes the reader aware of what is happening is popular plot tradition. For example, the reader knows, through narrative tradition, that character X must be the child of character Y. But Y cannot know this, since he has not read serial fiction.

A typical case is that of Rodolphe of Gérolstein in *Les mystères de Paris*. Rodolphe has met La Goualeuse, otherwise known as Fleur-de-Marie, a sweet, defenseless prostitute, and as soon as we are told that his daughter, whom he had had with Sarah McGregor, was taken away from him when she was very young, we immediately guess that Fleur-de-Marie can only be his daughter. But why should Rodolphe imagine he is the father of a young girl he comes across by chance in a sordid tavern? He will find out, quite rightly, only at the end. But Eugène Sue knows we will already suspect something, and reveals the answer at the end of the first installment: this is a typical case of subjection of the plot to the rules of literary tradition and commercial distribution. Literary tradition ensures that the reader already knows what is the most probable solution, whereas the weekly distribution of the feuilleton, with the story that continues for an endless number of installments, requires that the reader not be kept in suspense for too long, for fear of losing track of the story. Sue is therefore obliged to close that question so that he can open others without overburdening the reader's memory and capacity for suspense.

In narrative terms, he commits one suicide while keeping his best card for the second round. But the suicide occurred as soon as he chose to move according to obvious narrative solutions: the popular novel cannot be complex, not even in the invention of plot.

There is a last device in the category of pointless anagnorisis: the *topos of the false stranger*. At the beginning of a chapter, the popular novel often introduces a mysterious character who is unfamiliar to the readers. But a little further into the action they are told, "The stranger, whom the reader will have recognized as our X . . ." Here again we have a feeble narrative expedient through which the narrator introduces once again, in a cheap way, the pleasure of revelation. Note here that the anagnorisis is not directed at the character (the stranger knows perfectly well who he is, and generally appears in a dark alleyway, or in a private room, without the others having yet seen him). And if the reader is familiar with feuilletons, he understands straightaway that the stranger is a false stranger and can generally guess immediately who he is. But the author insists, nevertheless, on trying to make him play the role of village idiot—and perhaps with some readers he succeeds.

Although, from the point of view of plot style, these cheap devices constitute narrative padding, from the point of view of psychological enjoyment and success they work wonderfully—the laziness of readers demands that they be blandished with mysteries they have already solved or can solve easily.

Having reached this point, we might indeed ask whether, resorting to such well-worn ploys, the anagnorisis found in the feuilleton still has the narrative power that it once had. Well, yes. A friend of mine used to say, "When I see a flag fluttering in a film, I start to cry, and it doesn't matter whose country it belongs to." Someone wrote, in a review of the film *Love Story,* that you need a heart of stone not to burst out laughing at Oliver and Jenny's situation. Wrong. Even with a heart of stone, there will still be a tear in our eyes—there is a chemistry of passions, and when narrative ploys are designed to make us cry, then they always do make us cry, and the most cynical snob can at most pretend to scratch his nose to dry away a furtive tear. We can watch *Stagecoach* (or even one of its more slapdash remakes) countless times and yet, when the Sixth Cavalry arrives with the sound of the bugle, charging with sabers drawn to devastate Geronimo's mob on the verge of victory, even the most perverse heart pulses away under a fine lawn shirt.

So let us freely abandon ourselves to the pleasure and excitement of anagnorisis, even if we already know who has to recognize whom, and let us marvel aghast at the many techniques with which this narrative archetype continues to reappear throughout the history of the feuilleton:

> "Oh!" said Milady, rising to her feet, "I defy you to find the court which pronounced the infamous sentence against me. I defy you to find he who carried it out." "Silence!" said a voice. "It is for me to reply to that." And the man in the red cloak came forward in his turn. "What man is that? What man is that?" cried Milady, overcome by terror, her hair falling loose and rising above her livid countenance as if it were alive. "Who are you then?" cried all the witnesses of this scene. "Ask that woman," said the man in the red cloak, "for you may plainly see she knows me!" "The executioner of Lille, the executioner of Lille!" cried Milady, a prey to insensate terror, and clinging to the wall to avoid falling. And this man who for thirty years had bowed his head before André, stood up to his full height and, indicating the corpse of the father to the degenerate son, then the doorway and the man who had remained on the threshold, he said: "Monsieur Vicomte, your father murdered your mother's first husband, then cast your elder brother into the sea. But this brother is not dead: here he is." And he pointed to Armand, while André stepped back, terrified. "Your father," Bastien continued, "repented at the last minute and has restored to your brother the inheritance he had stolen from him and had sought to leave to you. This is no longer your house, but that of Comte Armand de Kergaz." "Begone!" Armand had spoken as master and André, perhaps for the first time in his life, obeyed. He moved slowly like a wounded tiger that retires backward and, as it retires, still menaces. Having reached the doorway, glancing back toward the window from where he had watched Paris illuminated by the

first rays of dawn, almost as if to hurl at Armand a terrible and supreme challenge, he exclaimed: "So alas for both of us, virtuous
brother! We shall see who will be the winner: you the philanthro-
pist, I the bandit, you the heavens, I the underworld . . . Paris shall
be our battle ground." He left with his head high and an infernal
smile on his face and, without shedding a tear, left the house no
longer his, like a godless Don Giovanni. He stopped once again
and allowed his gaze to wander over those present. The guests listened in silence and their smiles disappeared from their faces.
"Well," he continued, "this thief, this murderer, this torturer of
women . . . I found him this evening, an hour ago . . . he is here
among us: here he is!" And with his hand outstretched, he pointed
to the viscount. While the viscount leapt onto his seat, the speaker's mask fell off. "Armand, the sculptor!" someone said. "André!"
exclaimed Armand in a thunderous voice. "André, you recognize
me?" But at that moment, while the guests sat motionless listening
to the abrupt and terrible conclusion to the story, the door opened
and a man appeared, dressed in black. Like the old servant who
went to surprise Don Giovanni during an orgy to announce his father's death, this man, without any concern for the guests, went
straight up to André, saying, "The general, Count Felipone, your
father, who has been ill for some time, is sick and wishes to see you
on his deathbed." But the man who had brought the news, catch-
ing sight of Armand, who had rushed up from behind André to
stop him, shouted, "Good heavens, the living image of my colonel!" A man appeared at the doorway of the room where the married couple were to be found. At the sight of him, Count Felipone
drew back horrified. The new arrival was a man of around thirty-
six, tall in stature and dressed in a long blue uniform decorated
with a red stripe, of the kind worn by imperial soldiers during the
time of the Restoration. His eyes shone with a dark light that gave
his face, pale with anger, an expression of disdain. He took three
steps toward Felipone, who stepped back in fear, pointed an accus-
ing finger at him, and said, "Murderer! Murderer!" "Bastien!" mur-
mured Felipone, aghast. "Yes," replied the hussar. "Yes, I am Bas-

tien, whom you thought you had killed, but who is not dead . . .
Bastien, who an hour later was found by the Cossacks drenched in
blood; Bastien, who after forty years in prison has come to seek
amends for the blood of his colonel with which you stained your
hands." While Felipone, dumbfounded, continued to move back at
that terrible sight, Bastien turned to the countess, saying, "Madame, this man, this wretch, is the murderer of your son just as he
was the murderer of his father." The countess, who one instant earlier had been helpless and mad with grief, threw herself like a tiger
upon the killer of her son to rip him to pieces with her claws. "Murderer! Murderer!" she shouted. "The gallows await you . . . I myself shall deliver you to the executioner!" But at that very moment,
as the villain continued to retreat, the mother felt something moving within her. She let out a cry and stopped, pallid, reeling, bro-
ken-hearted . . . The man she wanted to consign to justice for its
vengeance, the man she wanted to drag to the gallows, this
wretched vile man was the father of her other child, who was beginning to move about within her. "It is she! It is she!" exclaimed
the old man, turning his gaze from Marzia to Virginia. He alone
had correctly interpreted the sad cry of the woman who had
fainted—and she fell into her habitual stupor, then gradually reviv-
ing, as if she had an important confession to make—and a tear finally bathed that cheek that had been dry for so long, through time
and suffering. Old Elias, who for some time had been beside himself with consternation, took advantage of an instant in which the
women raised the countess's head to help her drink, to hold before
her a gold necklace, with a beautiful cross in the same metal, en-
crusted with costliest diamonds of dazzling splendor. In doing so,
the old man added the following names: "Virginia and Silvia!" "Silvia!" exclaimed the countess, and her glassy eyes stared at the precious jewelry as if it were a talisman, and her fine head fell back
upon the pillow, like a flower in the blazing desert wind that drops
upon its stem, never to straighten again. But the final hour of that
beautiful victim of betrayal had not yet struck. She stirred a moment later, as if touched by an electric current, opened her eyes,

and turned to Marzia with such an ardent expression of love that only a mother can understand and cherish. "My daughter!" she exclaimed, and fell back again. At that very moment, a man with a bandaged face hurried precipitously into the room, kneeled between the two beds of the wounded women, and cried desperately, "Forgive me! Forgive me!" Countess Virginia was electrified by that cry. She sat up with extraordinary speed and glancing down upon the prostrate wretch, exclaimed in a heart-rending voice, "Marzia! Marzia! That villain is your father!" Étienne drew his wallet from his pocket, took from it a letter sealed with a large black seal, and gave it to Georges, adding: "My dear son, read this letter . . . Read it aloud . . . and you, Lucie Fortier, listen . . ." Georges Darier took the letter with trembling hand. He seemed not to have the courage to break the seal. "Read!" repeated the artist. The young man ripped open the envelope and read, "My beloved Georges. In the month of September 1861, a poor woman, with a child in her arms, presented herself at my house at Chevry. That poor woman had been persecuted, spied upon, victim of the triple accusation of murder, theft, and arson. Her name was Jeanne Fortier . . ." These words were followed by a triple exclamation made simultaneously by Georges, Lucie, and Lucien Labroue. "I . . . I . . . ," said Georges, confused. "I am the son of Jeanne Fortier, and Lucie . . . Lucie . . . is my sister!" At the same time he held his arms out to the young girl. "My brother! . . . My brother! . . . ," exclaimed Lucie, throwing herself toward Georges, who held her in a tight embrace. "Yes . . . yes . . . ," he then exclaimed. "This is the proof of the crime! Oh! Mother! . . . Mother! God has finally then been moved to pity! But this final proof, which was thought to have been lost . . . where was it?" "In the side of the small papier-mâché horse you were carrying when you and your mother arrived at Chevry," replied Étienne Castel. "Can you prove it?" "This is her death certificate . . . the real Paul Harmant, the millionaire, the great industrialist, former associate of James Mortimer, is none other than Jacques Garaud!" Marius abruptly drew his chair closer to Thénardier's, who noted this movement and continued with the deliberation of an orator who holds his interlocutor and feels his adversary palpitating under his words: "This man, forced to conceal himself for reasons, moreover, which are foreign to politics, had adopted the sewer as his domicile and had a key to it. It was, I repeat, the sixth of June, toward eight in the evening. Do you understand now: the person who carried the corpse was Jean Valjean, the one who had the key is speaking to you at this moment; and the piece of the coat . . ." Thénardier completed the phrase by drawing from his pocket at eye level, nipped between his two thumbs and his two forefingers, a strip of torn black cloth, covered with dark spots. Marius had sprung to his feet, pale, hardly able to draw his breath, with his eyes riveted on the fragment of black cloth, and without uttering a word, without taking his eyes from that fragment, he re-treated and fumbled with his right hand along the wall for a key that was in the lock of a cupboard near the chimney. He found the key, opened the cupboard, and plunged his arm into it without looking, and without his frightened gaze quitting the rag, which Thénardier still held outspread. But the other continued. "Monsieur le Baron, I have the strongest of reasons for believing that the assassinated young man was an opulent stranger lured into a trap by Jean Valjean, and the bearer of an enormous sum of money." "The young man was myself, and here is the coat!" cried Marius, and he flung upon the floor an old black coat all covered with blood. Then, snatching the fragment from the hands of Thénardier, he crouched down over the coat, and laid the torn piece against the tattered skirt. It fitted exactly, and the strip completed the coat. "Good heavens!" exclaimed Villefort, stepping back fearfully. "Surely that is not the voice of Abbé Busoni." "No!" The abbé threw off the false tonsure, shook his head, and his hair, no longer confined, fell in black masses around his manly face. "It is the face of the Count of Monte Cristo!" cried Villefort, with a haggard expression. "You are not exactly right, Monsieur Procureur; you must go farther back." "That voice, that voice! — where did I first hear it?" "You heard it for the first time at Marseille, twenty-three years ago, the day of your marriage with Mademoiselle de

Saint-Méran. Refer to your papers." "You are not Busoni?—you are not Monte Cristo? Oh, heavens—you are then some secret, implacable, and mortal enemy! I must have wronged you in some way at Marseille. Oh, woe to me!" "Yes; you are right," said the count, crossing his arms over his broad chest; "search, search." "But what have I done to you?" exclaimed Villefort, whose mind was balancing between reason and insanity, in the cloud that is neither a dream nor reality; "what have I done to you? Tell me, then! Speak!" "You condemned me to a horrible, slow death; you killed my father; you deprived me of liberty, of love, and happiness." "Who are you, then? Who are you? Good Lord!" "I am the specter of a wretch you buried in the dungeons of the Chateau d'If. When he at length issued from his tomb, heaven gave him the mask of the Count of Monte Cristo, enriched him with gold and diamonds, and led him to you." "Ah, I recognize you, I recognize you!" exclaimed the king's attorney. "You are . . ." "I am Edmond Dantès!" The Count of Monte Cristo turned dreadfully pale; his eye seemed to burn with a devouring fire. He bounded toward a dressing room near his bedroom and in a trice, tearing off his cravat, his coat, and waistcoat, he put on a sailor's jacket and hat beneath which rolled his long black hair. He returned thus, formidable and implacable, advancing with his arms crossed on his breast, toward the general who was waiting for him, and who, feeling his teeth chatter and his legs sink beneath him, drew back a step, and only stopped when he found a table to support his clenched hand. "Fernand," cried he, "of my hundred names I need only tell you one to overwhelm you! But you guess it now, do you not?" The general, with his head thrown back, hands extended, gaze fixed, looked silently at this dreadful apparition; then seeking the wall to support him, he glided along close to it until he reached the door, through which he went out backward, uttering this single mournful, lamentable, distressing cry—"Edmond Dantès!" Then, with sighs that were hardly human, he dragged himself as far as the porchway of the house, across the courtyard like a drunken man, and fell into the arms of his manservant. "Do you repent?" asked a deep, solemn voice, which caused Danglars's hair to stand on end. His feeble eyes endeavored to distinguish objects, and behind the bandit he saw a man wrapped in a cloak, half hidden by the shadow of a stone column. "Of what must I repent?" stammered Danglars. "Of the evil you have done," said the voice. "Oh, yes; I repent, I repent!" exclaimed Danglars. And he struck his breast with his emaciated fist. "Then I forgive you," said the man, dropping his cloak and advancing to the light. "The Count of Monte Cristo!" said Danglars, more pale from terror than he had been just before from hunger and misery. "You are mistaken: I am not the Count of Monte Cristo." "Then who are you?" "I am he whom you sold, betrayed, dishonored; I am he upon whom you trampled that you might raise yourself to fortune; I am he whose father you condemned to die of hunger; I am he whom you also condemned to starvation; and who yet forgives you, because he too hopes to be forgiven: I am Edmond Dantès!" Then he burst into a frightening laugh and began to dance before the body. He had gone mad.[1]

Oh, the delights of anagnorisis and the false stranger! Nor have they been rejected by Achille Campanile, who employed them, though with surreal good sense, at the beginning of his novel *Se la luna mi porta fortuna* (1928):

Anyone, on that gray morning of the 16 December 19 – . . . , furtively entering, and at their own risk and peril, the bedroom where the opening scene of our story takes place, would have been exceedingly surprised to find a young man with curly hair and pale cheeks, pacing nervously backward and forward; a young man whom no one would have recognized as Doctor Falcuccio, first of all because he was not Doctor Falcuccio, and, in the second place, because he bore not the slightest resemblance to Doctor Falcuccio. We observe, in passing, that the surprise of anyone furtively enter-

---

1. This collage contains passages, in the following order, from Alexandre Dumas, Ponson du Terrail, Giuseppe Garibaldi, Xavier de Montépin, Victor Hugo, Dumas again, and Carolina Invernizio.

ing that room to which we refer is wholly unjustified. That man was in his own home and had every right to pace about in whatever way he pleased. (From *Opere: Romanzi e racconti, 1924–1933*)

[Published in the *Almanacco del bibliofilo – Biblio nostalgia: Divagazioni sentimentali sulle letture degli anni più verdi,* edited by Mario Scognamiglio (Milan: Rovello, 2008).]

Ulysses: That's All We Needed . . .

A STRANGE NOVEL (novel?) came out a few years ago, from the pen of Giacomo Yoyce, or Ioice as Guido Piovene calls him, or Joyce. Few have read it, since it is written in English, a little used language. In attempting to describe it (now that the French translation is available for more educated readers), I feel such a confusion, victim of feelings as incoherent as the work that inspires them, that I shall proceed by way of observations here and there, notes for further development, which I propose to number so as not to give the impression that these paragraphs are intended to follow each other in any logical or consistent order.

1. This work, like Joyce's other books, was known in Italy only to a few, and most of them had heard about it from others, since there were rumors about it in artistic gatherings and intellectual salons. A few rare copies of this *Ulysses* (later translated as *Ulisse,* since that is the name of Homer's hero in the English language) were thus passed about from hand to hand, loaned reluctantly, desperately sought to be understood, leaving a confused and murky impression of scandal, of monstrous chaos.

2. There again, having already read his previous book, *A Portrait of the Artist as a Young Man,* we realize that at the end of the book every-

thing falls to pieces, and the writing as well as the ideas explode into damp fragments, like wet gunpowder.

3. Let us say straightaway, after a first, laborious reading and without further ado, that *Ulysses* is not a work of art.

4. In his approach to the novel, Joyce has brought a kind of psychological and stylistic pointillism that never adds up to anything, which is why not only Joyce but those like him, such as Proust and Svevo, are faddish phenomena destined not to last.

5. It is no surprise that Joyce, a second-rate Irish poet living in Trieste, says it was he who discovered Svevo (another author who writes atrociously). In any event Svevo is perhaps the Italian writer who has come closer than anyone else to that passively analytical literature that reached its culmination in Proust; and it is second-rate art if art is the work of keen and active men, if a painter is worth more than a mirror.

6. Joyce is basically one of those called to perpetuate the bad taste of the worst kind of Italian bourgeoisie. But thank God and Mussolini, Italy is not all bourgeois, in thrall to Europe and Paris.

7. But so be it, seeing that someone on the banks of the Seine has decided to translate this work. And anyone who reaches the last page arrives shocked and nauseated, as if emerging from an interminable tunnel piled full of garbage and inhabited by monsters. Joyce is a shower of ash that suffocates everything. The Romantics made you aspire to being a fallen angel, and now this relentless confessor convinces you that you are an idle animal with erotic tendencies and with some vague ambition toward the most seedy and feral kind of magic. Your very dreams, of which you were rather proud, are none other than realistic nocturnal sabbaths, a delirium of matter seeking to indulge in the orgy of your thoughts. Once again, there is no escape . . . In his works there is certainly an enormous patience, almost insane, almost intelligent, though uninspired, but Joyce's truth is a secondary, transitory truth, too closely bound up with our empirical existence.

8. It seems that Ungaretti, one of those so-called hermetic poets, has seen a relationship between Joyce and Rabelais. There is certainly a parallel disunity in the well-defined structure of the two worlds (of

Rabelais and Joyce); there is the systematic disorder from which gush forth, in one, the classic forces of the imagination, of poetic representation, of myth, and in the other, those forces of modern intelligence, taste, human representation, and psychology. There is, I repeat, the disunity that, in Rabelais, turns an epic subject into a grotesque, absurd, metaphysical film, a subject that is fluid and formless, loose, dissonant, yet concise; and he transforms a flamboyant crowd of characters, who could all be brave heroes of classical poetry, into abnormal, nightmarish, outlandish types. But Joyce, over a simple event, over an almost sentimental, simply psychological situation, which is a man waking up in the morning, produces detailed and infinitesimal effects, divisionistic impressions, dark illusions in reverse, in a fantastic array of calculations directed at the atom, at the cell, at the essentially chemical composition of thought. In short, the former enters a realm of superhuman absurdity, relying upon an architecture of absolute fantasy, the latter a continent of subhuman reverie that can only be penetrated with the scalpel, magnifying glass, and tweezers of *dernier cri* cleverness.

9. Joyce might perhaps be counted as a writer of the so-called literature of psychoanalysis, but he exhibits qualities that exclude him even from this genre of literature. He embraces man as he is, a rough formation of feelings, a profundity that can also be called shallowness and, as already suggested, a mixture of stupidity, prejudice, vague cultural recollections, shabby sentimentalism, and sexual arrogance. Psychoanalysis offers him, moreover, a method that he would have been better off using far less, without straying in any way from his purpose and from his descriptive results. In this respect his testimony is merely scientific, not literary. And it ought to be clear that in the history of literature he belongs to a well-worn, well-rehearsed tradition, according to which he must certainly resign himself to being a late and slight imitator, beside the honored places of Dostoyevsky, Zola, and, to some degree, Samuel Butler.

10. Some regard Proust or Joyce as leading figures in the historical moment of which they are clearly the product. But we are bound

to say that, for us, they do not represent the spirituality of today: their vision of the world, that particular and general *Weltanschauung* expressed in them is, for us, worthless, precisely because it relates to the mentality of the society that has produced them. But when we call for a "collectivist novel" we are asking to be given, at last, a novel in which human relationships, society, love, and our whole life are seen from that new viewpoint that constitutes for us the new morality and a new way of living. We have already indicated how this new ethic of ours becomes a part, a necessary corollary, of what is taking place, of the social and human phenomenon of the Corporations we so fervently support,[1] as a new approach to our life, and we have already indicated that for this very reason we oppose all forms of decadent individualistic and bourgeois novels (autobiographies, self-referential diaries, psychologisms of self-awareness).

11. The truth is that writers from beyond the Alps, such as Giacomo Joyce, Davide Erberto Lawrence, Tommaso Mann, Giuliano Huxley, and Andrea Gide, have sacrificed their poetic truth and integrity to petty, elegant acrobatics . . . Each and every one of these so-called European artists have on their faces the devilish smile of someone who, from time to time, holding a paramount truth, starts playing about with it. The truth they hold, and with which they play such dangerous games, is poetic truth, their genuine feelings. They all manhandle this supreme gift by mutual agreement. It seems they intend to erect a tower of intellectual falsehood, each in their own way, but each taking the same liberty. And that is why Joyce's work lacks measure, like a goat forced to give birth to a dog.

12. Joyce has obviously been taken by the devil of allusion and free association, and the idea of composing a page of prose like a page of actual music is a stupidity introduced into literature by the Wagnerian fashion that raged at the end of the nineteenth century. Joyce interweaves leitmotifs rendered unrecognizable by a dense counterpoint of allusions. But what is more, he seeks to match his episodes with color

---

1. *Translator's note:* Fascist organizations of workers and employers.

tones: the prevailing color will be red here, green there, and so forth. It is the confusion of the arts that began timidly with Baudelaire and became a commonplace of the decadent movement, after Rimbaud's famous sonnet on the colors of vowels. Colored hearing, verbal orchestrations . . . That path, as we know, brought us to pictures made from bits of newspaper and bottle ends. The language of Joyce is a deliquescent language, and—allow me here to use a Joycean pun—a delinquent language . . . Joyce has allowed himself to be tempted by the demon of Esperanto.

13. The problem is that we must get beyond the communistic novels of Tommaso Mann. Joyce has simply transformed the interior monologue modestly invented by Dujardin into verbal diarrhea, thus tainting the fine, succinct, dynamic, simultaneous *parole in libertà* boldly invented by our futurists, those true artists of the Regime.

14. The spirit of nationhood must not be abandoned. Joyce, eager for success, very soon adapted to the new artistic internationalism, abandoning the reality of true feeling and formulating in his new works the most wrongful act of rebellion against the national spirit from which he had sprung, mocking the nationhood, language, and religion of his country. From *A Portrait of the Artist* onward, vilifying his humanity, he reverted to chaos, to confused dreaming, to the subconscious. He died strangled by his own baleful demon, and all that remained were the sterile pedantic audacities of a sort of psychoanalysis that grafts itself onto Freud's method with the violence of his arbiters. A fragmentary spirit, more interested in the transient than the durable, the Irishman's attitude is feminine, not for the open gentleness that must always pervade the Hellenic spirit of an artist, but for the indifferent pose of the pseudo-intellectual with one foot in physiological corruption and the other in the madhouse. One cannot but declare all of this to be an example of work in decline, worthy at most of a pornographic trader in junk novels. Joyce is a typical exponent of modern decadence, a festering and infectious cell even in our own literature. Why? Because, with his anticlassicism, he stands in opposition to the figures of ancient and modern Latin civilization, against whom

he has taken a satirical attitude. He confers an impure and subversive character to his revolt by removing Universal Rome from the altar and replacing it with the gilded idol of Jewish internationalism – an internationalism that for many years has supported too many currents of modern thought. The fact is that Joyce has played court to that organization of Jews, proponent of men and ideas, which has especially held the field in Paris. Joyce is against all that is Latin, whether it be imperial civilization or Catholic civilization. He is anti-Latin *for an ulterior motive*. His jibes against Rome and the papacy, made in a clownish and shameful manner, would be less irksome if it were not apparent that concealed in them was a form of enticement toward the children of Israel.

15. But does the contemporary novel really have to descend from the pond to the sewer, and here in Italy of all places, crucible of moral renewal and spiritual restoration? Must Joyce be taken as a model, an author in whom morality, religion, sense of family and society, virtue, duty, beauty, courage, heroism, sacrifice – in other words, Western civilization as well as genuine humanity – are all lost and the Jewish worm destroys everything?

16. This is the truth, and little weight should be given to defenses of Joyce from the pens (sold to whom?) of Corrado Pavolini, Annibale Pastore, or Adelchi Baratono, not to mention Montale, Benco, Linati, Cecchi, or Pannunzio. And it is easy for Pannunzio to say that "the real problem for Italian literature is to become European once and for all, to graft itself onto the powerful trunk of foreign literature and to be truly original in doing so, to have something of its own to say, through observation, love, suffering, in our own reality that we find around us, which is not the usual repetition of the far-from-pitiful tales of Aunt Teresa or Uncle Michele and, worse still, the pseudo-poetical description of fantastic journeys, pointless returns, tram rides in suburbia (how much travel there is in this literature!)."

17. The real attack on the spirit of new Italy is in narrative prose itself, where a whole miserable net has been woven, from Italo Svevo, a Jew thrice over, to Alberto Moravia, a Jew six times over, to fish out

from the murky depths of society repugnant figures of men who are not "men" but inert beings, besmirched with base and repugnant sensuality, physically and morally sick . . . And the masters of all these narrators are those pathological lunatics named Marcello Proust and Giacomo Joyce, foreign names and Jews right to the bone, and defeatists to the roots of their hair.[2]

[Appeared in *Almanacco del bibliofilo — Recensioni in ritardo: Antologia di singolari e argute presentazioni di opere letterarie antiche e moderne, famose, poco note, e sconosciute,* edited by Mario Scognamiglio (Milan: Rovello, 2009).]

---

2. Apart from passages that link paragraphs, the various judgments are taken from articles that appeared in the 1920s and '30s, in the following order: (1.) Carlo Linati, "Joyce," in *Corriere della Sera,* August 20, 1925; (2.) Report on reading the manuscript of *A Portrait of the Artist as a Young Man,* 1916; (3.) Santino Caramella, "Anti-Joyce," in *Il Baretti,* vol. 12, 1926; (4.) Valentino Piccoli, "Ma Joyce chi è?" in *L'Illustrazione Italiana,* vol. 10, 1927, and "Il romanzo italiano del dopoguerra," in *La Parola e il Libro,* vol. 4, 1927; (5.) Guido Piovene, "Narratori," in *La Parola e il Libro,* vols. 9–10, 1927; (6.) Curzio Malaparte, "Strapaese e stracittà," in *Il Selvaggio,* vol. 4, no. 20, 1927; (7.) G. B. Angioletti, "Aura poetica," in *La Fiera Letteraria,* July 7, 1929; (8.) Elio Vittorini, "Joyce e Rabelais," in *La Stampa,* August 23, 1929; (9.) Elio Vittorini, "Letteratura di psicoanalisi," in *La Stampa,* September 27, 1929; (10.) Luciano Anceschi, "Romanzo collettivo o romanzo collettivista," in *L'Ambrosiano,* May 17, 1934 (in consideration of the man who was to become the leading light behind some of the most radical movements in postwar Italian culture, we should not forget that he was twenty-three at the time, and only ten when Fascism had begun to educate him); (11.) Vitaliano Brancati, "I romanzieri europei leggano romanzi italiani," in *Scrittori nostri* (Milan: Mondadori, 1935); (12.) Mario Praz, "Commento a *Ulysses,*" in *La Stampa,* August 5, 1930; (13.) Filippo Tommaso Marinetti et al., *Il romanzo sintetico,* 1939 (now in *Teoria e invenzione futurista* [Milan: Mondadori, 1968]); (14.) Ennio Giorgianni, "Inchiesta su James Joyce," in *Epiloghi di Perseo,* vol. 1, 1934; (15.) Renato Famea, "Joyce, Proust, e il romanzo moderno," in *Meridiano di Roma,* April 14, 1940; (16.) Mario Pannunzio, "Necessità del romanzo," in *Il Saggiatore,* June 1932; (17.) Giuseppe Biondolillo, "Giudaismo letterario," in *L'Unione Sarda,* April 14, 1939.

For all of these sources I am indebted to Giovanni Cianci, *La fortuna di Joyce in Italia* (Bari: Adriatica, 1974).

Why the Island Is Never Found

U TOPIAS ARE FOUND on islands (with a few rare exceptions, such as the realm of Prester John). The island is thought of as inaccessible, a non-place where you land by chance, and once you have left, you can never return. So only on an island can a perfect civilization be created, and we discover it only through legends.

The Greek civilization lived on archipelagos and ought to have been quite used to islands, yet it is only on mysterious islands that Ulysses meets Circe, Polyphemus, and Nausicaa. There are those islands we read about in Apollonius of Rhodes's *Argonautica;* there are the Blessed or Fortunate Islands where Saint Brendan lands during his voyage; Thomas More's city of Utopia is on an island, and there are those perfect, thriving unknown civilizations dreamed about in the seventeenth and eighteenth centuries, such as Foigny's Terra Australis and Vairasse's island of Sevarambes. The mutineers from the *Bounty* search for the lost paradise on an island (without finding it); Verne's Captain Nemo lives on an island; both Stevenson's and the Count of Monte Cristo's treasures lie hidden on an island, and so on until we reach the dystopias, from the island of Doctor Moreau's Beast Folk to the island of Doctor No, where James Bond lands.

What is the fascination of islands? It is not so much that they are places cut off from the rest of the world. Marco Polo or Giovanni Pian del Carpine found places far away from human society by crossing endless tracts of terra firma. Until the eighteenth century, when it became possible to calculate longitude, mariners would come across an island merely by chance, and, like Ulysses, would escape from it, but there was no way of finding their way back there. From the time of Saint Brendan (and even up to Gozzano) an island was always an *insula perdita*, a lost island.

This explains the success and fascination of that highly popular genre of island stories in the fifteenth and sixteenth centuries, which provide a record of all the islands in the world – known islands as well as those about which there were just a few vague legends. The island stories, in their own way, provided as much geographical accuracy as possible (unlike the tales of fabulous lands in earlier centuries) and were a blend of folk tales and traveler's accounts. Sometimes they were wrong. It was thought, for example, that there were two islands, Taprobane and Ceylon, whereas in fact (as we know) there was just one – but so what? They represented a geography of the unknown or, at least, the little-known.

Later came the journals of the eighteenth-century travelers – Cook, Bougainville, La Pérouse . . . They too were looking for islands but were careful to describe only what they saw, no longer relying on folk traditions – and that was quite a different matter. But still they went off looking for islands that didn't exist, such as Terra Australis (which appeared on all atlases), or for an island that someone had once discovered but had never been found again.

This is why, still today, our fantasies drift between the myth of *an island that doesn't exist,* or the myth of absence; that of *one island too many,* or the myth of excess; that of *the undiscovered island,* or the myth of inaccuracy; or that of *the un-rediscovered island,* or the myth of the *insula perdita,* the lost island – four quite different stories.

The first is a legendary story. Legends about islands are generally divided into those that require us to pretend the island exists (asking us to suspend our belief) – as with the islands of Verne or Stevenson – and those that describe an island that does not exist by definition and have the sole purpose of reaffirming the power of legends — as with Peter Pan's Neverland. The island that, by definition, does not exist is of no interest to us, at least today. The reason is simple: no one goes looking for it — children don't go to sea looking for Captain Hook's island, nor do adults go in search of Captain Nemo's island.

Likewise, I will pass over the *one island too many,* not least because there is, I believe, only one case of this phenomenon of excess — the duplication of Ceylon and Taprobane. This story has been told in much detail in an article on island stories by Tarcisio Lancioni[1] to which I refer you. In fact, what interests me today is that unfortunate love for an island that can no longer be found, whereas Taprobane was always being found, even when no one was looking for it, and therefore, in terms of sexual exploits, we might say it was not so much a

1. Tarcisio Lancioni, *Almanacco del bibliofilo — Viaggio tra gli isolari* (Milan: Rovello, 1992).

story of hopeless passion as one of Don Giovanni–like incontinence, where the number of maps showing Taprobane had already reached *mille e tre*.

According to Pliny, Taprobane was discovered during the time of Alexander the Great, and prior to that had been generally indicated as the land of the Antichthones and considered "another world." Pliny's island could be identified as Ceylon, and this can be seen from Ptolemy's maps, at least in the sixteenth-century editions. Isidore of Seville also places it to the south of India and confines himself to saying that it is full of precious stones and has two summers and two winters each year. Marco Polo's *Travels* doesn't give the name Taprobane but refers to Ceylon as Seilam.

The duplication of Ceylon and Taprobane appears quite clearly in Mandeville's *Travels*, which describes them in two different chapters. He doesn't say exactly where Ceylon is located but states that it is "well a 800 miles about" and is

> full of serpents, of dragons and of cockodrills, that no man dare dwell there. These cockodrills be serpents, yellow and rayed above, and have four feet and short thighs, and great nails as claws or talons. And there be some that have five fathoms in length, and some of six and of eight and of ten. And when they go by places that be gravelly, it seemeth as though men had drawn a great tree through the gravelly place. And there be also many wild beasts, and namely of elephants. In that isle is a great mountain. And in mid place of the mount is a great lake in a full fair plain; and there is great plenty of water. And they of the country say, that Adam and Eve wept upon that mount an hundred year, when they were driven out of Paradise, and that water, they say, is of their tears; for so much water they wept, that made the foresaid lake. And in the bottom of that lake men find many precious stones and great pearls. In that lake grow many reeds and great canes; and there within be many cocodrills and serpents and great water-leeches. And the king of that country, once every year, giveth leave to poor men to go into the lake to gather them precious stones and pearls, by way of alms,

for the love of God that made Adam. And all the year men find enough. And for the vermin that is within, they anoint their arms and their thighs and legs with an ointment made of a thing that is clept lemons, that is a manner of fruit like small pease; and then have they no dread of no cockodrills, ne of none other venomous vermin . . . In that country and others thereabout there be wild geese that have two heads. (*The Travels of Sir John Mandeville,* chapter 21)

Taprobane, on the other hand, according to Mandeville, is under the rule of Prester John. Mandeville had not yet sited Prester John's realm in Ethiopia, as he would later do, and it was still in the area of India — though Prester John's India was often confused with the farthest Orient, the land of earthly paradise. In any event, Taprobane is to be found in the vicinity of India (and he names the point where the Red Sea flows into the ocean). Like Isidore's account, the island has two summers and two winters and there are enormous mountains of gold guarded by pismires, or giant ants:

These pismires be great as hounds, so that no man dare come to those hills for the pismires would assail them and devour them anon. So that no man may get of that gold, but by great sleight. And therefore when it is great heat, the pismires rest them in the earth, from prime of the day into noon. And then the folk of the country take camels, dromedaries, and horses and other beasts, and go thither, and charge them in all haste that they may; and after that, they flee away in all haste that the beasts may go, or the pismires come out of the earth. And in other times, when it is not so hot, and that the pismires rest them not in the earth, then they get gold by this subtlety. They take mares that have young colts or foals, and lay upon the mares void vessels made there-for; and they be all open above, and hanging low to the earth. And then they send forth those mares for to pasture about those hills, and with-hold the foals with them at home. And when the pismires see those vessels, they leap in anon: and they have this kind that they let nothing be empty among them, but anon they fill it, be it what manner of thing that it be; and so they fill those vessels with gold. And when that the folk suppose that the vessels be full, they put forth anon the young foals, and make them to neigh after their dams. And then anon the mares return towards their foals with their charges of gold. (*The Travels of Sir John Mandeville*, chapter 33)

From this point onward, from one map to the next, Taprobane moves about from one place in the Indian Ocean to another, sometimes alone, sometimes duplicating Ceylon. For a certain period it is identified with Sumatra, but sometimes we find it between Sumatra and Indochina, close to Borneo.

Thomas Porcacchi, in *Isole più famose del mondo* (1572), tells us about a Taprobane full of riches, about its elephants and its immense turtles, as well as the characteristic attributed by Diodorus Siculus to its inhabitants — a kind of forked tongue ("double as far as the root and divided; with one part they talk to one person, with the other they talk to another").

After having recounted various folk stories, he then apologizes to readers for the fact that he has found no exact reference as to its geographical position, and concludes, "Although many ancient and modern writers have referred to this island, I find no one however who indicates its boundaries: hence I too will have to be excused if in this my usual order is lacking." As for the island of Taprobane's identification with Ceylon, he is doubtful: "She was first (according to Ptolemy) called Simondi, and then Salice, and finally Taprobane; but people nowadays conclude that today she is called Sumatra, though there are also those according to whom Taprobane is not Sumatra but the island of Zeilam . . . But some people now suggest that none of the ancients have positioned Taprobane correctly: indeed they hold that where they have put it there is no island at all that can be believed to be that."

From being *one island too many,* Taprobane therefore slowly became an *island that doesn't exist.* Thomas More would treat it thus when he situated his Utopia "between Ceylon and America," and Tommaso Campanella was to use Taprobane as the place where he built his City of the Sun.

Let us now turn to islands whose absence has encouraged (sometimes sporadic) research and an enduring nostalgia.

Ancient epics, of course, tell us about islands that may or may not have existed, so that the isles visited by Ulysses have produced a scholarly literature aimed at establishing which actual places they refer to. And the myth of Atlantis has led to an investigation that is not yet over (judging from the number of mystery magazines and second-rate television programs). But Atlantis was regarded rather more as an entire continent, and the idea was immediately accepted that it had sunk into the sea. It is therefore the subject of legend rather than research.

Navigatio Sancti Brendani was perhaps the first account of the quest for an island.

Saint Brendan and his mystical mariners visited many: the island of birds, the island of hell, the island reduced to a rock on which Judas is chained, and that bogus island that had already deceived Sinbad, on which Brendan's ship lands — not until the following day, when the ship's crew light fires and see the island stir in annoyance, do they re-

alize it is not an island but a terrible sea monster called Jasconius.

But the island that excited the imagination of those in later times is the Isle of the Blessed, a sort of earthly paradise on which our mariners land after seven years of adventure:

> A land more precious than all the others for its beauty, for the marvelous and gracious and agreeable things within it, such as its beautiful and clear and precious rivers with waters most sweet and fresh and gentle, and trees most precious in every way with precious fruits, and many roses and lilies and flowers and violas and herbs and all things sweet-smelling and perfect in their bounty. And there were songbirds of every agreeable nature and all sang harmoniously in sweet and gentle song: and the climate seemed truly agreeable like sweet springtime. And there were roads and paths of every kind, precious stones, and there was so much good that greatly cheered the heart of all those who saw it with their own eyes, and there were tame and wild animals of every kind, and they moved about and lived at their own ease and as they pleased, and lived together in domesticity without wishing to cause any harm or disturbance to the other; and there were birds of the same kind who lived together similarly. And there were vineyards and pergolas always well supplied with fine grapes that its goodness and beauty exceeded all others.

The island paradise visited by Saint Brendan awakens a desire (something that hadn't happened with Atlantis, Ogygia, or the island of the Phaeacians). Throughout the Middle Ages and during the Renaissance there is a firm belief that it exists. It appears on maps, such as the Ebersdorf globe. On a map prepared by Toscanelli for the king of Portugal, it appears in the middle of the sea, toward Japan, to be reached *buscando el levante por el poniente,* approaching the East via the west — and lies almost prophetically where America would later be discovered.

It is sometimes on the same latitude as Ireland, though on more modern maps the island moves farther south to the latitude of the Canaries or the Fortunate Isles, and sometimes the Fortunate Isles are confused with the island called Saint Brendan. Sometimes it is identified with Madeira and sometimes with another nonexistent island such as the mythical Antillia, as it was called in the sixteenth-century *Arte del navegar* by Pedro da Medina. In Martin Behaim's globe of 1492 it was positioned much farther west, close to the equator. And it now had the name Lost Island, Insula Perdita.

Honorious of Autun, in his *De imagine mundi* (twelfth century), had described it as the most pleasant of islands, unknown to humans, which even when it had been found, had not been found ("Est quaedam Oceani insula dicta Perdita, amoenitate et fertilitate omnium rerum prae cunctis terris praestantissima, hominibus ignota. Quae aliquando casu inventa, postea quaesita non est inventa, et ideo dicitur Perdita"); and in the fourteenth century, Pierre Bersuire spoke in the same terms about the Fortunate Isles.

It is apparent from the Treaty of Évora of June 1519 that the Lost Island was expected to be rediscovered one day. Under the treaty, King Manuel I of Portugal passed all rights over the Canary Isles to Spain, and the terms of the treaty expressly included a Lost or Hidden Isle. In 1569, Gerardus Mercator still marked the mysterious island on his map, and in 1721 the last explorers set off in search of it.[2]

Saint Brendan's island is not *an island that doesn't exist* — someone has actually been there, but it is lost since no one has succeeded in returning to it. For this reason it becomes the subject of an unfulfilled desire and its story is an allegory of every real love story, the story of a Brief Encounter, of a mystical Doctor Zhivago who has lost his Lara. The agony of love is not the love we dream of that never happens (the island that we know doesn't exist, the illusion of love for adolescent lovers), but the love that, having once happened, then vanishes forever.

But how did islands come to be lost?

From earliest antiquity, ships had no points of reference other than the stars. Using instruments like the astrolabe or the cross-staff, sail-

---

2. On this whole question, see Arturo Graf, *Miti, leggende, e superstizioni del Medio Evo*, chapter 4 (Turin: Loescher, 1892–93).

ors could fix the height of a star from the horizon and calculate the distance from the zenith point; once they knew the declination, they knew on what parallel they were, given that the zenith distance plus or minus declination gives latitude. They therefore knew how far north or south they were from a given point. But to get back to an island (or any other point) the latitude was not enough—the longitude was also needed. We know that New York and Naples are on the same latitude but we also know they are not in the same place—their longitude is different and they are therefore on a different degree of the meridian.

And this is the problem that navigators faced until almost the end of the eighteenth century. There were no certain means for determining longitude, for saying how far east or west they were from a given point.

This is what happened with the Solomon Islands (an extraordinary example of *insulae perditae*). Álvaro de Saavedra Cerón went in search of these legendary islands in 1528, hoping to find King Solomon's gold, but was sailing about between what are now called the Marshall and the Admiralty Islands. Álvaro de Mendaña arrived there, however, in 1568 and christened the Solomon Islands. But, after that, no one managed to find them again, not even Mendaña himself when he went back with Queiros, almost thirty years later, in search of them, though he only just missed them, landing instead on the island of Santa Cruz, to the southeast.

And the same happened to others after him. The Dutch set up their East Indies Company at the beginning of the seventeenth century and created the city of Batavia in Asia as a point of departure for many eastbound expeditions. They landed at a place they called New Holland, but never reached the Solomon Islands. Other lands, probably to the east of the Solomon Islands, were similarly discovered by English pirates whom the Court of Saint James hastened to reward with noble titles. But no one was able to find any trace of the Solomon Islands, and for a long time many believed them to be only a legend.

Mendaña had landed on them but had incorrectly fixed their longitude. And even if, through some celestial guidance, he had managed to fix them correctly, then other navigators looking for that longitude (and he himself on his second voyage) could not be entirely sure of their own longitude.

For several centuries the great European maritime powers strove to discover a way of establishing the *fixed point* — the *punto fijo* that Cervantes had joked about — and were prepared to pay enormous sums to anyone who found an effective method. Navigators, men of science, and cranks came up with all kind of answers — there was the method based on lunar eclipses, one that examined the variations of a magnetized needle, and the *loch,* or Dutchman's log method; Galileo proposed a technique based on the eclipses of the satellites of Jupiter, which are so frequent that they can be seen several times each night.

But all turned out to be inadequate. There would, of course, have been one sure method: to keep a clock on board that tells the time at one known meridian, then to find out the time at place X at sea and, by working on the basis that the globe has been subdivided since antiquity into 360 degrees of longitude and that the sun moves 15 degrees in one hour, to work out the longitude of point X from the difference. In other words, if the clock on board showed that it was, let us say, noon in Paris, and that in place X it was six in the afternoon, by translating every hour of difference into 15 degrees, we would have known that the longitude of place X was 90 degrees from the Paris meridian.

Although it was not difficult to work out the time at the place where the calculation was being made, it was practically impossible to keep a mechanical clock on board that would function perfectly after months of sailing and the inevitable jolts, through winds and waves; hourglasses and water clocks were, of course, out of the question since they need to work on a flat motionless surface. And any clock would have to be of an extremely high precision: an error of four seconds would produce an error of one degree of longitude.

One suggestion mentioned in various chronicles of the time was the use of Powder of Sympathy.

This was a miraculous compound that, when applied to the weapon that had caused a wound, acted (through a sort of almost atomic continuity) on the particles of blood released into the air over the wound, even if the weapon and the injury were a great distance apart. This would heal the wound, allowing time to take its course, but as an immediate reaction it would cause irritation and pain.

It was therefore decided to wound a dog, to be kept on board the ship during the journey, and to rub the miraculous compound over the weapon each day at the same hour. The dog would have reacted with a whimper of pain and that was how they would know aboard ship what time it was at that moment at the point of departure.[3]

I dealt with this story in my novel *The Island of the Day Before,* so allow me to quote one passage since, after all, on such uncertain information, this is the only document that suggests what must have occurred.

Finally one morning, taking advantage of a sailor's bad fall from a yardarm, which fractured his skull, while there was great confusion on the deck and the doctor was summoned to treat the unfortunate man, Roberto slipped down into the hold. Almost groping, he managed to find the right path. Perhaps it was luck, or perhaps the animal was whimpering more than usual that morning: Roberto, more or less at the point where later on the *Daphne* he would find the kegs of aqua vitae, was confronted by a horrid sight. Well shielded from curious eyes, in an enclosure made to his measure, on a bed of rags, lay a dog.

He was perhaps of good breed, but his suffering and hunger had reduced him to mere skin and bones. And yet his tormentors

---

3. Although a great deal was written at the time about Powder of Sympathy, in particular in the writings of Sir Kenelm Digby (for example, *Theatrum sympatheticum, in quo Sympathiae Actiones variae, singulares & admirandae tàm Macro – quam Microcosmicae exhibentur, & Mechanicé, Physicé, Mathematicé, Chimicé & Medicé, occasione Pulveris Sympathetici, ita quidem elucidantur, ut illarum agendi vis & modus, sine qualitatum occultarum, animaeve Mundi, aut spiritus astralis Magnive Magnalis, vel aliorum Commentariorum subsidium ad oculum pateat* [Nuremberg, 1660], the story about the dog is perhaps legendary. More recent references to it include Dava Sobel, *Longitude* (London: Fourth Estate, 1996).

showed their intention to keep him alive: they had provided him with abundant food and water, including food surely not canine, subtracted from the passengers' rations. He was lying on one side, head limp, tongue lolling. On that exposed side gaped a broad and horrible wound. At once fresh and gangrenous, it revealed a pair of great pinkish lips, and in the centre, as along the entire gash, was a purulent secretion resembling whey. Roberto realized that the wound looked as it did because the hand of a chirurgeon, rather than sew the lips together, had deliberately kept them parted and open, attaching them to the outer hide.

Bastard offspring of the medical art, that wound had not only been inflicted but wickedly treated so it would not form a scar and the dog would continue suffering — who knows for how long. Further, Roberto saw in and around the wound a crystalline residue, as if a doctor (yes, a doctor, so cruelly expert!) every day sprinkled an irritant salt there.

Helpless, Roberto stroked the wretch, now whimpering softly. He asked himself what he could do to help, but at a heavier touch, the dog's suffering increased. Moreover, Roberto's own pity was giving way to a sense of victory. There was no doubt: this was Dr. Byrd's secret, the mysterious cargo taken aboard in London.

From what Roberto had seen, from what a man with his knowledge could infer, the dog had been wounded in England, and Byrd was making sure he would remain wounded. Someone in London, every day at the same, agreed hour, did something to the guilty weapon, or to a cloth steeped in the animal's blood, provoking a reaction, perhaps of relief, but perhaps of still greater pain, for Dr. Byrd himself had said that the Weapon Salve could also harm.

Thus on the *Amaryllis* they could know at a given moment what time it was in Europe. And knowing the hour of their transitory position, they were able to calculate the meridian! (translated by William Weaver)

If the story about the dog seems fanciful, in the same novel I described an instrument proposed by Galileo in a letter of 1637 (to Lorenzo Realio). Galileo thought of fixing longitude by observing the positions of Jupiter's satellites. But once again, on a ship at the mercy of the waves, it would be difficult to point the telescope accurately. And here Galileo suggested an extraordinary solution. To enjoy its comedy, we need not read the humorous account in my novel — it is enough to read Galileo himself:

> As for the first problem, this is certainly the most difficult, but I think I have found a remedy for this, at least for the ordinary movements of the ship; and this should be enough since, during great storms and tempests, which normally prevent the sun and other stars being seen, all other observations cease, as indeed do all mariner's duties. But during ordinary movements I think it is possible to reduce the state of the person who has to make the observations to a tranquility similar to that of the peace and calm of the sea; and to achieve this benefit I have thought of placing the observer in a specially prepared part of the boat so that he does not feel either the movements from bow to stern or the rocking from side to side: and my thinking is based on this. If the ship is always in calm waters and without waves, there is no doubt that the use of the telescope would be just as easy as on land. Now, I want to place the observer in a small boat placed inside the large boat, the small boat being in such necessary quantity of water as I will explain below. Here, first of all, it is clear that the water contained in the small vessel will remain in equilibrium, even when the large boat inclines and reclines to right and left, forward and backward, without any part of it being raised or lowered, but will always remain parallel to the horizon; so that if in this small boat we build another smaller boat, floating in the water contained within it, it would find itself in an extremely calm sea, and would therefore stay there without moving: and this second boat is the place where the observer must be placed. I therefore want the first vessel, which has to contain the water, to be like a large semi-spherical basin, and that the smaller vessel is similar to it, except that it is smaller, and that the space between its convex surface and the concave inner surface of the container is no more than the thickness of a thumb; so that a very small quantity of water will be enough to float the inner vessel,

as if it were floating in the wide ocean . . . The size of these vessels must be such that the inner and smaller vessel can hold the weight of the person making the observations without sinking, as well as his chair and the other equipment on which the telescope is fixed. And in order to keep the smaller vessel separate from the outer one so as not to touch it, so that it cannot be influenced by the motion of the ship in the same way that the larger one is, I want the internal concave surface of the inner vessel to be held with several springs, eight or ten in number, which stop the two vessels from touching each other, but do not prevent the inner vessel from not responding to the raising and lowering of the sides of the outer container: and if, rather than water, we wish to use oil, that would be even better, nor would the quantity be great, since two or three barrels would be enough . . .

I have already made a kind of curved helmet on the same principle, for the use of our galleys, which, when placed on the head of the observer, and a telescope being placed upon it, adjusted in such a way that it was always directed towards the same point at which the other free eye was looking, without doing anything else, the object that he was looking at with his free eye was always to be found through the telescope. A similar machine could be built which is not just held on the head but over the shoulders and bust of the observer, on which is fixed a telescope of the size necessary to clearly distinguish the stars of Jupiter.

In order to resolve the problem—with all due respect to Galileo, whose extraordinary invention no one had the courage to finance, and to the whole plethora of inventors of other extraordinary methods for fixing longitude—we had to wait for Harrison's invention of the marine chronometer, or rather, his final version in the 1770s. From then on, even during storms, the clock would keep the correct time for the point of departure. But before that moment the *insulae* were fatally *perditae*.

Before then, the history of Pacific exploration is the history of people forever discovering lands they were not looking for. Abel Tasman,

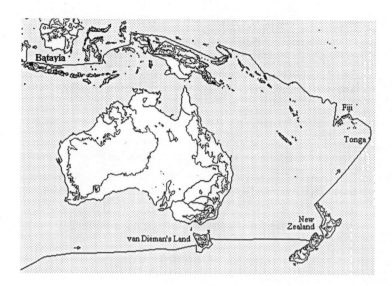

for example, while searching for the Solomon Islands in 1643, arrives at Tasmania (which is forty-two degrees latitude farther south, as if that were nothing), sees New Zealand, passes Tonga, arrives in Fiji without disembarking, where he sees only a few small islands, and reaches the coast of New Guinea, without realizing that inside that loop he had made stood Australia. No mean achievement. He had gone from point to point like a billiard ball, and for many years after, other navigators came extremely close to Australia without seeing it.

In short, it was a madcap voyage between islands, coral reefs, and continents, without any apparent plan. And poor them. We can set a course today using the maps created after Cook, but they were all basically wandering about like Captain Bligh, in a ship's launch, heading toward the Moluccas, and the most important thing was not to bump into the *Bounty* again.

But even after the problem of longitude had been solved, it was still easy for ships to lose themselves among such islands. Look at the voyages of Corto Maltese and Rasputin in *Ballad of the Salt Sea*. The characters in the *Ballad* are avid readers. At one point, Pandora seems

to be happily immersed in the complete works of Melville while Cain is reading Coleridge, the author of another ballad, the one about the Ancient Mariner—curiously he finds it on the German submarine of Slütter who, when he dies, will also leave his copies of Rilke and Shelley at Escondida. And toward the end, Cain quotes Euripides.

And even an old jailbird like Rasputin, at the very beginning, is reading *Voyage autour du monde par la frégate du roi* La Boudeuse *et*

la flûte L'Étoile. I can guarantee that this is not the first edition of 1771, which does not carry the author's name on the title page and is not in three columns.

The book is open about halfway through and, at least in the original edition, of the same size, this is the point where chapter 5 begins: "Navigation depuis les grandes Cyclades; découverte du golfe de la Louisiade . . . Relâche . . . la Nouvelle Bretagne."

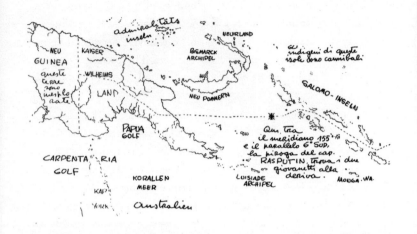

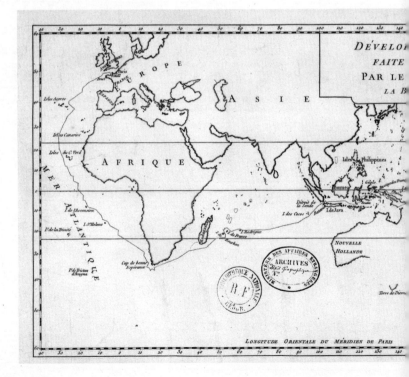

If he was up-to-date with the techniques of 1913, Rasputin ought to know that he is on the 155-degree meridian west (according to Hugo Pratt's map), but if he relies on Bougainville he should be on the crucial 180-degree meridian, the date line. There again, Bougainville referred to the "Isles Salomon dont l'existence et la position sont douteuses."

When the Dutch cargo ship meets Rasputin's catamaran, the first thing the officers and the Fijian sailor notice is that the boat seems rather off course for a Fijian vessel, since the Fijians usually head east and south. And this is what they should have done, as we shall see later, since the Monk's island is much farther southeast.

Tell me why Corto should find Slütter's submarine below the western point of New Pomerania — he is sailing west, having departed from

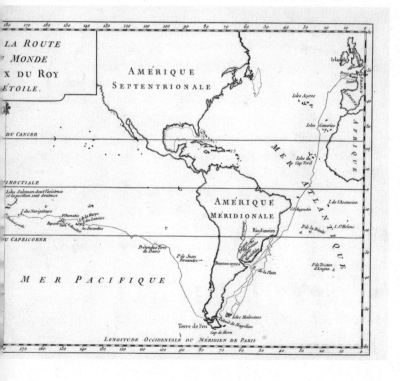

Kaiserine, whereas the submarine's destination is Escondida, and the Monk's island of Escondida (19 degrees south and 169 west) ought to be south of the Solomon Islands and west of Fiji. A German naval officer who sails toward New Guinea to get to Escondida and says (as he does) "We'll be arriving shortly at Escondida" (which is 20 degrees away) is caught in Rasputin's net, a dreamer who has confused the frontiers of space. The fact is that Rasputin or Pratt, or both, are also trying to confound the frontiers of time.

Cain and Pandora are captured by Rasputin on November 1, 1913, but they all arrive at Escondida after August 4, 1914 (the Monk tells them that war has broken out on that date), at some time between September and the last ten days of October, when the English appear on the scene. After two pages of Coleridge and a few discussions with Slütter, a year has passed, during which time the submarine navigates vague routes, with the curious indolence, the thirst for drifting, of seventeenth-century buccaneers, the Ancient Mariner, and Captain Ahab.

All of the main characters in the *Ballad* act as though they are liv-

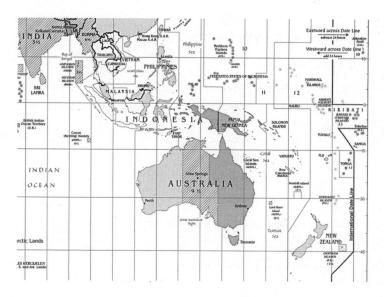

ing in the times of Bougainville, or even Mendaña: they travel in the archipelago of uncertainty.

The fascination of islands is precisely that of losing ourselves. Heaven help us if we find our way straight back, like taking one of those wretched ferry crossings from Manhattan to Ellis Island. The eternal fascination of the island is still that celebrated by Guido Gozzano.

> But more beautiful than all, the Island Never Found:
> The one the king of Spain had from his cousin
> the king of Portugal with sealed signature
> and papal bull in Gothic Latin.
> The Infante sailed off for the legendary realm,
> saw the Fortunate Isles: Iunonia, Gorgo, Hera,
> and the Sargasso Sea and the Dark Sea
> searching for that isle . . . But the island was not there.
> In vain the round-bottomed sailing galleys,
> in vain the caravels armed their bows:
> with due respect to the pope, the isle is hidden,

and Portugal and Spain still search for it.
The isle exists, appearing sometimes from afar
between Teneriffe and Palma, suffused in mystery:
" . . . the Island Never Found!" From the high peak of Teide
the good Canarian points it out to the foreigner.
Marked on the ancient maps of the corsairs.
. . . *Hifola* to — be found? . . . *Hifola* pilgrim? . . .
The magic isle that glides over the seas;
mariners sometimes see her near . . .
And point their bows toward her blessed shore:
Among unfamiliar flowers soar lofty palms,
The divine aromatic forest, thick and lush,
Weeping cardamom, seeping rubber sap . . .

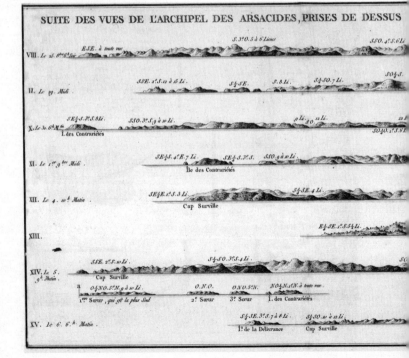

Herald like the arrival of a perfumed courtesan,
the Island Never Found . . . Yet, if the pilot draws closer,
it rapidly fades away, like a vain shadow,
tinged with the azure color of faraway . . . ("La più bella")

I don't suppose Gozzano had in mind some of the maps we find in eighteenth-century books on sea travel, but this idea of the island that "fades away, like a vain shadow, tinged with the azure color of faraway" makes us think about the way in which, before the problem of longitude had been solved, islands were identified using drawings of their profiles as they had been seen for the first time. Arriving from a distance, the island (whose shape did not exist on any map) was recog-

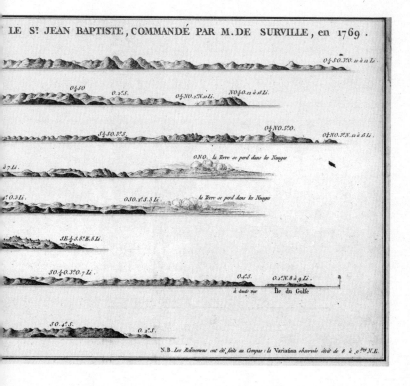

nized from its *skyline,* as we would say of an American city today. And what happened if there were two islands with very similar skylines, as if there were two cities, both with the Empire State Building and (at one time) the Twin Towers south of it? They would land on the wrong island, and who knows how many times this happened.

Moreover, the profile of an island changes with the color of the sky, the haze, the time of day, and perhaps even the time of year, which alters the appearance of the vegetation. Sometimes the island is tinged with the azure color of faraway, it can disappear in the night or in the mist, or clouds can hide the shapes of its mountains. There is nothing more elusive than an island about which we know only its profile. Arriving on an island for which we have neither map nor coordinates is similar to moving about like one of Edwin Abbott's characters in Flatland, where there is only one dimension and we see things only from the front, like lines with no thickness — with no height and no depth — and only someone from outside Flatland could see them from above.

And it was said, in fact, that the inhabitants of the islands of Madeira, La Palma, La Gomera, and El Hierro, deceived by the clouds or by the mirages of the fata morgana, sometimes thought they had seen the *insula perdita* toward the west, shimmering between the water and the sky.

Thus, in the same way that an island that didn't exist could be sighted among the reflections of the sea, so it was also possible to confuse two islands that *did* exist, or never to find the one that was the intended destination.

And that is how islands become lost.

And why islands are never found. As Pliny said (book 2, chapter 96), some islands are forever wavering.

[Published in the *Almanacco del bibliofilo — Sulle orme di san Brandano* (Milan: Rovello, 2011) and based on a paper given at a conference on islands held in Carloforte, Sardinia, in 2010.]

Thoughts on WikiLeaks

I N TERMS OF CONTENT, WikiLeaks has turned out to be a false scandal, but in terms of its formal implications, it has been, and will prove to be, something more. As we shall explain, it marks the beginning of a new chapter in history.

A false scandal is one in which something becomes public that everyone had known, and had been talking about in private, and that, so to speak, was only being whispered about out of hypocrisy (for example, gossip about adultery). Everyone knows perfectly well — not just those well-informed about diplomatic matters but anyone who has ever seen a film about international intrigues — that embassies have lost their diplomatic role since at least the end of the Second World War, in other words since the time when heads of state could pick up the telephone or fly off to meet each other for dinner (was an ambassador sent off in a felucca to declare war on Saddam Hussein?). Except for minor tasks of representation, they have been transformed, more overtly, into centers to gather information on the host country (with more competent ambassadors playing the role of sociologist or political commentator) and, more covertly, into full-blown dens of espionage.

But now that this has been openly declared, American diplomacy has had to admit that it is true, and therefore to suffer a loss of image in formal terms — with the curious consequence that this loss, leak, flow of confidential information, rather than harming the supposed victims (Berlusconi, Sarkozy, Gaddafi, or Merkel), has harmed the supposed perpetrator, in other words, poor Mrs. Clinton, who was probably just receiving messages sent by embassy staff carrying out their official duties, as this was all they were being paid to do. This, from all the evidence, is exactly what Assange wanted, since his grudge is against the American government and not against Berlusconi's government.

Why have the victims not been affected, except perhaps superficially? Because, as everyone realizes, the famous secret messages were simply "press echo," and did no more than report what everyone in Europe already knew and was talking about, which had even appeared in America in *Newsweek*. The secret reports were therefore like the clippings files sent by company press offices to their managing director, who is too busy to read the newspapers.

It is clear that the reports sent to Mrs. Clinton are not about secret dealings — they were not spy messages. And although they dealt with apparently highly confidential information, such as the fact that Berlusconi has private interests in Russian gas deals, even here (whether true or false) the messages would have done no more than repeat what had already been talked about by those who in Fascist times were branded café strategists, in other words, those who talked politics at the bar.

And this goes to confirm another well-known fact, that every dossier compiled for the secret service (in whatever country) consists entirely of material already in the public domain. The "extraordinary" American revelations about Berlusconi's wild nights reported what could have been read months earlier in any Italian newspaper (except the two controlled by the premier), and Gaddafi's satrapic follies had for some time been providing — rather stale — material for cartoonists.

The rule that secret files must contain only information already known is essential for the operation of a secret service, and not just in this century. Likewise, if you go to a bookshop specializing in esoteric publications, you will see that every new book (on the Holy Grail, the mystery of Rennes-le-Château, the Knights Templar, or the Rosicrucians) repeats exactly what was written in earlier books. This is not simply because occult writers are averse to carrying out new research (nor because they don't know where to go looking for information about the nonexistent), but because followers of the occult believe in only what they already know, and in those things that confirm what they have already learned. It is the formula behind the success of Dan Brown.

The same happens with secret files. The informant is lazy, and the head of the secret service is either lazy or blinkered—he only regards as true what he already recognizes.

Given that the secret services, in any country, aren't able to foresee events like the attack on the Twin Towers (in some cases, being regularly led astray, they actually bring them about) and that they file only what is already known, it would be just as well to be rid of them. But in present times, cutting more jobs would indeed be foolish.

I have suggested, however, that while in terms of its contents it was a false scandal, in terms of its formal implications, WikiLeaks has opened a new chapter in history.

No government in the world will be able to maintain areas of secrecy if it continues to entrust its secret communications and its archives to the Internet or other forms of electronic memory, and by this I mean not only the United States but even San Marino or the Principality of Monaco (and perhaps only Andorra will be spared).

Let us try to understand the implications of this phenomenon. Once upon a time, in Orwell's day, Power could be seen as a Big Brother who monitored every action of every one of its subjects, particularly when no one was aware of it. The television Big Brother is a poor caricature because everyone can follow what is happening to a small group of exhibitionists, assembled for the very purpose of being seen—and therefore the whole thing is of purely dramatic and psychiatric relevance. But what was just a prophecy in Orwell's time has now actually come true, since the Power can follow people's every movement through their mobile telephones, through every transaction, hotel visit, and motorway journey carried out using their credit card, through every supermarket visit followed on closed-circuit television, and so on, so that the citizen has fallen victim to the eye of a vast Big Brother.

That, at least, is what we thought until yesterday. But now it has been shown that not even the Power's innermost secrets can escape a hacker's monitoring, and therefore the relationship of monitoring ceases to be one-directional and becomes circular. The Power spies on every citizen, but every citizen, or at least the hacker appointed as avenger of the citizen, can find out all the secrets of the Power.

And even though the vast majority of citizens are unable to examine and evaluate the quantity of material that the hacker seizes and makes public, a new rule of journalism is taking shape and is being put into practice at this very moment. Rather than recording the important news — and once upon a time it was governments who decided what items were really important, whether it was declaring war, devaluing a currency, signing a treaty — the press now decides independently what news ought to be important and what news can be kept quiet, even negotiating with the political power (as has happened) over which disclosed "secrets" to reveal and which to keep quiet.

(Incidentally, given that all secret reports fomenting government hatred or friendship originate from published articles, or from confidential information given by journalists to embassy officials, the press is coming to assume another purpose — at one time it spied on foreign embassies to find out about secret plots, but now it is the embassies that are spying on the press to find out about events in the public domain. But let us get back to the point.)

How can a Power hold out in the future, when it can no longer keep its own secrets? It is true, as Georg Simmel once said, that every real secret is an empty secret (because an empty secret can never be revealed) and holding an empty secret represents the height of power; it is also true that to know everything about the character of Berlusconi or Merkel is in fact an empty secret, so far as secrets are concerned, because it is material in the public domain. But to reveal that Hillary

Clinton's secrets were empty secrets, as WikiLeaks has done, means removing all power from the Power.

It is clear that countries in the future will no longer be able to hold secret information online — it would be just the same as posting it on a street corner. But it is equally clear that with current surveillance technology there is no point in hoping to carry out confidential transactions by telephone. And nothing is easier, moreover, than to find out where and when a head of state has flown off to meet a colleague . . . not to mention those popular jamborees for demonstrators that are the G8 meetings.

How then can private and confidential relationships be carried on in future? What reaction might there be to the irresistible triumph of Complete Openness?

I am well aware that for the time being my prediction is science fiction and therefore fanciful, but I cannot help imagining government agents riding discreetly in stagecoaches or calèches along untrackable routes, along the country roads of more desolate areas — and those not blighted by tourism (because tourists use their mobile phones to photograph anything that moves in front of them) — carrying only messages committed to memory or, at most, hiding a few essential pieces of written information in the heel of a shoe.

It is most appealing to imagine envoys from the Glubbdubdrib Embassy meeting the messenger from Lilliput on a lonely street corner, at midnight, murmuring passwords in their brief furtive encounter. Or a pallid Pierrot, during a masked ball at the Ruritanian court, who draws back from time to time to where the candles have left an area of shadow, and takes off his mask, revealing the face of Obama to the Shulamite who, swiftly drawing aside her veil, we discover to be Angela Merkel. And there, between a waltz and polka, the meeting will at last take place, unbeknownst even to Assange, to decide the fate of the euro, or the dollar, or both.

All right, let us be serious. It won't happen like that. But in some way or other, something very similar will have to happen. In any event, information, the recording of a secret interview, will then be kept as a single copy or manuscript, in a locked drawer. Just think: ultimately, the attempted espionage at the Watergate Complex (which involved forcing open a cupboard and a filing cabinet) was less successful than WikiLeaks. And I recommend this advertisement to Mrs. Clinton. I found it online:

> Matex Security has been in existence since 1982 to protect your property. With made-to-measure furniture for the home, with secret compartments to hide your valuables and documents, where no intruder will ever find them even if they search your whole house or offices or boats of whatever make or model. These works are carried out in the greatest confidentiality and made to the specifications and instructions of the client, built exclusively by our cabinetmaker and our highly dependable staff.

Some time ago, I wrote that technology moves like a crayfish, in other words, backwards.[1] A century after wireless telegraphy revolutionized communications, the Internet has reestablished a telegraphy that runs on (telephone) wires. Videocassettes (which are analog) enabled film buffs to explore a film step by step, moving backward and forward and discovering all the secrets of how it was put together, whereas DVDs (which are digital) allow us only to jump from chapter to chapter, in other words, only by macro-leaps. High-speed trains now take us from Milan to Rome in three hours, while flying there, all in all, takes at least three and half. It is not so extraordinary, then, that even politics and government communication techniques should return to the times of the horse-drawn carriage, meetings in the steam room of a Turkish bath, or messages left in an alcove by some Mata Hari.

[Reworking of two articles that appeared in *Libération* (December 2, 2010) and *L'Espresso* (December 31, 2010).]

---

1. *Turning Back the Clock* (London: Harvill Secker, 2007).

www.vintage-books.co.uk